SHAKESPEARE, CHAPMAN AND
SIR THOMAS MORE

CROSS INN, OXFORD.

SHAKESPEARE, CHAPMAN
AND
SIR THOMAS MORE

Providing a more definite basis
for biography and
criticism

BY

ARTHUR ACHESON

AUTHOR OF "SHAKESPEARE AND THE RIVAL POET"
"MISTRESS DAVENANT, THE DARK LADY OF SHAKESPEARE'S SONNETS"
"SHAKESPEARE'S LOST YEARS IN LONDON"
"SHAKESPEARE'S SONNET STORY"

AMS PRESS
NEW YORK

PR
2894
.A25

Reprinted from the edition of 1931, London
First AMS EDITION published 1970
Manufactured in the United States of America

International Standard Book Number: 0-404-00278-1

Library of Congress Catalog Card Number: 72-113536

AMS PRESS, INC.
NEW YORK, N.Y. 10003

CONTENTS

CHAP.		PAGE
I.	INTRODUCTORY	1
II.	SHAKESPEARE AS A SERVING MAN	16
III.	AN UNKNOWN COMPANY IDENTIFIED	42
IV.	SHAKESPEARE AND PEMBROKE'S COMPANY	54
V.	SHAKESPEARE, CHAPMAN, AND *SIR THOMAS MORE*	99
VI.	GREENE'S COLLABORATION WITH LODGE AND NASHE	135
VII.	STAGE HISTORY OF KYD AND HIS PLAYS	184
VIII.	CHAPMAN AS A PRE-SHAKESPEAREAN	220
IX.	PEELE'S HAND IN *SIR THOMAS MORE*	265
	With reproductions of his handwriting	
	INDEX	274

And when it cometh, all things are,
And it cometh everywhere.

SHAKESPEARE, CHAPMAN AND *SIR THOMAS MORE*

CHAPTER I

INTRODUCTORY

THOUGH Shakespeare's life in London covered a period of approximately twenty-four years, *i.e.* from about 1586–7 until 1610–11, no poems nor plays of his composition that we now possess—with the probable exception of two of the sonnets written to the " dark lady "—can be dated upon any reasonable grounds earlier than the spring of 1591, nor later than 1611. While it is not yet generally recognised, however, we have practically conclusive circumstantial and inferential evidence in a number of scurrilous allusions by Robert Greene and Thomas Nashe to several persons—whom I find to have been connected with the theatrical interests of James Burbage—which were made in publications issued between 1588 and 1591, that even at this early period Shakespeare had written " ballads," and engaged in dramatic revision or composition ; and that he had also at this time attained to a position of critical authority in Burbage's theatrical organisation.

In the two decades between 1591 and 1611 Shakespeare

produced three long poems, over one hundred and fifty sonnets, and thirty-one plays; besides revising or re-writing portions of a number of old plays by other hands, the reversion of which he or the Burbages had bought for the use of their company. In this collection of poems and plays we have all that deeply interests the world in Shakespeare. Had these been missing, the hazy conjectures and distorted traditions recorded by his biographers concerning his early and late Stratford years, which are so utterly destitute of any spiritual significance, would never have been rescued from oblivion.

Taken as a whole, in the poems and plays produced by Shakespeare during these two decades, we possess not only the life's work of one of the greatest minds and rarest spirits in recorded history, but when this work is chronologically synchronised with his life and times, and studied biographically as the steadily developing expression of the growth of this spirit and mind in their reaction upon experience, we have also, in the transcendent vision of life which it reveals, the most interesting human document in our literature.

Whatever other merits have been claimed for Shakespeare's art, or however it has been questioned by those who have viewed it astigmatically through academic lenses, all critics of the drama admit the life-likeness of his characterisation and action. By certain scholastic and theoretical critics this naturalness has from time to time been challenged as a derogation from what they appear to have regarded as infallible and immutable dramatic laws, enunciated over two thousand years ago. Such anti-climactic lapses from tragic intensity as the porter's soliloquy in *Macbeth*, and the garrulity of the clownish

INTRODUCTORY

countryman with the asp in the catastrophic scene of *Antony and Cleopatra*, have by such critics been condemned or patronisingly condoned as art, though admittedly level with life, in which tragedy and comedy are inextricably mixed. For these and similar reasons Shakespeare has been accused of " carelessly extending to art the boundless freedom of life itself," a charge which—omitting the carelessness—the living Shakespeare would, no doubt, have regarded as a compliment—as this, modified by his own proper judgment, was apparently his intention.

From the time that we first begin to gain glimmerings of knowledge concerning Shakespeare's earliest dramatic activities in the supercilious and abusive allusions of Greene and Nashe, in their publications from 1588 to 1592, the analytical student may apprehend him as already at odds with contemporary interpretations of classical dramatic conventions, and working consciously upon naturalistic lines. Thomas Nashe, in his *Anatomy of Absurdity*, in 1589, following up his and Greene's combined attack upon Burbage's stage in Greene's *Menaphon*, published earlier in the same year, writes of " these upstart reformers of arts," and again—using the plural but with a singular intention, and, alluding to Shakespeare—" they contemn arts as unprofitable, contenting themselves with a little *country grammar school knowledge*." In *Love's Labour's Lost* a few years later, when Shakespeare challenges pedantry and its " learned fools," with their " base authority from others' books," and champions the study of life and nature, we get some idea of his anti-scholastic attitude that called forth these earliest attacks. Several years later still, when Chapman, Marston, and Jonson, combining against him, challenged his art with Aristotelian standards, he answered them in *Hamlet*, definitely proclaiming as his dramatic gospel, " the purpose of playing, whose end both at the first and now was, and is, to hold as it were the mirrour up to nature, to show virtue her own feature, scorn her own image, and the very age and body of the time his form and pressure." And even towards the close of his dramatic career, though then in a more serene and persuasive mood, we find him still maintaining the same naturalistic thesis when, in *A Winter's Tale*, the grave and ageing Polixenes instructs the youthful Perdita that

> . . . nature is made better by no mean.
> But nature makes that mean : so, over that art
> Which you say adds to nature, is an art
> That nature makes. . . .
> . . . This is an art
> Which does mend nature,—change it rather; but
> The art itself is nature.

This, clearly, is not the attitude of ignorance, nor yet is it the expression of a " capricious and unsystematic artist," however fortified by alleged " temperament " or " instinct," but of a creative and judicious master of his art, then standing on the top of twenty years of the most successful practical experience on record, and calmly sensible of the excellence of its results when compared with the best efforts of his scholastic critics, and of all other dramatists combined, during that prolific period. The cumulative verdict of the greatest minds during the centuries that have since elapsed has so accentuated the surpassing degree of this excellence, that no dramatic work produced then or since, in England or elsewhere, appears now so surely destined as his to endure as living art into a remote future.

INTRODUCTORY

Life and nature, then, being Shakespeare's avowed models, the creation and presentation of the drama his vocation, and the centre of English literary, social, and political life the scene of his activities, it appears evident that he would view this life—the only life that came into his experience—with eyes and mind awake to its dramatic aspects. It is impossible that his plays—vitalised into imperishable art from crude sources or lifeless originals—should not, in this vitalising process, have taken on some recognisable analogy to the life he observed and lived during the two decades of their production, even though such analogy should be unconscious. But when we remember the topical and polemical nature of the Elizabethan stage—influenced as it was by the political or factional interests of the noblemen licensing or patronising the companies or their writers; by the literary hostilities between the stage poets and their academic competitors—the self-called "Gentlemen-Poets"—as well as by the business and histrionic rivalry of competing theatrical interests—it appears opposed to reason that the most popular dramatist of the time, writing for the most popular company, could for a period of twenty years pursue a serenely detached and unswervingly objective course, uninfluenced by such prevailing conditions. It is much more probable, and may in fact appear, that Shakespeare's and his company's pre-eminence and success made them at times the very storm-centre of such polemics, compelling Shakespeare, despite his reputed gentleness and his acknowledged dramatic objectivity, frequently to enter the lists, either in his patron's personal or factional interests, or in his own or his company's defence. The masterly suggestive art by which as a rule he accomplished his double purpose, and at the same time protected himself and his company from an observant and arbitrary censorship, is displayed by the fact that the majority of his reputed critics are still oblivious to or sceptical of this phase of his work.

While Shakespeare is never obviously didactic, no one has better realised the power of suggestion, as well as its enhanced effectiveness by indirection. It is most unlikely, then, that he, the favourite Court dramatist, patronised by and sympathising with the leaders of the popular faction during years of intense factional rivalry, and making, as he does, one of his dramatic characters conceive that

> ... the play's the thing
> Wherein I'll catch the conscience of the king,

should not himself upon occasion have made indirect but intentional use of this effectively suggestive instrument to influence the minds and consciences of others.

For critical purposes it has been aptly said, " Shakespeare's work differs from that of more erudite authors much in the manner that a lake differs from a river ": theirs we may at times consider as a whole; his, to appraise judiciously, we are forced to regard as a progressive development. As we trace the stages of this development in his work we become increasingly conscious of the rapid and continuous growth of power and insight in the mind and spirit behind it; and synchronising the work with the facts of his life and environment, we are led to realise in the transfigured reflections of concurrent life which we find mirrored in his great mind something of the functioning, as well as of the limitations, of what we call creative genius,

INTRODUCTORY

in the fact that with him, as with lesser men who have sailed their course upon " the river of time "—

> As what he sees is
> So have his thoughts been;
>   .   .   .   .   .
> As is the world on its banks
> So is the mind of the man,

but in his case, viewed with a vision more attentive, more perceptive, more comprehensive, and withal glorified by the splendour of his imagination, and imperishably vitalised by the magic of his art. I cannot conceive that genius differs from normality in any other manner than in its greater natural capacity, through finer sensibilities, to absorb knowledge from observation and experience and concomitant fineness of judgment and imagination to use this knowledge creatively.

Nothing approaching finality in criticism can be attained that is based upon the spiritually irrelevant traditions and trivial details of extant biography, and which does not take into consideration with Shakespeare's work the necessity for enlarging our knowledge of the man himself, and of his times and environment, in order to gain a clearer conception of the *underlying spiritual causes of the vastly differing spiritual effects exhibited in the drastic changes in the character of his work with the passing years;* lacking this, criticism at its best is mere opinion.

In any endeavour made to establish a more definite and logical basis for biography and criticism it is primarily essential that we acquire a much clearer conception than now generally prevails amongst scholars of Shakespeare's beginnings, by seeking more definite knowledge of his theatrical and dramatic affiliations from the time he left

Stratford until we find him associated with the Burbages as a sharer in the Lord Chamberlain's company in December 1594.

The next, and an equally if indeed not more important essential, is a correct understanding of the biographical value of the Sonnets, as well as of their literary and critical values, when their dates of production and the manner in which the personal experiences they reveal are co-ordinated chronologically, with tacit reflections of these experiences in Shakespeare's concurrent dramatic work, between 1591 and 1598.

A third biographical requisite, as revealing the venomous odds against which he was compelled to struggle from the very inception to the end of his London career, is a clearer and more extended knowledge of his relations with his jealous academic competitors. The critical aspects of such knowledge are also of value in accounting frequently for things that have been regarded as "incongruities in his art," by what has gravely been termed "an instructed modern criticism."

In the following chapter I purpose to epitomise and simplify a more extended argument, first published in *Shakespeare's Lost Years in London,* in 1920, showing that Shakespeare began his theatrical career, in from 1586 to 1587, as a bonded serving man for a period of two years to James Burbage, who at that time, as the owner of the Theatre and of the Lord Chamberlain's company (which comprised his theatrical employees and musicians), was affiliated with Edward Alleyn and the Lord Admiral's company. This affiliation continued until 1589, when a reorganisation of these and other companies took place, resulting in the formation of Lord Strange's company,

INTRODUCTORY

which, with the Admiral's company, continued under the auspices of Burbage and Alleyn until late in 1590, when Alleyn, the Admiral's company, and the majority of Strange's company left Burbage for Henslowe and the Rose Theatre. Shakespeare, who remained with Burbage, now co-operated with his old chief in forming the Earl of Pembroke's company, becoming its leader and principal playwright, continuing in this capacity until the spring of 1594, when a new general reorganisation took place—the majority of Strange's men returning to Burbage and Shakespeare, and the rest remaining with Alleyn and Henslowe, who, with accretions from the Queen's and Sussex's companies, re-established the Admiral's company as an independent unit. This company thereafter for many years continued to be the Burbages' leading competitor for Court and public favour.

In the epitome to follow I will also endeavour to make clear that the invidious allusion to Shakespeare in Robert Greene's posthumously published *A Groat's-worth of Wit*, in September 1592, was not the first nor an isolated attack upon the poet, but was Greene's last and expiring effort in a series of equally scurrilous but less literally recognisable attacks, made by him in conjunction with Thomas Nashe, against Shakespeare and the Burbage organisation during the past three to four years. As most of these attacks challenged Shakespeare's criticism and revision of dramatic work written by their fellow scholars, it is significant that all logical evidence places the date of Shakespeare's revisionary work in *Sir Thomas More* at this exact period. *It is historically impossible that his revision of this play could have been made at any other time.* I will also demonstrate the new and interesting fact that it was the collaborative work of his future arch-enemy, George Chapman, in this play, that Shakespeare now revised, thereby accounting for what I have sought for over thirty years—the inception of Chapman's bitter and prolonged hostility.

In the slurring allusions made by Greene and Nashe in their publications between 1588 and 1591 to Shakespeare and others connected with the Burbage-Alleyn interests, both of these scholars resent the presumption of the " idiot art-masters " of this company in daring to question or revise the work of " scholars." They refer to the " scorn " of " the arts " exhibited by these " upstart reformers of arts," and censure their desire to have plays suited to stage requirements or to the popular comprehension and taste. When the critical attitude of the " scholars " is coupled with the fact that James Burbage was then the oldest and most experienced theatrical manager in England, and withal, as shall be shown, " a stubborn fellow," holding decided opinions of his own, we gain a new and interesting sidelight upon Burbage's managerial methods, which suggests that Shakespeare's early success as a practical playwright was probably, in no small measure, due to the technical guidance of his experienced chief during the formative period of his work. It appears very probable also that his connection with the Burbages, from the beginning to the end of his London career, was the result of what now appears to have been for years one of Burbage's managerial policies—which was, to retain within his own organisation as reader, critic, and writer, a producing playwright of his own technical training. *It will become evident that Marlowe immediately preceded Shakespeare with Burbage in this capacity, and that Kyd preceded Marlowe.*

INTRODUCTORY

However new and startling this theory may at first appear, a careful examination of all sources of information will reveal the fact that no evidence exists to show that Kyd, after 1582, or that Marlowe or Shakespeare ever wrote or revised a play for any company other than those working under Burbage's auspices, though certain plays written or revised by all three of them for Burbage and Alleyn were later acted, in still further revised forms, upon other stages.

All of Marlowe's known work, and possibly some unknown work, composed before 1591, was written for the Burbage-Alleyn interests; and all of his work after this date, when Burbage and Alleyn parted, was written for Pembroke's company, under Burbage and Shakespeare.

While our past limited knowledge of Kyd's dramatic work makes all theories regarding him and his work rather indefinite, new evidence to be presented points to prolonged relations with the Burbage-Alleyn interests preceding Marlowe's appearance upon the scene, and of a nature similar to those sustained with them later by Marlowe and Shakespeare, as the company poet.

It would be difficult to select three contemporary dramatists differing so distinctly in temper, spirit, and mind as Kyd, Marlowe, and Shakespeare, yet each in his heyday attained a dramatic prestige and popularity greater than that of any of his dramatic competitors. Assuming for the present their successive connection with Burbage, may we not reasonably infer that Burbage's stagecraft and training were in some measure responsible for their preponderant popularity; and that his managerial methods of adapting his presentations to his stage, his time, and existing taste and manners, which were so superciliously contemned by Greene and Nashe, proved more effective in practice than the more "learned" theories of the scholars applied upon other and more officially favoured stages? Within four years of the junction between Burbage and Alleyn, in 1585, they had largely supplanted the Queen's company for Court performances, for which specific purpose that company had been organised in 1583—and two years later had completely ousted them. It was their steady growth in Court and public favour and the consequent decline of the Queen's company, for which Greene wrote, that aroused his jealousy at this time.

Incidentally, the argument and evidence for this theory will serve also to identify Lord Hunsdon as Kyd's hitherto unknown patron, referred to as "my Lord" and "his lordship" in Kyd's letter to Lord Keeper Puckering concerning his acquaintance with Marlowe, which was written shortly after Marlowe's death in June 1593, and may also account for Kyd's evident animus against Marlowe, as well as for Burbage's loss of Lord Hunsdon's protection from 1589 until 1594, when—nearly a year after Marlowe's death—his patronage was restored.

At the present time there is as little definitely known concerning the company and dramatic affiliations of Greene, Peele, Marlowe, Lodge, Nashe, Chapman, Kyd, and Munday during the seven years preceding 1594, as has hitherto been known regarding Shakespeare's status and whereabouts during these, his first seven years in London. In the following pages, besides clarifying Shakespeare's theatrical connections during these seven years, new and revelatory light will be thrown upon the concurrent company affiliations of all the other writers mentioned.

It will appear evident that Robert Greene was con-

INTRODUCTORY

tinuously connected with the old Queen's company, from the time he left Cambridge in 1583 until the end of 1590, when this company disrupted, its men and properties being then largely absorbed by Strange's and Pembroke's companies, while a portion of its membership formed a new Queen's company, which affiliated with Sussex's men for the following three to three and a half years; Greene continuing to write for this united company until shortly before his death in 1592.

It will also be shown that Thomas Lodge wrote for Burbage and Alleyn between about 1585 and 1587, and was connected with the old Queen's men, as a collaborator with Greene, from about 1588 at the latest until the end of 1590; and that he wrote independently for the new Queen's and Sussex's men between the beginning of 1591 and August in that year, when he left England on a voyage to the South Seas.

Though it is at present known that Thomas Nashe collaborated with Greene in other than dramatic work as early as 1589, nothing is known of their dramatic collaboration except Greene's possible reference to Nashe as "young Juvenal," "who lastly with me together writ a comedy," in his *A Groat's-worth of Wit*, published after Greene's death in 1592. It will here be shown that Nashe collaborated with Greene in at least two plays for the new Queen's and Sussex's men between the beginning of 1591 and about the middle of 1592, that one of these plays was the play referred to by Greene, and that Nashe *was* "young Juvenal."

It will also become apparent that Marlowe was connected with Burbage and Alleyn between about 1586–7 and the end of 1590, when Burbage and Alleyn parted; and that he then continued his connection with Burbage and Shakespeare, as a writer for Pembroke's company, until his death in the middle of 1593.

Nothing is at present definitely known of Peele's theatrical affiliations from the beginning until the end of his career, except that in 1581 his *Arraignment of Paris* was presented by the Children of the Chapel. It is probable that he wrote other plays for this company, or for Oxford's company, between 1581 and 1589. It will be indicated by the allusions of Greene and Nashe, in 1589, to Alleyn and Peele, as well as by the later possession by Alleyn and Henslowe's companies of Peele's early work, that Peele became connected with the Burbage-Alleyn interests as a writer for the Admiral's company in this year. Peele's hand in the revision of the *First Part of Henry VI.*, and in *Titus Andronicus*, indicates that, when Burbage and Alleyn parted in 1590, he accompanied Alleyn to Henslowe. His later hand in the Admiral's *Henry V.*, upon which it will be shown that Shakespeare's *Henry V.* is based, reveals him as a writer for the Admiral's company as late as 1595. It is probable that he continued in this connection until his death in or shortly before 1598.

The new and interesting fact will also be demonstrated that George Chapman, instead of beginning his dramatic career in from 1593 to 1594, as is now generally supposed, was already engaged in dramatic collaboration with Anthony Munday, for Oxford's company, as early as from 1581-2, and as late as from 1586-7, and probably as late as 1589, when he and Munday became connected with the Admiral's company under Edward Alleyn.

The historical facts and deductions to be presented concerning the theatrical affiliations of these early contemporaries of Shakespeare's, in conjunction with new

INTRODUCTORY

critical light correcting the misascription of a number of plays of this period, will serve to clarify our present very nebulous ideas of the relations of these writers for the dramatic companies, to each other and to Shakespeare, to dissipate much current critical error, as well as to reveal the inception of the jealous hostility with which Chapman, and those he later influenced, pursued Shakespeare until the end of his dramatic career.

CHAPTER II

SHAKESPEARE AS A SERVING MAN

THE following summarised chronicle — based upon documentary, circumstantial, and collateral evidence — of Shakespeare's theatrical experience from the time he came to London until the first documentary evidence of his connection with the interests of James Burbage appears in 1595, differs very materially from all other accounts of him and his connections during this period. Nearly all recent attempts to trace his history during these early years have been made upon the erroneous assumption that his first theatrical connection was formed in the capacity of an actor with the Earl of Leicester's company, with which company, under its supposed later titles, he is alleged to have been continuously connected until the end of his London career.

As Shakespeare's twin children, Judith and Hamnet, were born early in 1585, we may naturally infer that he did not leave Stratford for London before, or even shortly after, this event. Further on I will indicate by new evidence that his connection with the Burbages was formed, at the latest, before the autumn of 1587.

The first specific record of Shakespeare's connection with a company of players is a mention of his name, in conjunction with those of William Kempe and Richard

SHAKESPEARE AS SERVING MAN 17

Burbage, on March 15, 1595, in the accounts of the Treasurer of the Chamber, as receiving payment for two comedies presented by the Lord Chamberlain's company before the Court at Greenwich on the 26th and 28th of the previous December. This record establishes the fact that Shakespeare was connected with the Burbages at that time as a sharer in the Lord Chamberlain's company. As we possess conclusive evidence that he continued to be connected with the Burbages thereafter until he retired from London, it has naturally been inferred, and it may now appear correctly so, that he began his theatrical career also in their service.

Most of the ambiguity which exists at present among scholars regarding Shakespeare's connections between the time he came to London and December 1594 is due to lack of knowledge of Burbage's company affiliations during these years, it being nebulously assumed that he was somehow a member, or the manager, of both Leicester's and the Queen's companies during part of this period; when he is erroneously alleged also to have managed the Queen's company at the Curtain, as well as Leicester's at the Theatre. No explanation whatever is offered by biographers or critics for his activities or whereabouts between 1591 and 1594, during which interval his son, Richard, was working with the Strange-Chamberlain company under Henslowe and Alleyn at their theatres.

Though the exact date of the inception of Shakespeare's relations with the Burbages is not, and probably never shall be, known, a consideration of new facts concerning Burbage's theatrical affiliations between 1582 and 1589 credibly infers that they commenced some time between 1586 and 1587.

To whatever prestige and reputation Shakespeare

may have attained in later years, when he came to London as a youth of from twenty-two to twenty-three, he bore no stigmata of dramatic genius that would lead an experienced theatrical manager, such as James Burbage, to afford him terms of employment differing materially from those upon which he, and others in his position, engaged young and inexperienced employees. Henslowe's *Diary* supplies evidence of the fact that the theatrical business, like all other businesses at that period, demanded indentures and bonds for stated terms of service from apprentices and serving men. In Shakespeare's case, even though we lacked the tradition handed down by the Stratford parish clerk, William Castle, that Shakespeare became connected with the Theatre as a servitor, we could not logically form any other conclusion in view of the business and legal usages of that period.

The term " servitor " has been misunderstood by many critics, who have supposed that it signified a specific capacity in a company of players, when, in fact, it applied to Shakespeare's legal and business relations with James Burbage, who, at the time Shakespeare came to London, was the owner and manager of a playhouse. Being then, as it was, the only capacity in which a youth of Shakespeare's poverty, social condition, and lack of technical experience could very well become connected with the theatrical business or the dramatic profession, it may be made evident that Castle's tradition is literally true. As I will later adduce cumulative inferential evidence linking logically with Robert Greene's accepted allusion to Shakespeare as " Shakescene," in his *A Groat's-worth of Wit* in 1592, that Thomas Nashe, collaborating with Greene in an attack upon Burbage's organisation in 1589, alludes to Shakespeare *as a recently emancipated serving man*, we may reasonably infer that his servitorship with Burbage had its inception in from 1586 to 1587, Henslowe's *Diary* affording conclusive evidence that the usual term of such servitorships covered a period of two years.

At this time—1586-7—James Burbage was unquestionably the manager of the Lord Chamberlain's company, and evidently had been its manager under its earlier title of Lord Hunsdon's company since 1582, when, we may judge, this company was formed, as it appears in that year for the first time in both Court and provincial records.[1]

The evidence for Burbage's connection with Lord Hunsdon's company at this period, while of a documentary nature and historically most important, has been badly misconstrued by Halliwell-Phillipps, and distorted by others who have followed him in his error.

William Fleetwood, one of Lord Burghley's gossips, and the Recorder of the City of London, in a weekly report upon affairs in the city to Lord Burghley, dated June 18, 1584, writes as follows: " Upon Sondaie My Lord sent two aldermen to the Court, for the suppressing and pulling downe of the theatre and curten for all the Lords agreed thereunto, saving my Lord Chamberlayn and Mr. Vice-Chamberlayn ; but we obtained a letter to suppresse them all. Upon the same night I sent for the Quene's players, and my Lord of Arundell his players, and they all well nighe obeyed the Lord's letters. The chiefest of her Highnes' players advised me to send for the owner of the theatre, who was a stubborne fellow, and to bynd him. I dyd so. He sent me word that he was my Lord of Hunsdon's man. and that he would not come to me ; but

[1] *English Dramatic Companies*, John Tucker Murray, vol. i. p. 379.

he would in the morning ride to my Lord. Then I sent the under-sheriff for hym, and he brought him to me ; and at his coming he showted me out very justice. And in the end, I showed hym my Lord his master's hand, and then he was more quiet. But to . . . . for it he wold not be bound. And then I mynding to send hym to prison, he made sute that he might be bounde to appeare at the oier and determiner, the which is to-morrowe, where he said that he was sure the court wold not bynd hym, being a counsellor's man. And so I have graunted his request, where he is sure to be bounde, or els is lyke to do worse."

As James Burbage was unquestionably the owner of the Theatre from the time he built it, in 1576, until his death in 1597, there is no possible reason to doubt that Fleetwood referred to Burbage, with whose independent character and pugnacious spirit the incident aptly fits. The gratuitous assumption that Fleetwood referred to John Hyde, to whom Burbage had mortgaged *the lease* of the Theatre five years before, is due apparently to lack of knowledge of the nature of a lease mortgage, which certain former critics appear to have regarded in the light of a pawnbroking transaction, in which the mortgagee, like the pawner, loses the use and possession of his property during the period of hypothecation. As Burbage's mortgage to Hyde was for a ten years' period, at the end of which the mortgage was satisfied and taken over by Cuthbert Burbage, it is very evident that James Burbage did not forgo to the mortgagor the use and possession of his only means of livelihood during the ten years' life of the mortgage, nor for any portion of it.

Recorder Fleetwood was one of the best-informed men of the time regarding affairs in the City, and was also an

SHAKESPEARE AS SERVING MAN

exact and legal-minded official who was not likely to use loosely such an expression as "the owner of the theatre" in his report to his chief, under whose instructions, his letter implies, the Lord Mayor was working at this time in his attempt to suppress the theatres. Neither Halliwell-Phillipps nor his followers appear to have been aware that this letter of Fleetwood's was one of his regular weekly reports upon affairs in the City to Lord Burghley, nor to have recognised the fact that Fleetwood was the Recorder of the City of London.

Had this palpable piece of evidence regarding Burbage's company connections in 1584 been recognised at its face value by Halliwell-Phillipps, the mystery of Shakespeare's lost years in London might have been solved three quarters of a century ago.

A backward glance, in the records of the dramatic companies, of two years from the date of Fleetwood's letter referring to the owner of the Theatre as a Hunsdon's man, shows that Lord Hunsdon's company was established in 1582. As the Earl of Leicester who, previous to this date, had been Burbage's protector, left England in this year for a prolonged stay upon the Continent, it appears evident that James Burbage, with such contingencies in mind as the one that had now arisen, transferred the protection of his theatrical interests to Lord Hunsdon, to whom he could appeal directly and personally in the event of such constantly recurring trouble with the authorities. In spite of Fleetwood's avowed confidence in the success of his suppressive efforts, we know that Burbage was not suppressed nor the theatres pulled down at this time, and that Lord Hunsdon's protection proved effective.

The later history of Lord Hunsdon's company, and of

the companies affiliated with it between 1584 and 1590, substantiates Burbage's identity as the " owner of the theatre " mentioned in Fleetwood's letter, as well as the fact that he was then, and later, the manager of Lord Hunsdon's company. In 1585, Lord Hunsdon becoming Lord Chamberlain, his company took on this new title.

In this same year the Earl of Leicester's company, which, since 1576, had been Burbage's permanent customer at the Theatre, was temporarily disrupted, seven of its members — including, apparently, all of the sharers — departing for the Continent, where they remained until July 1587.

Immediately after their departure Burbage supplied their place by combining with the Lord Chamberlain's company at the Theatre the newly established Lord Admiral's company, under the leadership of Edward Alleyn, thus fortifying his defence against the attacks of the municipal authorities, by securing the added protection of the Lord Admiral, who, in the preceding year, in his then capacity of Lord Chamberlain, had, as I have shown, in company with the Vice-Chamberlain, disagreed with the remainder of the Lords of the Council in their proposed action against the Theatre and the Curtain.

Edward Alleyn and a number of his associates in the new Lord Admiral's company had previously been members of the Earl of Worcester's company, which, through the ill-behaviour of some of its members, had lost this nobleman's protection. This title for a company of players now disappears from the records for five years, and is not restored until after the death of the old Earl of Worcester, in 1589, when a new company, containing some of the

SHAKESPEARE AS SERVING MAN

old members, again appears under the patronage of his son and heir.

The remainder of the men forming the Admiral's company in 1585 came no doubt from Lord Sheffield's company, as John Alleyn, who was previously with this company—which in this year disappears also from the records—joined his brother, Edward Alleyn, at this time, and continued to be affiliated with him in business until 1590 and possibly later.

As the combination between the Lord Chamberlain's men and the Lord Admiral's men continued until 1589, when a new reorganisation took place, and Lord Strange's company was formed by incorporating a number of younger men from Lord Strange's company of acrobats, the Lord Chamberlain's company, and the recently disbanded Leicester's company, it is possible that there may also have been a few Oxford's men in this new company, as, while still retaining Oxford's licence for protective purposes, it submerges its identity in that of the new Worcester's company in this year.

It is now evident that if Shakespeare became bonded to Burbage in from 1586 to 1587, he would at that time have been regarded as a Lord Chamberlain's man.

Thus we find him from the beginning of his theatrical career associated in his work with Richard Burbage and Edward Alleyn, two young actors already making names for themselves, and, within a decade, recognised as the leading actors of rival companies, which were then, and for years afterwards, regarded as the most prominent companies in England.

At about the same time that Shakespeare, as Burbage's serving man, became associated with Richard Burbage

24 SHAKESPEARE AS SERVING MAN

and Edward Alleyn, he must also have begun his acquaintance with Christopher Marlowe, who, in 1587, produced upon Burbage's stages his first known play—*Tamburlaine* —and who, I now find, from this time onward until his death in 1593, continued to be connected as a dramatist *with the Burbage interests, and with no others.*

Though much baseless assumption exists to the contrary, I confidently affirm that, with the exception of *Queen Dido,* which was presented by the Children of the Chapel, but which was left unfinished at Marlowe's death, being completed and, in fact, practically written by Nashe, no evidence exists to show that Marlowe, during his short known dramatic career of six years, ever wrote or revised a play for any company other than those performing under Burbage's auspices. *The Tragedy of the Guyes*—evidently *The Massacre at Paris*—presented by Strange's company under Henslowe and Alleyn at the Rose, in January 1593, as a new play—was doubtless, like Greene's *Henry VI.*, Kyd's *Titus Andronicus,* and several other plays presented as " ne " on Henslowe's boards, merely a revision by Peele or others of an older play, by Marlowe, held by Strange's men as company property when they parted from Burbage late in 1590. It was evidently originally written by Marlowe for Burbage and Alleyn, in 1589, shortly after the assassination of Henry III. of France, and while public interest was still fresh in that tragic affair.

Assuming, then, for the present that Shakespeare joined Burbage in London some time in 1586 or 1587, we find him at the beginning of his career associated with the two most promising actors in London, and also with the outstanding figure among the dramatic writers of the period. It is not surprising then to find that a theatrical company, backed by the matured experience of James Burbage, and having in its membership, or associated with it in dramatic work, four young men such as William Shakespeare, Christopher Marlowe, Edward Alleyn, and Richard Burbage, soon won such Court favour and popular regard as to excite the jealousy of competing theatrical and dramatic interests.

At the same time that Marlowe produced *Tamburlaine* on Burbage's stages, Robert Greene held similar dramatic relations with the Queen's company, which was then, and had been since 1583, regarded as the most powerful and popular theatrical company in London. The pronounced success of Marlowe's *Tamburlaine* so greatly enhanced the steadily growing prestige of Burbage's organisation, that it began now to challenge the predominance of the Queen's company, both in Court favour and popular regard, while Marlowe's fame commenced to dim, by comparison, the reputation of Greene and others who wrote for it. To the steady growth, during the next five years, of a resentment and jealousy now aroused in Greene by Marlowe's success with *Tamburlaine*; and to the resulting abuse which he and his vitriolic collaborator, Nashe—in their publications issued between 1588 and 1592—heap upon Marlowe and others who wrote for Burbage, as well as upon Burbage's theatrical associates, including Shakespeare, and, in a less critical tone, Edward Alleyn, we owe most of the light that it is possible to cast upon Shakespeare's career, from the time he came to London until his name appears in print for the first time, subscribed to his dedication of *Venus and Adonis* to the Earl of Southampton, in 1593; and to the continued attacks of an augmenting scholastic clique, who took their cue from Greene and Nashe, we owe most of our knowledge of his personal life from 1593 until the end of his London career.

Though Mr. Richard Simpson, in his *School of Shakespeare*, recognised the fact that Greene's now generally accepted allusion to Shakespeare as "Shakescene" and "Johannes factotum" in his posthumously published *A Groat's-worth of Wit*, in 1592, was not a bolt out of the blue, but that it had been preceded in Greene's and Nashe's earlier publications by equally slurring though less literally indicative allusions, he was frequently led astray in his identification of persons, owing to the nebulous nature of extant knowledge of the dramatic companies, and of their various combinations and transmutations at the time he wrote; while the new light I have been enabled to shed upon Burbage's company connections from 1582 onwards, and upon his association with Edward Alleyn between 1585 and 1590, compels me to differ with Mr. Simpson's identifications in many instances, I do so with due acknowledgment of the fact that he first blazed the path I follow.

Shortly after the production of *Tamburlaine* upon Burbage's boards, Robert Greene, emulating and imitating Marlowe's heroic style and subject, produced upon the Queen's company's boards his *Alphonsus of Arragon*, which, it appears, from his subsequent attempt at apology and defence, was unsuccessful in its public appeal, and also excited ridicule upon rival stages.

Though Greene, in nearly all of his publications issued since 1585, had been girding at certain theatrical interests, whose identities we may now readily infer from his later more definitely indicative allusions, he makes his first easily recognisable point at the Burbage-Alleyn interests,

SHAKESPEARE AS SERVING MAN 27

by attacking Marlowe and his recent success with *Tamburlaine*, in his *Perimedes the Blacksmith*, issued in 1588. Here he attributes his own recent failure to the lack of blasphemy in his lines, and in the words " Merlin " and " that atheist Tamburlaine " alludes to Marlowe, whom he charges with atheism and impiety. It appears very likely that this spiteful and sinister imputation, first given publicity by the jealous Greene, and later evidently retailed by Kyd to Lord Hunsdon, within a few months lost Burbage that nobleman's patronage; and that it also was the foundation of the charges of atheism against Marlowe exploited by Government spies and informers, both before and after his shocking and mysterious murder five years later.

The title-page of the earliest known publication of *Tamburlaine*, in 1590, reads: " Divided into two Tragical Discourses, as they were sundrie times shewed upon Stages in the Citie of London. By the right honorable the Lord Admyrall, his servauntes." This company was continuously with Burbage at the Theatre in Shoreditch in summer, and evidently at the Crosse-Keys in Grace Church Street in winter, from 1585 until 1589, working in conjunction with the Lord Chamberlain's men, who were Burbage's theatrical employees and musicians, and never anything more, from the time Burbage secured Lord Hunsdon's patronage in 1582 until he lost it in 1589, when Lord Strange's company was formed. Though the name of Lord Hunsdon's company, or of the Lord Chamberlain's company, appears occasionally in the provincial records in these years, these men were always accompanied by another regular company of actors, whose title is also frequently recorded at the same place and date.

When Lord Strange's new company of adult actors was

28 SHAKESPEARE AS SERVING MAN

formed in 1589 and took the place of the Chamberlain's men, it was enlarged to the full proportion of a regular company, which played under Burbage and Alleyn at the Curtain from 1589 till the end of 1590; while the Admiral's men continued to play under Burbage and Alleyn at the Theatre; this powerful organisation having appropriated the use of the largest two theatres in London. Surprising as this statement may appear to scholars, I will further tax their credulity by stating that a somewhat similar condition had previously existed between these two theatres and Burbage and Alleyn since 1585. I will devote the next chapter to elucidating this theory.

The inroads which the combination of companies playing at the Theatre and the Curtain, under one general management, must have begun to make, as early as 1585, upon the popularity and the receipts of the Queen's company, added to the strong probability that the Queen's company was now ousted by a Burbage-Alleyn company from the Curtain, marks the inception of Greene's resentment against this organisation at this time, though he does not yet begin to attack the writers for the company.

In *Shakespeare's Lost Years in London*, I have shown that Greene, in his *Planetomachia*, published in 1585, makes the first of his steadily continued attacks upon actors and actor-managers. As it will become evident that all of his later attacks were made against the Burbage-Alleyn organisation, it is clear that the present attack is directed at the greater prominence they attained in the theatrical world in this year by their control of both the Theatre and the Curtain.

Greene centres his attack upon Valdrako, an actor in *Venus Tragedy*, one of the tales in his *Planetomachia*.

SHAKESPEARE AS SERVING MAN 29

Greene describes this actor as "stricken in age, melancholic, ruling after the crabbed forwardness of his doting will . . . politic because experienced, familiar with none except for his profit . . . skilful in dissembling, trusting no one, silent, coveteous, counting all things honest that were profitable." It is clear that an ordinary actor is not here indicated, but one who is prominent in his profession, who has financial dealings with writers for the stage, and who, when such writers prove unreliable and dishonest—as Greene admits himself to have been—is not easily imposed upon. This characterisation and description of the methods of an aged and powerful London theatrical manager in the year 1585 fits no one but James Burbage. The only other person to whom it might possibly apply at this period is Philip Henslowe, who, if he was then engaged in the theatrical business, as I shall show good reason to believe that he was, could not at this time truthfully be described as either aged or as an actor. The words "ruling after the crabbed forwardness of his doting will" give a recognisable characterisation, by a prejudiced writer who had failed to get the better of him, of the pugnacious, wilful, and stubborn old actor and actor-manager, James Burbage, in the year 1585.

New fuel was added to the fire of Greene's jealousy of Marlowe and Burbage's stage with the formation of the reorganised Lord Strange's company, in 1589. In this year Greene published his *Menaphon*, to which he induced his friend Nashe to prefix an Epistle, addressed "To the Gentlemen Scholars of both Universities." As Nashe had just returned from the Continent, after an absence of two years, and could not from his own observation and knowledge have been as intimately aware of conditions in

London theatrical and dramatic circles as his Epistle shows him to have been, it appears evident that Greene primed him for the effort. As Mr. Simpson long ago pointed out, " The identity of idea as well as of phrase between Nashe's Epistle and things which Greene subsequently published prove this assumption to be correct."

When Greene's past allusions to Marlowe and *Tamburlaine* in 1588, shortly after the success of this play on Burbage's boards, and his later allusion in 1592 to Shakespeare as " Shakescene," are borne in mind, it becomes apparent that Nashe's similar allusions in his Epistle to Greene's *Menaphon* in 1589 are also to persons connected, or who had been connected, with Burbage's stage. Nashe mentions *Hamlet*, and alludes to its author as making use of " English Seneca."[1] Mr. Simpson supposed that this referred to Shakespeare, but Mr. Fleay more logically suggests it to be an allusion to Thomas Kyd. Modern criticism is now generally agreed that the old *Hamlet* was a work of Kyd's. Nashe's allusion in this Epistle to a follower of " English Seneca " leaping " into a new occupation," and translating " twopenny pamphlets from the Italian without knowledge even of the articles," is apparently directed at Kyd's translation from Tasso, entitled *The Householder's Philosophie*, which was published a few months earlier in 1588. A critical examination of all of Kyd's known work, and of work attributed to him, made with the object of ascertaining the companies for which they were written, combined with the undoubted fact of his connection with the Burbage-Alleyn interests preceding the advent of Marlowe in 1587; and this knowledge, linked with Burbage's demonstrated method of

[1] *Seneca, his Tenne Tragedies.* 1581.

SHAKESPEARE AS SERVING MAN 31

retaining a company poet, leads me to infer that Kyd became connected with Burbage in this capacity in or about 1583, shortly after Burbage first secured Lord Hunsdon's patronage, and that he continued in this capacity until 1587, when he was supplanted by Marlowe, *Kyd in the same year entering into the personal service of Lord Hunsdon.* There is no evidence that Kyd produced any dramatic work for the stage after 1587; while an examination of the history of his known and traceable dramatic work infers that after 1582 all of such work belonged to companies working under or affiliated with Burbage, or to companies later inheriting Burbage properties. In order not to involve the present argument, more definite evidence of the above inferences will be presented later.

In his Epistle to Greene's *Menaphon* Nashe gives further evidence that Burbage's stage is the object of his attack by alluding to the *The Taming of a Shrew,* and parodying certain of its phrases. He also alludes to *Edward III.,* by a play upon the word " horizon," which is there used in the manner he criticises. I have elsewhere demonstrated, by the collocation of significant passages from *Edward III.* with passages from Marlowe's *Edward II.,* that the former play, though revised by Shakespeare after Marlowe's death in 1593, was an early work of Marlowe's.[1]

All three of the above-mentioned plays were afterwards revised by Shakespeare, and two of them are mentioned in Henslowe's *Diary* as properties of the Lord Chamberlain's company, in June 1594, when that company was reorganising to leave Henslowe for Burbage, while no mention of them appears in the *Diary* during the company's

[1] *Shakespeare's Sonnet Story*, p. 170. Bernard Quaritch, London 1922.

32 SHAKESPEARE AS SERVING MAN

two to three years' previous connection with Henslowe's stage. This naturally infers that they were in other hands during this period, and their preceding owners are plainly revealed by the facts that *The Taming of a Shrew* was entered upon the Stationers' Registers five weeks before it is mentioned in Henslowe's *Diary* as a Chamberlain property, and that it was published later in the year with a title-page reading : " As it was sundry times acted by the Right Honourable the Earle of Pembrook his servants." This clearly implies, that though the play is called *The Taming of a Shrew* in the *Diary,* Shakespeare, while still with Pembroke's company, was already working upon his first revision of this play for, and in anticipation of uniting with, the Lord Chamberlain's company, and that his revised *Taming of the Shrew* is indicated in the *Diary.* Were this otherwise, the name of the Lord Chamberlain's company, which presented a play under the old title on June 11, 1594, would undoubtedly have been mentioned with Pembroke's company on the title-page of the 1594 issue, as were those of Pembroke's, Derby's, and the Lord Chamberlain's companies mentioned with the Earl of Sussex's company on the title-page of *Titus Andronicus,* published in the same year, and under similar circumstances. This also gives added evidence, were it needed, that Shakespeare had no hand in the composition or revision of *Titus Andronicus* in the form in which it was published in 1594, which version is practically identical with that of the First Folio.[1] As *Titus Andronicus* was acted—as we learn on the title-page of the Quarto of 1594—by the Earl of

---

[1] The only difference being the addition of Scene iii. Act. ii. to the Folio. A critical analysis of the style of this Scene infers a common authorship with the remainder of the play.

SHAKESPEARE AS SERVING MAN 33

Pembroke's company, the Earl of Derby's company, and the Lord Chamberlain's company, *in the same form as it was presented as a new play by Sussex's company, on January 23, 1594*; and as Shakespeare had no connection then, nor afterwards, with either Sussex's company or Henslowe, literary history and textual criticism alike preclude Shakespeare's connection with the play, either as an author or reviser.

I find, as a rule, that old plays which continued upon the boards in revised forms were generally entered upon the Stationers' Registers or published at, or about, the same time that such revisions were made and staged. The revised forms of such plays were seldom published, but were at times used as the bases for other plays upon the same subjects. It will later be argued that this was so in the cases of the origins of Shakespeare's *Two Gentlemen of Verona, Richard III.*, and *Henry V.*

In Nashe's allusions to *The Taming of a Shrew*, when it was a Burbage property in 1589, its entry for publication as a Pembroke property in 1594, and its mention in Henslowe's *Diary* later as a Lord Chamberlain's property at the time that this company was returning to Burbage, we have conclusive evidence that this play and its revision were continuously Burbage properties from 1589 to 1594.[1] This illustrates the desirability of students basing their investigations upon the larger and more permanent theatrical interests, such as those of Burbage and Henslowe, rather than depending so largely upon temporary and mutable company titles, which so frequently covered members of two or more companies who still retained the

---

[1] Between 1589 and 1590 it was in the hands of the Admiral's company at the Theatre.

licences of their former patrons. Though the occasional use or mention of such tacit or dormant licences in the records has been a fruitful source of critical error, a correct understanding of their occasional, accidental, or intermittent mention will aid greatly in clarifying the present very nebulous and distorted histories of the dramatic companies.[1]

In the *Menaphon* Epistle Nashe also alludes to what he calls the "idiot art-masters" of the new and popular Lord Strange's company. He writes: "This affectation of actors and audience is all traceable to their idiot art-masters that intrude themselves . . . as the alchemists of eloquence, who—mounted on the stage of arrogance—*think to outbrave better pens with the swelling bombast of bragging blank verse,* indeed it may be the engrafted overflow of some kill-cow conceit that overcloyeth their imagination with more than drunken resolution . . . amongst this kind of men that repose eternity in the mouth of a player, I can but engross some deep read schoolmen or grammarians, who have no more learning in their skulls than will serve to take up a commodity *nor art in their*

---

[1] Between 1585 and 1589 all references to the Lord Admiral's company and the Lord Chamberlain's company refer to Burbage's men. In the same years all references to Oxford's men include old Worcester's men, and between 1589 and 1603 all references to Worcester's men include Oxford's men. Between 1591 and 1593 all references to Strange's men include Admiral's men, and *vice versa*. Between 1591 and 1594 all references to Pembroke's men refer to Burbage's company, with which Shakespeare was connected during these years. Between the beginning of 1589 and the end of 1590 Lord Strange's and the Admiral's men were separate companies, but both working under Burbage-Alleyn management, the Admiral's men performing at the Theatre and Strange's men at the Curtain, though the two companies combined for Court presentation. Between 1591 and 1594, all references to the Queen's company include Sussex's company, and *vice versa*.

brains than was nourished in a serving man's idleness, will take upon them to be the ironical censurors of all, when God and Poetry doth know they are the simplest of all." The first passage I have italicised above is paraphrased by Greene two and a half years later, when he alludes to Shakespeare in his *A Groat's-worth of Wit* : " For there's an upstart crow, beautified with our feathers, that with his tyger's heart wrapt in a player's hide, supposes he is as well able to bombast out a blank verse as the best of you."

The allusion above to the " idiot art-master," whose art was " nourished in a serving man's idleness," implies, in the use of the past tense, that the person indicated had recently completed his term of service. It is now fairly apparent that Greene's and Nashe's strictures, quoted above, are directed at Burbage's theatrical organisation. As it is not at all likely that Burbage had more than one serving man at this immediate period who had recently ended an initial term of service, and who was also of such critical ability and authority in the company as to incur the heated disapproval of these alleged scholars by challenging the dramatic excellence of, as well as by revision greatly bettering, their work—Shakespeare's revision of *Sir Thomas More* being clearly indicated at this immediate period—and as Nashe's collaborator, Greene, identifies Shakespeare, and also alludes to Marlowe as connected with him in practically identical phrases two and a half years later, the conclusion that Shakespeare also is indicated in 1589 appears now to be fully warranted. Shakespeare's term of service ending some time late in 1588 or early in 1589, and a two-year period being the conventional term of such service, clearly indicates the inception of his connection with Burbage some time between the beginning of 1586 and the middle of 1587.

In the same Epistle to Greene's *Menaphon* in which he indicates and abuses Shakespeare, Nashe also alludes to the leading actor of the Burbage-Alleyn organisation—who was Edward Alleyn—under the name of " Roscius," but in terms more complimentary than he uses in his allusions to Shakespeare. He refers to Roscius as the company's " Cæsar," " whose deserved reputation is of force to enrich a rabble of counterfeits " ; having previously mentioned George Peele as " the chief supporter of Pleasaunce now living, the Atlas of Poetry, and the *Primus verborum artifex.*"

In the same year that *Menaphon* with Nashe's Epistle was published Nashe also published his *Anatomy of Absurdity*, in which he repeats similar slurring allusions to the same persons as he indicated in his Epistle. He refers to " unlearned sots," " who contemn arts as unprofitable, contenting themselves with a little country grammar school knowledge." This evidently reflects Shakespeare's objection, as Burbage's reader, to the manner in which the scholars interlarded their plays with irrelevant and obscure classical allusions, which would, as a rule, be lost upon the great body of the London theatre-frequenting public. In revising such plays Shakespeare always eliminated, or greatly minimised, such classical allusions, and probably advocated the writing of plays better suited to the public understanding. Greene and Nashe consequently accuse him of " affecting his audience," and contemning " arts as unprofitable."

It may be seen in Shakespeare's early revisionary work that he eliminates such allusions, and in his early plays that he eschews their use. Had he not revised Marlowe's *Edward III.* and *Richard III.*, instead of finding from three to four simple classical allusions in each, we would probably find from thirty to forty, as we do in *The True Tragedie, The Contention,* and *Edward II.*, all three of which we may therefore assume remain in, or near, to the forms in which Marlowe left them. The utter absurdity of regarding the *Second* and *Third Parts of Henry VI.*, in the forms we now possess them, as Shakepeare's revisions of *The Contention* and *True Tragedie,* becomes apparent when the preponderance of classical allusions is noted in the former plays. *The Contention* and *True Tragedie* are certainly condensations and revisions of older plays upon these subjects, made for Pembroke's company between 1590 and 1593, the older plays being, like *The Troublesome Raigne of King John,* old Queen's company's properties, and approximating closely to the plays we now know as the *Second* and *Third Parts of Henry VI.*, when we eliminate from them certain passages by Marlowe, mostly incorporated from *The Contention* and *True Tragedie,* and some slight revisions made by Shakespeare after the death of Marlowe.

As Nashe referred to Peele as the " Atlas of Poetry," and alluded to Alleyn as " Roscius " in his Epistle to Greene's *Menaphon,* so in his *Anatomy of Absurdity* he writes of " stage players who, to win credit to their names, encounter with those on whose shoulders all arts do lean." This obviously alludes to an alleged encounter between Alleyn and Peele—the " Atlas of Poetry "—when compared with a similar allusion made by Greene in the following year, in his *Never Too Late,* and both allusions collated with a letter, quoted below, which is preserved among Alleyn papers at Dulwich College. This letter was written to

Alleyn by one of his admirers, referring to this alleged "encounter." It specifically mentions Peele. In his *Never Too Late*, published in 1590, Greene, continuing personal allusions to members of Burbage's organisation and writers for his stage, writes as follows : " In the days of Tully one Roscius grew to be of such exquisite perfection in his quality that he offered to contend with the orators of the time in gesture as they did in eloquence, boasting that he would express a passion in as many sundry actions as Tully could discourse it in a variety of phrases. . . . It chanced that Roscius and he met at dinner, both guests unto Archias, the poet, where the proud comedian dared to make comparison with Tully, which insolence made the learned orator grow into these terms, ' Why, Roscius, art thou proud with Æsop's crow, being pranked with the glory of others' feathers ? Of thyself thou canst say nothing, and if the cobbler hath taught thee to say *Ave Cæsar*, disdain not thy tutor because thou pratest in a King's chamber, what sentence thou utterest on the Stage, flows from the censure of our wits, and what sentence or conceit of the invention the people applaud for excellent, that comes from the secrets of our knowledge. I grant your action, though it be a kind of mechanical labour, yet well worthy of praise, but you worthless, if for so small a toy you wax proud."

The " *Ave Cæsar* " quoted above alludes to *Edward III.* and the " cobbler " to its author, Marlowe, his father having been a shoemaker. Greene's allusions inform us that Alleyn took the heroic part of the Black Prince in *Edward III.* The expression " *Ave Cæsar* " does not appear in any other known play of the period, and is used by Prince Edward in *Edward III.* The " Roscius " mentioned by Greene as challenging competition with Tully is the same person as the " stage player " mentioned in the preceding year by Nashe, in his *Anatomy of Absurdity*, as encountering " with those on whose shoulders all arts do lean " ; he had previously mentioned Peele in his *Menaphon* Epistle in the same year as the " Atlas of Poetry." It becomes obvious, then, that Peele, who is the " Atlas of Poetry," is also " those on whose shoulders all arts do lean," as well as Greene's " Tully," and that the following undated letter, written by W. P. to Edward Alleyn, pertains to this period, and refers to Alleyn's alleged encounter with, or challenge to, Peele, which, however, is shown by the letter to be distortion of the facts, which probably were that Alleyn's friend W. P., in order to provide after-dinner amusement for a coterie of friends, proposed a competition of some nature between Alleyn and Peele, he wagering on Alleyn, and Alleyn declining for fear of giving offence to Peele.

" Your answer the other night so well pleased the gentlemen, as I was satisfied therewith, though to the hazard of the wager ; and yet my meaning was not to prejudice Peele's credit ; neither would it, though it pleased you so to excuse it ; but being now grown further into question, the party affected to Bentley (scorning to win the wager by your denial) hath now given you liberty to make choice of any one play that either Bentley or Knell[1] played ; and lest this advantage agree not with your mind, he is contented both the play and the time shall be referred to the gentlemen here present. I see not how you can any

[1] As Bentley was a member of the Queen's company, it appears probable that Knell was also a Queen's man.

40 SHAKESPEARE AS SERVING MAN

way hurt your credit by this action; for if you excel them, you will then be famous, if equal them; you will win both the wager and the credit, if short of them; we must and will say Ned Alleyn still. Your friend to his power,

"W. P."

Alleyn's object in preserving this letter for so many years was probably as evidence of the misconstruction of the affair which had been given such widespread publicity by Greene and Nashe.

In view of the fact that the strictures of Greene and Nashe against dramatic writers, actors, and their "idiot art-masters" were all directed against Burbage's stages, Mr. Simpson's suggestion that Mullidor, the clown of the second part of Greene's *Never Too Late*—which was published in 1590—was intended as caricature of Shakespeare, takes on greatly added significance. Greene writes, describing Mullidor: "He is said to be a fellow that was of honest parents, but very poor; and his personage was as if he had been cast in Æsop's mould: his back like a lute, and his face like Thersites', his eyes broad and tawny, his hair harsh and curled like a horse-mane, his lips were of the largest size on folio. . . . The only good part that he had to grace his visage was his nose, and that was conqueror-like, as beaked as an eagle. . . . Into his great head (nature) put little wit, that he knew rather his sheep by the number, for he was never no good arithmetician, and yet he was a proper scholar, and well seen in ditties." A comparison of the face, head, and figure here suggested with the Chandos portrait of Shakespeare, or with the Drœshout engraving — making due allowance for the animus of this spiteful, ill-bred, and by no means truthful

SHAKESPEARE AS SERVING MAN 41

writer—reveals a striking resemblance between these pictures and the description. It is quite apparent that Greene is not sketching a fanciful picture of a purely imaginary creation, but is endeavouring to give a recognisable description of some one of the several persons whom he and Nashe have been indicating in their literary diatribes for the past three years. The simple, unlearned, and country-bred Mullidor matches only the provincial, grammar-school youth and late serving man out of the several persons whom these scholars have been attacking. This brings us to the end of the year 1590.

Some time in the eight days between the 16th and the 24th of November 1590 a portion of Lord Strange's company, as well as the Admiral's men, separated from Burbage to attach themselves to Henslowe. That the Admiral's men did not part amicably is revealed by legal records concerning Burbage's affairs in 1590, discovered by Professor C. W. Wallace, amongst which a deposition made by John Alleyn in 1592, but relating to 1590—in which he describes himself as an Admiral's man, and also as a servant to James Burbage—shows that upon 16th November this company was still playing under Burbage at the Theatre, but that by the 24th they had parted. John Alleyn, and several of his fellows of the Admiral's company, on the latter date sought a settlement with Burbage at the Theatre for money due them, which Burbage denied them, whereupon John Alleyn threatened to complain to the Lord Admiral, and was told by that "stubborn fellow" Burbage that he "did not care for any three lords of them all."[1]

[1] "The First London Theatre," *The University Studies of the University of Nebraska*, vol. xiii.

CHAPTER III

AN UNKNOWN COMPANY IDENTIFIED

IN a former publication I have shown that when Burbage lost the services of Leicester's company, in 1585, owing to the departure of their sharers for the Continent, he replaced them at the Theatre with the Lord Admiral's company, which had apparently been organised with this intention, as the first knowledge of their existence we possess is a record of their junction with the remnant of Leicester's company in the middle of June 1585, at Dover.[1] It appears evident that these men had accompanied their departing members to this port, and that they met the Admiral's men there by appointment. That such an arrangement had been made between Alleyn and Burbage is evidenced by the facts that the next mention of the Admiral's men in the records of the dramatic companies shows them performing with the Lord Chamberlain's men before the Court a few months later, and that they were thereafter continuously with Burbage until 1590, when, as I have shown above, they left him for Henslowe.

When Edward Alleyn left Worcester's company in

[1] *Shakespeare's Lost Years in London*, pp. 54–55. Bernard Quaritch, London, 1920.

A COMPANY IDENTIFIED 43

1585, though he was then a sharer in the company, its leader was Robert Browne. From the slight but significant glimpses we get of Browne's personality in the records, it seems probable that the troubles in which Worcester's company became involved in the preceding year or two—resulting in the loss of the old Earl of Worcester's patronage—were due to Browne's unruly spirit, or lack of managerial ability, and that under these circumstances he would find it difficult to secure a new patron. It is unlikely that all of the men previously with Worcester's and Sheffield's companies would be absorbed by Alleyn into the Admiral's company, and still less likely that Browne, the leader of Worcester's men, would join the then very youthful Alleyn in a subordinate capacity; yet, less than four years later—at the time Lord Strange's company was organising, in 1589—we find that some unnamed company, in which Edward Alleyn, John Alleyn, Robert Browne, and Richard Jones were joint sharers, was liquidating its assets, Edward and John Alleyn absorbing the shares of Browne and Jones. That this unnamed company was not a temporarily quiescent Worcester's company is apparent from the fact that John Alleyn, who was never connected with Worcester's company, was one of its four sharers. This unknown company, then, would date from 1585, if it was a new company.

There is no record of any new London company in this year, with the exception of the Admiral's company. We are faced now by two hypotheses, either of which may appear to account for this unknown company: one, that in 1585, Edward Alleyn, John Alleyn, Richard Jones, and Robert Browne united in forming the Lord Admiral's company, and that Edward Alleyn—whom Nashe alludes to when

44   A COMPANY IDENTIFIED

Strange's company was formed in 1589, as the company's "Cæsar"—had with his brother bought out Browne's and Jones's interests in the Admiral's company, in order to secure a controlling interest in the new Lord Strange's company. We know that both Browne and Jones joined the resuscitated Worcester's company at this time, and I have shown that John Alleyn continued as an Admiral's man until the end of 1590.

This hypothesis, while apparently plausible, is not the true solution of the question. It appears certain that when Edward Alleyn joined Burbage in 1585, and combined selected men from Sheffield's and Worcester's companies to form the Lord Admiral's company, a number of men from both companies were left patronless, and that these men were joined with another London company possessing assured patronage and title, and worked under this patronage and title until 1589, when Robert Browne and Richard Jones and their fellows re-established Worcester's company; Edward Alleyn in the intervening years, while managing the Admiral's men, retaining with his brother a half-interest in the unknown company, until 1589, when he and his brother bought Browne's and Jones's shares. While this theory appears less obvious than the former, it is the true solution of the enigma.

Before inquiring into the identity of the unknown company, I will draw the student's attention to a curious but significant arrangement that was made at this immediate period between Henry Laneham, the owner and manager of the Curtain, and James Burbage of the Theatre, which implies that somewhat similar relations were established at the same time between the shareholders of the two companies playing at the Theatre and the Curtain,

A COMPANY IDENTIFIED 45

and, in fact, that it was owing to such relations first established between the companies that the theatre-owners were led to form similar co-operative plans.

In a Court deposition made by Henry Laneham, the owner of the Curtain, in a suit concerning Burbage in 1592, we learn that an arrangement was made between him and Burbage in 1585, by which the Curtain was to be used as an easer to the Theatre, *i.e.* for overflow business, and that in consideration of this Laneham and Burbage agreed to divide equally the profits of the performances in both houses.[1]

As this arrangement between the theatre-owners was evidently based upon identity of financial interest between the leaders or sharers of the two companies using the two theatres, the seven-year term of the contract implies an expectation of permanency on the parts of Burbage and Laneham in the use of their houses by these companies. We may then safely assume that the company using the Curtain was, like the company using the Theatre—the Admiral's—a permanent and adult London company. Such companies not being numerous, a process of elimination may aid us in its identification.

Neither the Children of St. Paul's nor the Children of the Chapel appear to have operated continuously between

[1] " About seven years now shalbe this next winter, they, the said Burbage and Braynes, having the profits of playes made at the Theatre, and this deponent having the profits of playes made at the Curtain, as an esor [easer] to their playhouse, did of their own motion move the deponent, that he would agree that the profit of the said two playhouses might for seven years space be in dyvydent between them, whereunto this deponent, upon reasonable conditions and bonds, agreed and consented and so continueth to this day. February 1592." " The First London Theatre," *The University Studies of the University of Nebraska*, vol. xiii. pp. 148–50.

1582 and 1588,[1] as there is no mention of either company in Court or London records during these years; these companies may therefore be eliminated. The only permanent and adult London companies during this period were the Queen's, the Admiral's, Leicester's, and Oxford's companies. The bitter rivalry that developed between Greene—who wrote for the Queen's company during this period—and the writers and actors for Burbage, quite precludes co-operative relations with the Queen's company. Leicester's company—except for a remnant which spent most of this period in the provinces—was absent from England from 1585 to 1587. We are then left with Oxford's company. Surprising as it may appear, the facts lead to the conclusion that when Alleyn joined Burbage in 1585, taking with him men from Worcester's and Sheffield's companies, to form the Admiral's company, he, with his brother John Alleyn, Robert Browne, and Richard Jones, combined the remainder, or part of the remainder, of the two companies with Oxford's company; this amalgamation working under Oxford's title in summer at the Curtain, and probably at the Boar's Head in winter, until 1589, in which year Oxford's company disappears from all theatrical records, not appearing again for thirteen years, and then appearing united and performing with Worcester's men at the Curtain and the Boar's Head.

In January 1589 Edward and John Alleyn, through the purchase of Browne's and Jones's shares in Oxford's company, came into possession of the properties of this amal-

[1] On April 26, 1585, Thomas Gyles, the Master of Paul's boys, was granted a writ to "take up . . . apte and meete children" for the "Church of St. Paul's." The first record of Gyles's success in forming this company is its appearance before the Court in 1588. In 1589 an allusion in Lyly's *Pap with a Hatchet* shows it as performing at St. Paul's.

A COMPANY IDENTIFIED 47

gamation, which included old plays written by Anthony Munday as early as 1579, and plays written by Munday and Chapman in collaboration, as early as about 1581 to 1582, and as late as from 1586 to 1587, and possibly as late as 1589.

When Worcester's company was re-established in 1589, while Oxford's title disappears from the records for many years, later records show that Worcester's men were joined, in 1589, by Oxford's men, who, while still retaining the licence of the Earl of Oxford, submerged their identity and played thenceforth as Worcester's men at the Boar's Head. Though they played for several months, in 1602 and 1603, under Henslowe at the Rose, a letter from the Lords of the Council to the Lord Mayor, in 1602, shows that they still used the Boar's Head as winter quarters, and that Oxford's and Worcester's men were still combined in the company. This letter requests the Lord Mayor to permit the servants of the Earls of Oxford and Worcester to play at that house. Late in 1603 these titles disappear and the company becomes Queen Anne's company. An undated draft of their patent as Queen Anne's men, which appears in Collier's *Annals* [1] (1879, i. p. 336), again records the fact that Worcester's men included men from Oxford's company, and mentions the Curtain and the Boar's Head as "their usual playing places." The validity of this draft, which has been questioned, appears to be demonstrated by the foregoing history, of which Collier, as well as all other past critics, have been unaware.

It is evident that the new Worcester's company did not

---

[1] Whether or not Collier's draft is an authentic paper, the information it gives is verified by the State Papers. *Calendar of State Papers* (Domestic Series), vol. 1623-5, Addenda 530.

play at the Curtain between 1589 and 1592, during which years Laneham's reciprocal contract with Burbage was still in force. A portion of Worcester's company, under Robert Browne, played on the Continent in 1590, and again in 1592, while those who remained in England appear, from the provincial records, to have played principally in the provinces until about 1596 or 1597, at which time they probably renewed their connection with the Curtain. The expression used in the draft of their patent, "their usual playing places," implies a previous connection of some duration with these houses. The Curtain was used by Strange's company, and the Theatre by the Admiral's men, between the beginning of 1589 and the end of 1590, for summer and autumn performances; and the Crosse-Keys in Grace Church Street by Strange's company in the winter. Where the Admiral's company played during these two years in the City in winter-time is at present unknown. They probably, however, like Strange's company, had an inn for winter performances, though they may have united for winter performances, as they undoubtedly did for Court performances during this period.

The Elizabethan age appears to have been one of virile youth and early maturity. Sir Philip Sidney, of whom his friend, Foulke Greville, writes, "Though I lived with him and knew him from a child, yet I never knew him other than a man," was a figure of European note by his twenty-third year, and was with the immortals at thirty-two. Essex distinguished himself at Zutphen at nineteen, commanded an English army in France at twenty-five, and at thirty led the brilliantly successful expedition to Cadiz; while Marlowe, though done to death at twenty-nine, had, in six years of irregular and intermittent work, left an imperishable name in literary history. Edward Alleyn, in his humbler sphere as an actor and actor-manager, presents a still more precocious figure : at the age of sixteen we find him a leading sharer in the Earl of Worcester's company ; and at eighteen, not only the leader of the Admiral's company, but also the controlling factor in another company, which, with the Admiral's men, under his guidance, had now appropriated to their use the largest and most important two theatres in London. At twenty-three Nashe alludes to him as the " Cæsar " of what was then the most progressive and prosperous theatrical organisation in England, and three years later writes of him, " not Roscius nor Esope, those two tragedians admired before Christ was borne, could ever perform more in action than famous Ned Alleyn."

Though Alleyn was undoubtedly a great if somewhat robustious actor, he appears also to have been a business man of more than ordinary ability. In fact, in his case the man of affairs dominated the artist, as in Shakespeare's the artist overshadowed the business man ; yet to Shakespeare's four years' business association with Alleyn, between 1586–7 and 1590, and to his observation of Alleyn's managerial and financial methods, was probably in no small measure due the technical knowledge that enabled him to aid Burbage's organisation in recovering from the depths into which they were cast in 1590 by the loss of Strange's company ; and within a year or two to compete with Alleyn and Henslowe on even terms for Court and public favour ; and later still, to establish an unquestionable pre-eminence, the prestige of which maintained them and their successors in the lead for over forty years.

One of Alleyn's theatrical policies, copied and very

much bettered by Shakespeare in his inceptive, dramatic days, was to capitalise the extant or established knowledge and interest of the theatre-going public, by purchasing the reversion of popular but stage-worn plays, and rewriting or revising them for renewed presentations. As Shakespeare had not, to our present knowledge, written any of his known plays as early as 1588–90, the strictures of the scholars against him in these years was no doubt directed at his revisionary work in such plays, originally written by them or their fellows, which were owned or purchased by the Burbage-Alleyn interests. The heat that these strictures display was evidently due to the promise shown by this late serving man in these revisions. Very definite evidence will later be adduced, showing that the earliest knowledge we possess of Shakespeare as a writer reveals him as functioning in this capacity late in 1589, or early in 1590, and certainly before Burbage and Alleyn separated at the end of the latter year.

Though the first mention of Lord Strange's men in any of the records is upon November 5, 1589, the fact that Edward and John Alleyn bought Oxford's company's properties in January of this year, as well as the allusions of Greene and Nashe to the formation of a new and powerful company in the early months of the year, indicate its inception some time in the first quarter of 1589.

Later in the summer of this year plays reflecting some phases of the Martin Marprelate controversy were presented by the Children of Paul's, and by either the Admiral's or Strange's men at the Theatre in Shoreditch, infringing the law against the presentation of matters of Church or State upon the stage. This resulted in the summons of Strange's and the Admiral's men before the Lord Mayor

A COMPANY IDENTIFIED

when they returned to their winter quarters in the City, upon November 5, when they were ordered to discontinue playing until they received further permission to do so. Though the Admiral's men dutifully obeyed the Mayor's order, Strange's men, as the Mayor reported to Lord Burghley, " in very contemptuous manner departing from me, went to the Crosse-Keys and played that afternoon, to the great offense of the better sort." For this behaviour two of Strange's men were committed to " one of the compters." From the very divergent attitudes of the two companies at this time, we may judge that whatever interest " Cæsar " Alleyn may now have acquired in Strange's company, that the " stubborn fellow," James Burbage, was still responsibly interested in its management. It is not improbable that Alleyn's submission to, and Burbage's defiance of, the Mayor's, and, in fact, of Burghley's orders at this time, led directly or indirectly to Burbage's loss of Strange's company a year later, and to Alleyn's triumph for the following two to three years as the leader of the combined Strange's and Admiral's men, at this time the most favoured Court company in London.

This incident was followed a week later (November 12) by an order from the Privy Council to the Archbishop of Canterbury, the Lord Mayor, and the Master of the Revels, commanding that all plays be licensed by three persons appointed by them, and that this censorship be instructed to command all players and play-makers to appear straightway before them, bringing with them all the plays they were presenting, or proposed to present, in order that anything in them of an immoral or seditious nature might be reformed.

52 A COMPANY IDENTIFIED

Though this was a general order applying to all the London companies, it was directed more particularly at those that had been involved in the Martin Marprelate affair; and, as I have shown, one of the Burbage-Alleyn companies was an offender.

Bearing in mind the recent formation of Strange's company, by the union of leading actors from a number of other companies, some of them no doubt bringing with them, as properties, plays used by their former companies, and also the recent purchase by the Alleyns of all of Oxford's properties, in addition to their own old and current plays, it appears unlikely that any other London theatrical interests would provide Mr. Tilney and his fellow-censors with as much material to be examined at this time. It is interesting to find that of all the MS. plays examined by the censors upon this occasion, the only one surviving that bears on its face, and in its literary and stage history, assured evidence of the fact, is a MS. from the Burbage-Alleyn properties. It is still more interesting to know that this MS. contains three pages of Shakespeare's revisionary work, written in his own autograph, and evidently shortly after Tilney had censored the play, the revision being plainly intended to comply with his instructions, and also the only one of the several revisionary hands in the play that exhibits any attempt to comply with Tilney's orders. In view of Shakespeare's connection with the Burbage interests, and with no others from the beginning to the end of his London career, as well as of new and important light to be cast upon the authorship and history of *Sir Thomas More*, it will become evident that all theories dating Shakespeare's work in the *More* MS. later than November 1590 are erroneous.

A COMPANY IDENTIFIED

Before attempting to elucidate the history and authorship of this play and its bearing upon Shakespeare's history, I will, in the following chapter, continue a consideration of his theatrical affiliations, from the end of 1590 until the end of 1594, when he appears as a sharer in the newly reorganised Lord Chamberlain's company.

CHAPTER IV

SHAKESPEARE AND PEMBROKE'S COMPANY

AT about the time that Strange's and the Admiral's men left Burbage for Henslowe a drastic change took place in the comparative standing, personnel of its membership, and theatrical habitat of the hitherto dominant Queen's company. This company was established, under official direction, in 1583, with the professed object of providing an efficient company for Court performances. Between this date and 1591, when it was supplanted as the most favoured Court company by Strange's company, being a company of such unusual importance and official favour, it must have possessed strong financial and theatrical backing, and have had permanent summer and winter quarters in the Liberties and the City, as was the case with Oxford's company and the Admiral's company. Yet, at the present time, nothing is definitely known regarding the theatrical backer of the Queen's company nor of its playing places during these years. The very nebulous theory that Burbage managed or provided playing places for the Queen's company between 1583 and 1591 is now seen to be quite baseless. Who then was the Queen's company's financial angel and housekeeper during these years? All the evidence we possess, which

PEMBROKE'S COMPANY

is entirely inferential, points directly to Henslowe in this capacity, from at least 1585 to 1591, and probably from the company's inception in 1583. Whatever city headquarters in the winter-time the Queen's company may have had from 1583 to 1585, it appears probable that they played at the Curtain in the summer during these two years. If they did, their connection with that theatre ceased in 1585, when it was taken over by the Worcester-Oxford amalgamation. My reason for tentatively placing the Queen's company at the Curtain previous to 1585 is that it is one of the companies mentioned as playing at either the Theatre or the Curtain in Fleetwood's letter to Burghley of June 1584, quoted above. As Leicester's company when in London monopolised the summer use of the Theatre as late as 1585, it is evident that the Queen's company was not permanently established there in 1584. Its mention in Fleetwood's letter would indicate that it had occupied the Curtain on that date. John Laneham, who was formerly with Burbage and Leicester's men, and after 1583 a member, and probably the leader, of the Queen's company, may have been related to Henry Laneham, the owner and manager of the Curtain, and, through such a possible kinship, have also had theatrical relations between 1583 and 1585 with Henry Laneham's house, the Curtain.

The probability that the Queen's company played in summer-time at the Curtain from the time of its formation, late in 1582, until 1584-5, is further enhanced by the significant fact, hitherto unnoticed in this connection, that Henry Laneham is mentioned on November 28, 1583,[1] in a warrant signed by the Vice-Chamberlain, Sir Christopher Hatton,

[1] Accounts of the Wardens of the Tower.

as a "Yeoman of her Majesties Chamber." As Henslowe received a similar appointment in 1592, after he became housekeeper for Strange's men, it appears probable that Laneham also owed his office to his relations with the new, and officially fostered, Queen's company in 1583. Stowe reports that all of the new Queen's men in 1583 " were allowed wages and liveries as Grooms of the Chamber."

While we have no definite knowledge of Henslowe's connection with players or theatrical affairs earlier than 1587, when we find him contracting to sell to John Cholmley a half-interest in the profits of an unnamed theatre that he then had already started to build on the same property upon which we later find the Rose Theatre standing, we are assured by Henslowe's prudent and non-speculative nature, as well as by his careful financial and business methods, of the extreme unlikelihood that he would invest the large sum of money involved in this venture—over eight hundred pounds—in a business of which he had no previous personal experience. It is equally unlikely that John Cholmley or any other sane business man would pay, or consider paying, the large amount asked for the half-interest in the profits of a theatre—over eight hundred pounds—the investment value of which half-interest was purely hypothetical, or the management or conduct of which theatre was entirely in hope.

It is very evident, then, that when Henslowe built the Rose Theatre in 1587, he knew from past theatrical experience exactly what he was doing and why he was doing it; and that he was not then starting a new venture, but further developing a business in which he had for some years been already engaged. As a lease of the property upon which he built the Rose Theatre, in

PEMBROKE'S COMPANY

1587, was purchased by him early in 1585, it is not improbable that even at that time it was occupied by structures affording, or easily convertible for, theatrical accommodations. In the light of Henry Laneham's contract made with Burbage at this time, it also appears extremely probable that Henslowe purchased the lease of the Rose property in 1585, with the specific intention of providing a summer playing place for the Queen's company, which had been ousted by Burbage from the Curtain. The animus expressed by the Queen's company's poet, Robert Greene, in his *Perimedes*, in 1585, against the aged and grasping actor-manager, Valdrako, evidently reflected his resentment against Burbage's monopolistic arrangement with Laneham at this time.

It is impossible to account for the financing and housing of the Queen's company from 1585 to 1591 by any hypothesis other than a connection of this nature with Henslowe; did any other exist we should surely possess some chance record, hint, or suggestion regarding it; but all such available indications, and they are many and cogent, point clearly to Henslowe. Let us now consider these indications.

Though records of Henslowe's dealing with Lord Strange's company do not appear in his fortuitously preserved *Diary* until February 1592, it is now apparent that a connection was established between them at, or about, the time they left Burbage, in November 1590.

When Henslowe's records first begin, we find among the plays presented by Strange's company a number that shortly before had belonged to the Queen's company. At this time we also find several Queen's men among Strange's players. These facts have led former critics to the erroneous conclusion that a previous and prolonged connection had existed between Burbage and the Queen's company, as well as between Alleyn and the Queen's company, though how, when, and where have not been clear.

An examination of the membership and list of plays owned by the Earl of Pembroke's company at the same period reveals exactly the same conditions as are shown in the case of Strange's company and its plays, *i.e.* recent Queen's men in its membership, and recent Queen's plays in its possession. This naturally leads to the conclusion that the old Queen's company was dismembered at the same time that Strange's and the Admiral's men united under Alleyn and Henslowe, and that Pembroke's company was formed by Burbage and Shakespeare. It also infers that the Queen's plays, now in possession of these two companies, were either brought to them as properties by Queen's men who now joined them, or were sold to them or to the men joining them, by Henslowe, who had retained them for debts owed him by the old Queen's company.

As I find that all of the traceable plays that came into the hands of Pembroke's and Strange's men at the general reorganisation of companies, now indicated at the beginning of 1591, other than the plays inherited from the Burbage-Alleyn stock preceding that date, were old Queen's plays, there can now be little doubt that the originals of the *Three Parts of Henry VI.* came also from the Queen's company's stock; and as Robert Greene had a principal hand in nearly all of the Queen's plays now inherited by these companies, there can be little doubt that he also had a large share in the originals of the *Henry VI.* trio. In this light it becomes evident that neither Peele, Marlowe, nor Shakespeare had anything whatever to do with these three plays until after the beginning of 1591, when the

PEMBROKE'S COMPANY

First Part became a Strange's property, and the *Second* and *Third Parts* Pembroke's properties. It also becomes clear that all theories regarding collaboration between these poets, or between any of them and Greene, in these plays are entirely baseless.

The large number of Greene's plays taken over at this time by Pembroke's and Strange's men from the Queen's company implies a prolonged previous connection by Greene with that company, and also the strong probability that during these years he occupied the same relations with the Queen's company as company poet, that Kyd, Marlowe, and Shakespeare successively occupied with Burbage, and that Peele occupied with Alleyn from 1589 to about 1597 or 1598.

In 1592 we find the *First Part of Henry VI.* presented upon Henslowe's boards by Strange's company, after it had been revised by Peele, when both Peele's revision and Alleyn's probable presentation in the heroic part of Talbot are flatteringly commended by Nashe. At exactly the same period we find the *Third Part of Henry VI.*, as well as the *Second Part*, in the hands of Pembroke's company, which now presents the *Third Part* upon the boards, when Shakespeare, in the character of the Duke of York, is indicated and attacked by Greene in his *A Groat's-worth of Wit*, published several months later in the same year.

If these facts be combined with internal evidence in the stage directions of these plays, and with the definite knowledge we possess of the personnel of the membership of these two companies at this period, it becomes evident that Gabriel Spencer and Humphrey Jeffes—both members of Pembroke's company at this time—were recently Queen's men, and that John Sinclair and John

Holland, who were with Strange's company at this time, were also recently with the Queen's company. These facts also confirm the theory hitherto advanced by the present scribe that *The Contention* and *The True Tragedie* are condensations, for provincial presentations, of older plays, and that the plays we now know as the *Second* and *Third Parts* of *Henry VI.* do not necessarily present the final forms given to these plays by Shakespeare, but probably the forms given by the compilers of the Folio in 1623, who, incorporating matter by both Shakespeare and Marlowe—mostly taken from *The Contention* and *True Tragedie*—into the old plays, also retained in them some matter deleted by Marlowe between 1591 and 1593. The elimination of Marlowe's and Shakespeare's additions and overwriting, were it possible, would then leave these plays in, or near, to the forms in which they were originally received from the old Queen's company.

The stage directions of the *Third Part of Henry VI.* contain the names of Gabriel, Sinklo, and Humphrey, which Fleay identified as Gabriel Spencer, Humphrey Jeffes, and John Sinkler. The first two named were members of Pembroke's company from 1591 to 1594 and later, while Sinkler was with Strange's company from 1591 to 1594; though the play in which all three appear was a property of, and presented in a revised form by, Pembroke's company during these years. It is obvious then that the stage directions antedate the reorganisation of these companies in 1591, and pertain to presentations by the company formerly owning the play, which was clearly the Queen's company. So also in the *Second Part of Henry VI.*, which was condensed into *The Contention* for Pembroke's company between 1591 and 1593, the name of John Holland

PEMBROKE'S COMPANY

appears. As Holland was a member of Strange's company in these years, the stage directions must here also indicate the original state and ownership of the play. It now becomes apparent that Holland, Spencer, Jeffes, and Sinkler were Queen's men before 1591. These plays came into the hands of Strange's and Pembroke's companies late in 1590, or early in 1591, at the same time that the Admiral's and Strange's men were combined into one company under Alleyn and Henslowe, and that Pembroke's company was formed by Burbage and Shakespeare.

It will later be shown that in the form in which they came into the hands of Strange's and Pembroke's men, in 1591, the *Three Parts of Henry VI.* were undoubtedly written by Robert Greene and Thomas Lodge in collaboration. The title-page of *The Looking Glass for London* (1594) gives specific evidence that Lodge collaborated with Green in dramatic work at this period. Greene's, however, is still the principal hand in the *Second* and *Third Parts* of these plays, and Lodge's in the *First Part*, though both hands are much overwritten in the *First Part*, which was revised by Peele in 1592, and in a slight measure by Shakespeare late in 1594. Both hands are also overwritten by Marlowe in the *Second* and *Third Parts*, and some small additions made by both Marlowe and Shakespeare. These additions are largely borrowed from *The Contention* and *The True Tragedie*, though some of them which display Shakespeare's purpose of linking consecutively the whole series connected with the Wars of the Roses, by making this his linking theme, were evidently written by Shakespeare after the middle of 1594, when all three plays had become Chamberlain's properties. There is no trace of Marlowe's hand in the *First Part of Henry VI.*, which was in Alleyn's and

Henslowe's possession from 1591 until after Marlowe's death. Marlowe had no connection as a writer with Alleyn and Henslowe. When, about a year after Marlowe's death, the *First Part of Henry VI.* became a Burbage property for the first time, in about the middle of 1594, Shakespeare revised it slightly by re-writing, or incorporating, the Temple Garden scene, and a few linking passages.

When these three plays came from the Queen's to Strange's and Pembroke's companies in 1591, Greene was, and had for several years been, the chief writer for the Queen's company. In his *Strange News from Purgatory*, published in 1592, Nashe writes: " Greene being chief agent for the company for he writ more than four others, etc." That this referred to the Queen's company is apparent in the fact that no evidence exists to show that Greene ever wrote a play for any other company except Sussex's and the new Queen's company, while the voluminous nature of his known and traceable work for the old Queen's company infers a prolonged connection with them, and, in view of Nashe's phrase "chief agent," evidently in the capacity of company poet.

How long before 1591 Greene's connection with the old Queen's company began is at present unknown ; but new facts I have recently found infer that it began with the inception of this company in 1583. I find that the archaic play of *Sir Clyamon and Sir Clamydes*—at present ascribed to Peele—was in fact written by Greene, and that it is an early, if indeed not the earliest, play written by him for the Queen's company. It was evidently written at about the same period that Peele produced *The Arraignment of Paris* for the Children of the Chapel, and that Chapman and Munday produced *Fidele and Fortunio* for Oxford's

PEMBROKE'S COMPANY

company, all three plays displaying similar metrically archaic characteristics. As both Peele's and Chapman's plays, written largely in fourteeners, were published in 1584, their production is indicated about a year or two earlier. An analytical comparison of the diction, as well as of the relative poetical merits, of *Sir Clyamon and Sir Clamydes* and Peele's *Arraignment of Paris*, clearly demonstrates the fallacy of the ascription of the former play to Peele, and as plainly reveals in it Greene's apprentice dramatic hand.

I have recently found also that Greene, after the end of 1590, continued to write for the new Queen's company and its affiliated company—the Earl of Sussex's men—until shortly before his death in 1592; and that some time between the beginning of 1591 and the middle of 1592 he produced for Sussex's men, in collaboraton with Thomas Nashe, *The Old Wives' Tale*, another play at present ascribed to Peele, and upon equally uncritical grounds. This play obviously pertains to this period and to the quarrel of Lyly, Greene, and Nashe with Gabriel Harvey, who is here presented in the character of Huanebungo. The verse lines are nearly all Greene's, and a number of them are to be found repeated in his acknowledged work. It was evidently the presentation of this play that aroused Harvey's ire and led to the attack upon the anti-Martinist poets, including Lyly, Greene, and Nashe, in Harvey's *The Lamb of God* — mentioned by Nashe in his *Strange News from Purgatory* in 1592 — where Harvey refers to these poets as "piperly makeplays and make-bates." This in turn was answered by Greene in 1592 in his *Quip for an Upstart Courtier*. Shortly after the presentation of *The Old Wives' Tale*, Greene, in his *A Groat's-worth of Wit*, refers to Nashe and his share in this satirical anti-Harvey play. "With thee I join young Juvenal, that biting satirist, that lastly with me together writ a comedy"; the word "lastly" has been misunderstood by certain critics, who, in quoting this passage, usually change it to "lately." As the greater portion of Greene's *A Groat's-worth of Wit* was evidently a death-bed effort, Greene refers to his *last* dramatic collaborative work with Nashe. The fact that no comedy by Greene and Nashe has hitherto been known to exist led the brilliant and conscientious Fleay to assume that Greene's known dramatic collaborator, Lodge, is here indicated. As Lodge was as old, or older, than Greene, it is evident that the latter would not refer to him as "young Juvenal." When *The Old Wives' Tale* was written, Lodge was on the ocean, and well on his way to the South Seas. No evidence of any kind exists to show that either Lodge or Peele were in any way involved in the Greene-Harvey-Nashe quarrel.

The attribution of *The Old Wives' Tale* to Peele has been due altogether to the words "written by G. P." on the title-page of the Quarto, published in 1595. These words may be accounted for in the same way as the words "by W. S." printed by Creede on the title-page of *Locrine*, issued also in this year. Shakespeare, from 1591 until about the middle of 1594, was the "chief agent"—to use Nashe's phrase regarding Greene's connection with the Queen's company—for Pembroke's company, and, later in the year, for the Lord Chamberlain's company; as was Peele for the Lord Admiral's company. These publishers, to enhance the sale of their wares, evidently went as far as they dared, in using Peele's and Shakespeare's initials instead of their names. It will later appear, however, not improbable that in this instance Creede was authorised by Shakespeare to use the announcement he makes and his initials on this page.

The Old Wives' Tale became an Admiral's property at the time of the new organisation of companies in the middle of 1594, when some men and properties of its former possessors, the Queen's-Sussex's men, were absorbed by the Admiral's, Chamberlain's, and Queen's men. A comparison of the simple songs it contains with Nashe's lyrics in *Summer's Last Will* reveals his hand. That the remainder of the play is by Greene and Nashe will be demonstrated in a later chapter.

The elimination of Peele as the author of these two plays removes the only reason that has hitherto existed for his supposed connection with the Queen's company, and with Greene as a collaborator in plays for that company. Marlowe's continuous and exclusive connection with the Burbage interests, from 1587 until his death in 1593, eliminates him also as a pre-Shakespearean collaborator with Greene in the *Henry VI.* plays.

While Henslowe's *Diary* and other sources show a number of other old Queen's plays inherited by Strange's company in 1591, and also in 1594, nearly all of which were originally written by Greene and his collaborators before 1591, such as *Friar Bacon* (Greene's *Friar Bacon and Friar Bungay*), *Orlando Furioso, A Looking Glass for London*, and others, a larger proportion of their list was made up of old Burbage-Alleyn properties, written originally in the following chronological order, by Kyd, in or before 1586; by Marlowe, in or before 1590; by Peele, in 1589 to 1590; some of these being now revised by Peele and others—as in the case of the *First Part of*

Henry VI., and presented as " ne " (new) on Henslowe's stage.

In this number the following plays are all evidently revisions of old Kyd plays, produced before 1587, when he was supplanted by Marlowe as Burbage and Alleyn's stage poet: *Doneoracio* (*Don Horatio*, the same as *The Spanish Comedie*), *Jeronymo* (*The Spanish Tragedie*), *The Spanish Comedie* (the same as *Doneoracio*, a companion piece to Kyd's *Spanish Tragedie*, now extant in a much altered form as the *First Part of Jeronymo*), *Titus and Vespasian* (probably one of Henslowe's characteristic misnomers, and intended for *Titus Vespasian*. This is evidently Peele's first re-writing of the old *Titus Andronicus*, referred to by Jonson as having been produced in about 1585), *Titus Andronicus* (Peele's second re-writing and partial restoration of the old *Andronicus*, for Sussex's company, playing at this time under Henslowe and Alleyn).

The following are evidently all old Marlowe plays, written for the Burbage-Alleyn interests in or before 1590: *The Jew of Malta* (revised by Peele); *The Tragedy of the Guyes* (Marlowe's *Massacre at Paris*, revised by Peele or others); *Doctor Ffostes* (Marlowe's *Doctor Faustus*), *Tamberlen* (Marlowe's *Tamburlaine*).

We have also in this list at least two, and probably three, old plays written by Peele for the Admiral's company in, or before, 1590, and while they were still with Burbage, at which time Peele became company poet for the Admiral's company, Marlowe continuing with Burbage and Strange's men. Peele evidently continued with Alleyn in this capacity until his death, some time before September 1598. It is not improbable that he was succeeded for a short time in this capacity by John Marston, who worked

PEMBROKE'S COMPANY

in collaboration with Chapman at this time for Henslowe's stages. A note in Henslowe's *Diary*, under date of September 28, 1599, of a loan to " Mr. Maxton, the new poet," may refer to Marston as the company poet. A later reference by Henslowe to " Anthony, the poet," probably refers to Munday in the same manner, when he had succeeded to this position. It is improbable that the very literal Henslowe was using this word in a generic sense, while the close relations of Marston and Munday with other writers for Henslowe and Alleyn at these periods imply such a connection. The plays produced by Peele for the Admiral's company while they were still with Burbage are : *Longshankes* (Peele's *Edward I.*, now revised), *Muly Molloco* (Peele's *The Battle of the Alcazar*). It is also probable that *Mahomet*, mentioned in the *Diary*, is Peele's lost play, *The Turkish Mahomet and Hiren the Fair Greek*.

Of the Oxford properties purchased by the Alleyns in 1589—while there were probably others in Alleyn and Henslowe's hands—we can now definitely identify only two—*The Wise Man of Westchester* (a revision of *John-a-Kent and John-a-Cumber*) and *Sir Thomas More*, upon which —following Shakespeare's first revision in 1589 or 1590, while it was still a Burbage-Alleyn property—at least one, and possibly two, revisions were made ; one in 1595, and one shortly later in 1598-9. The year 1593 has been suggested for the production of *Sir Thomas More*[1] as a reflection of the alleged libels against the foreigners at that date. A correct historical understanding of social,

[1] *Shakespeare's Hand in the Play of Sir Thomas More*, by Alfred W. Pollard, W. W. Gregg, E. Maunde Thompson, J. Dover Wilson, and R. W. Chambers. Cambridge University Press, 1923.

theatrical, and especially of political conditions in London at this time will show the error of this assumption.

It is not improbable that, when Alleyn employed Peele as a writer for the Admiral's company in 1589, that he first considered using Greene, and entered into negotiations with him, which proved abortive owing to the resentment into which Greene had now worked himself against the Burbage-Alleyn players, coupled with his own admitted unreliability in his business dealings with them. It is to this year (1589) that his alleged double-dealing with the Queen's company and the Lord Admiral's company, regarding the sale of *Orlando Furioso* to each of them in turn, refers. If this transaction ever took place—and Greene appears not only to admit that it did, but even to boast of it in something of the same quizzically arrogant spirit as Falstaff's—

". . . What, ye knaves,
Young men must live . . ."

—it is apparent that he was then losing whatever moral balance he may have possessed, and going fast to the dogs.

It has long been recognised that many of Greene's pamphlets are fancifully autobiographical. In *A Groat's-worth of Wit* the experiences of Roberto so closely match facts in Greene's life that it is obvious the reflection is intentional. Roberto marries, deserts his wife, and takes up with a courtesan, who deserts him when his money is gone. At this stage, while sitting under a hedge bemoaning his fate, he is accosted by a player who offers to engage him in writing plays. This player, like Nashe's "Roscius" of three years before, is a large owner of theatrical property, and also famous for acting *Delphrygus* and *The King of the Fairies*. He informs Roberto that his share in playing

apparel " will not be sold for two hundred pounds."
"'But how mean you to use me?' says Roberto. 'Why, sir, in making plays,' said the other, 'for which you shall be well paid if you will take the pains.' Roberto, perceiving no remedy, thought it best to respect his present necessity, and to try his wit went with him willingly, who lodged him at the town's end in a house of retail. . . . But Roberto now famoused for an arch-playmaking poet, his purse like the sea sometimes swelled, anon like the same sea fell to a low ebb, yet seldom he wanted, his labours were so well esteemed. Marry this rule he kept, whatever he fingered beforehand was the certain means to unbind a bargain; and being asked why he so slightly dealt with them that did him good, 'it becomes me,' saith he, 'to be contrary to the world, for commonly when vulgar men receive earnest they do perform; when I am paid anything beforehand I break my promise.'"

This self-admitted dishonesty of Greene's appears to be referred to in 1592 in *The Defense of Cony-Catching.* " What if I should prove you a cony-catcher, Master R—— G——? Would it not make you blush at the matter? Ask the Queen's players if you sold them not *Orlando Furioso* for twenty nobles, and when they were in the country sold the same play to the Lord Admiral's men for twenty more." If·Greene sold this play to Alleyn under these circumstances in 1589, as Alleyn's possession of a fragmentary copy differing somewhat from the published play implies that he did, it appears to be the only play he ever sold the Burbage-Alleyn interests. All of his plays presented by Strange's men under Alleyn and Henslowe were old Queen's properties.

In the possession by both Strange's and Pembroke's

men at this period of plays recently owned by the Queen's company, and the presence of Queen's men in both companies, we have good evidence of a general reorganisation between the old Queen's company, the Admiral's, and Lord Strange's companies. This fact is further emphasised by the continued presence of Strange's men with, and the continued possession of old Burbage-Alleyn properties by, the Alleyn-Henslowe and the Burbage interests after Burbage and Alleyn parted at the end of 1590. Though we have no such specific records of the plays now retained, and later procured by Burbage and Pembroke's company, as Henslowe's *Diary* affords for Strange's men from 1591 to 1594, we have sufficient facts, and logical inferences therefrom, as well as occasional references and allusions, to enable us to show for Pembroke's company during this period, if not as long a list of plays, one superior in dramatic quality—when the plays produced by Marlowe and Shakespeare in these years are included—for both were certainly with Pembroke's company during this interval.

Much critical error has been caused and good work stultified by the unreasoning adhesion of scholars to the untenable theory of Shakespeare's connection with Henslowe's stage during these three years.

Some of the plays inherited by Pembroke's company from Strange's men at this time, as well as some now brought to them by Queen's men, were re-written during the following three years by Shakespeare and by Marlowe. There is no evidence to show that any writers other than Shakespeare and Marlowe revised old plays or produced new plays for Pembroke's company between 1591 and 1594.

From the fact that Greene's, Peele's, Marlowe's, and

PEMBROKE'S COMPANY 71

Shakespeare's hands are all recognisable in portions of one or more of the *Three Parts of Henry VI.*, it has been common with past critics to impute this to collaboration between these poets. The foregoing history of the companies, and of the writers for the companies owning these plays, automatically dispels this hoary illusion. There is no evidence whatever to show that Greene and Marlowe, Greene and Peele, or Peele and Marlowe ever collaborated in a play; while the facts of their histories, characters, and divergent interests and connections distinctly negative this idea. Neither does any evidence exist to show that Shakespeare ever collaborated with any of the three, though it seems possible, in the case of Marlowe, between 1591 and 1593. Yet I rather doubt that Shakespeare at this time would presume upon offering to collaborate with a scholar and playwright of Marlowe's then assured standing and reputation. It appears still more doubtful that Marlowe would invite such collaboration. The comparatively slight traces of Shakespeare's hand in *The Contention* and *True Tragedie* were probably written, as were his revisions of Marlowe's *Edward III.* and *Richard III.*, after the death of Marlowe in June 1593. Fleay's ascription of a share, and especially of a collaborative share, in the *Henry VI.* plays to Thomas Kyd is very wide of the mark, and was due to lack of knowledge of Kyd's history when he wrote.

The chances are extremely remote that Shakespeare ever at any time in his history invited, accepted, or tolerated collaboration by another writer in any of his own undisputed plays, though it is fairly evident that for strategical reasons he may have worked with Dekker in his rewriting of *Henry V.* in 1599, and in some of the *Troilus and Cressida–Agamemnon* presentations made upon Burbage's or Henslowe's boards during the dramatic recriminations between the theatres in the decade between 1599 and 1609. It seems practically certain also that Shakespeare collaborated at least once with Jonson, in *Sejanus*.

The recognised existence of extensive traces of other hands in certain of Shakespeare's plays is due, not to collaboration, but invariably either to the fact that such plays were older plays re-written by him, and in some cases only partially re-written; or else—and this is especially true in some of his later plays—they were revised by other hands between the time he retired from the stage and the issue of the First Folio in 1623. There are, however, a few notable instances where I find Shakespeare's hand superimposed upon very early originals, and, in some instances, both the old hand and Shakespeare's again partially overwritten by a post-Shakespearean reviser. I will later show the former to be the case with *The Comedy of Errors*, and the latter with *Timon of Athens* and *Macbeth*, by indicating the pre-Shakespearean authors. In the case of *Henry V.*, as will presently appear, I find three collaborative hands overwritten by Shakespeare and Dekker within four years of the production of the play of which it is a revision.

Continuing a consideration of the plays acquired by Pembroke's men from the old Queen's company in 1591, the fact that *The Troublesome Raigne of King John*—upon which Shakespeare's *King John* is based, and which was published in Quarto in this year—contains no mention of its presentation by Pembroke's men upon the title-page, where only the Queen's company is mentioned, clearly indicates it as a Queen's property now acquired by Pembroke's men, as well as the fact of its transformation

PEMBROKE'S COMPANY

at this time by Shakespeare into *King John* for Pembroke's company.

The coincident publication of an old play with the stage presentation of a new play upon the same subject occurs so frequently where we possess specific record of stage presentations, as we do in Henslowe's *Diary*, that we may safely apply the same general rule in the case of Burbage plays, where the actual record of stage presentations is lacking. I have already shown this to be so in the case of *The Taming of a Shrew*, and Shakespeare's revision of it, when, for a few days during the new reorganisation of companies in 1594, presentations by Burbage's men are temporarily recorded in Henslowe's *Diary*.

I have elsewhere given reasons for my belief that *The Troublesome Raigne of King John* was a political play, written for and presented by the Queen's company in 1588, in the interests of Sir John Perrot, a natural son of Henry VIII., whom the Queen, his half-sister, had appointed Viceroy of Ireland,[1] and who, early in 1588, was recalled upon charges of maladministration. As the Earl of Pembroke, and his father before him, were friends and partisans of Perrot's, it appears not unlikely that Shakespeare revised the old play into *King John* in 1591 at the instigation of his company's patron, as Perrot was arrested early in this year upon suspicion of treason, and confined at Burghley's house. Later in the year he was sent to the Tower, and early in the following year was tried upon the charge of high treason and condemned to death. It was rumoured at the time that the Queen intended to pardon him, but he died in the Tower before the pardon was granted

[1] *Shakespeare's Lost Years in London.* Bernard Quaritch, London, 1920.

and while still under sentence. Adherents of Hatton's were credited with poisoning him, but, as Hatton died before Perrot, this is very unlikely.

In re-writing this play, Shakespeare magnified and heightened the heroic character of Falconbridge. A comparison of the spiritual and physical characteristics of Perrot and Falconbridge, the royal parentage of both, as well as a striking similitude in their careers, render Shakespeare's personal and political intention practically certain.

Another play of the historical series, which served as a basis for Shakespeare's dramatic history of the Wars of the Roses, that came from the Queen's company to Pembroke's company in 1591, was *The True Tragedie of Richard III.* This play, or a play founded upon it, was originally re-written by Marlowe into *Richard III.* for Pembroke's company, and some time after the end of May 1593, when Marlowe was killed, and before June 1594, when Shakespeare and Burbage were rejoined by the Lord Chamberlain's company, was revised for the first time by Shakespeare for that company. Having appeared in this new form for about three years, during which it attained great popularity, it was again revised by Shakespeare in 1597, and published later in the year in the form we now possess it—which, even after these two revisions, still bears unmistakable evidence of Marlowe's as well as of still earlier hands.

From the rather slight, but none the less certain, use which Shakespeare made of the old Queen's play of *The Famous Victories of Henry V.* in his *Two Parts of Henry IV., Henry V.*, and the *Merry Wives of Windsor*, we are assured that this play was, at some period, a Burbage property. The fact that a play entitled *Henry V.* appeared upon

PEMBROKE'S COMPANY

Henslowe's boards on the 28th of November 1595, and thirteen times thereafterwards by the middle of 1596, makes it probable, if indeed not certain, that the old play was in the hands of the Admiral's company at this time, and that the play presented upon Henslowe's boards as "ne" on November 28, 1595, was a revision of the old play of *The Famous Victories*, now made for the Admiral's company. We know that *The Famous Victories* was an old Queen's play. It appears evident, then, that it came either to Henslowe's or Burbage's men at the time of the reorganisation, in 1591, when each of them secured so many old Queen's plays. Let us consider the evidence, to ascertain, if possible, the ownership of the old play, between the reorganisation of the companies in 1591 and 1598, when the play was published. Though it was not published until 1598, it was entered upon the Stationers' Registers along with Greene's *James IV.* and Wilson's *The Pedlar's Prophecy* on May 14, 1594, by Thomas Creede, the publisher, who, within two months, entered two other old Queen's plays—*The True Tragedie of Richard III.* on June 19 and *Locrine* on July 20. While the fact that Creede shortly before had entered and also published *A Looking Glass for London*—at that time undoubtedly a Henslowe property, as well as also an old Queen's play—might seem to imply that the other five plays entered by Creede three to four months later were also Henslowe's properties, other more cogent inferences indicate their ownership by the Burbages as discarded properties of the disintegrating Pembroke's company, a portion of which, including Shakespeare, was now in process of reuniting with the Chamberlain's men who rejoined Burbage at this time.

I have already, in the cases of *The Taming of a Shrew*

and *The Troublesome Raigne of King John*, and other plays, called attention to the significant fact, hitherto unnoticed by critics, that the entry upon the Stationers' Registers, or publication, of an old play, which remains upon the stage in a revised form, generally denotes the approximately concurrent date of its revision or re-writing. I will now give several other concrete instances of this usage.

The entry upon the Stationers' Registers and publication at this time of *The True Tragedie of Richard III.* by Thomas Creede, the publisher, evidently denotes Shakespeare's first revision of Marlowe's earlier *Richard III.*, based upon the old play; while Creede's entry upon the Stationers' Registers of *The Famous Victories of Henry V.* denotes Shakespeare's composition of the *First Part of Henry IV.*, in its early form, where the young and beautiful " hostess of the tavern " probably preceded the quaint and garrulous " Mistress Quickly " of the *Second Part* and Oldcastle anticipated Falstaff. Creede's entry, at the same time, of *James IV.*, from which Shakespeare took the idea of making dramatic use of Oberon and the fairies in *Midsummer Night's Dream*, also coincides significantly with the first appearance of this play, which I have elsewhere shown to have been written for presentation upon the occasion of the marriage of Sir Thomas Heneage to Lady Southampton, on May 2, 1594—less than two weeks before Creede's entry of *James IV.* on the Registers. Though there is no evidence that Shakespeare ever made dramatic use of *Locrine*, it becomes apparent that this also was one of the old Queen's plays secured by Pembroke's men in 1591, now sold for publication to Creede, who made the title-page read : " Newly set forth overseene and

PEMBROKE'S COMPANY

corrected by W. S."[1] In the light of these coincident facts it appears evident that all five plays entered by Creede upon the Stationers' Registers between May 14 and July 20, 1594, were old Queen's plays secured by Pembroke's company in the reorganisation of companies and properties in 1591.

While *no evidence whatever* exists for Shakespeare's assumed connection with Alleyn and Henslowe from 1591 to 1594, the evidence for his connection with Burbage and Pembroke's company during this period, while extensive and cumulative, is all of a circumstantial and inferential nature. In the entry upon the Stationers' Registers by Creede between May 14 and July 20, 1594, of the five Pembroke's properties mentioned above and the concurrent production of Shakespeare's *Richard III.*, *First Part of Henry IV.*, and *Midsummer Night's Dream*, coupled with the "W. S." printed by Creede upon the title-page of *Locrine*, we have still further and more direct evidence for Shakespeare's personal connection with the Burbage interests and Pembroke's company in the preceding three years.

In the possession by the Lord Chamberlain's men of *The Taming of a Shrew*, *Titus Andronicus*, and *Hamlet*, in June 1594, as appears in Henslowe's *Diary*, and their continued future possession of these plays, we are assured that they were then reorganising to rejoin Burbage, and that they had already absorbed certain of Pembroke's men as well as certain of their properties. The history of Pembroke's plays, so far considered, gives evidence that Shakespeare was kept fairly busy revising old, and writing

[1] It will appear later that Creede was probably authorised by Shakespeare to make this announcement.

new, plays during 1594 in anticipation of the new reorganisation at this time.

Before continuing a consideration of Pembroke's company's plays, I have yet to account for the evident possession and use of *The Famous Victories of Henry V.* by the Lord Admiral's company in 1595, when their play of *Henry V.* was written and staged.

Of the five Pembroke plays entered upon the Stationers' Registers by Creede in May to July 1594, three were published within a year, while neither *The Famous Victories* nor *James IV.* were published until 1598. I will now give my reasons for believing that Creede, instead of publishing these plays, or staying them for later publication, as the sellers of them apparently intended that he should, in the meantime fraudulently sold the stage reversion of *The Famous Victories*, and possibly of *James IV.*, to certain writers for Henslowe's stage; and that *The Famous Victories* was then re-written by two or more hands, among the number being George Chapman and George Peele, both of whom we know were then writing for the Lord Admiral's men. Chapman had recently written *The Blind Beggar of Alexandria* for them, and Peele was still working in the capacity he had now filled with them since 1589, as the company poet.

The presentation of this revision as a new play, under the title of *Henry V.*, is recorded in Henslowe's *Diary* upon November 28, 1595, and twelve times afterwards by July 1596. *It then disappears for ever from their records and properties.*

About eighteen months later, Shakespeare was forced by Cobham's protest to revise his (already probably twice revised) *First Part of Henry IV.*—which I have indicated

PEMBROKE'S COMPANY 79

as being originally written early in 1594, at about the same date as *The Famous Victories* was entered upon the Stationers' Registers. Shakespeare changed Oldcastle to Falstaff at this time. In the following year he wrote the *Second Part of Henry IV.* and *The Merry Wives of Windsor,* and *Henry V.* shortly afterwards. At about this same period *The Famous Victories,* upon which all of these plays are ultimately based, was finally let go to press. Though the date of this publication is 1598, all plays published before March 25, 1599, would bear the earlier date. The conclusion is obvious that the Lord Chamberlain's men, after a long delay, had regained the stage rights to this play — in the meantime evidently having prevented the publication.

I now find that when Shakespeare's company regained possession of *The Famous Victories,* they also secured with it its revision into *Henry V.*, produced for the Admiral's company late in 1595. All the evidence points to their recovery of these plays in about November or December 1598, about a year after Shakespeare made his last revision of *Henry IV. Part I.,* and less than a year after this play was entered upon the Stationers' Registers on February 25, 1598. Though Shakespeare, in this final revision of *Henry IV. Part I.,* incorporated a few significant links, which indicate that he then had the composition of a second part in mind, a critical comparison of the vocabulary, diction, construction, and characters of *Part I.* with those of *Part II.* and *Henry V.* clearly reveals the facts that the latter two plays were built upon a very different basis from *Henry IV. Part I.,* and evidently upon a dramatic and historical expansion of *The Famous Victories,* rather than upon that play itself; and that extensive substrata from this base still remain in *Henry IV. Part II.* and *Henry V.*; while *Henry IV. Part I.*, though revised only shortly before these other plays were written, stands out in Shakespearean atmosphere and flavour as probably the most characteristic of all his plays.

The long interval between the last presentation of *Henry V.* on Henslowe's boards in July 1596 and Shakespeare's composition of the *Second Part of Henry IV.* some time after the middle of 1598, implies that the repossession by the Burbages of *The Famous Victories*, and the acquisition of its revision, were the result of protracted legal action of some nature.

Bearing in mind the pugnacious character of the Burbages, and the irritating fraud practised upon them by Creede and the writers for the Admiral's company, it is altogether unlikely that they purchased these plays from the Admiral's men; and still more unlikely, considering the interval of two years, that the latter voluntarily parted with them to the Burbages; yet there can be no doubt, upon careful analysis of the matter, that Shakespeare used the Admiral's company's revised play as the basis for *The Second Part of Henry IV.* and for *Henry V.* as we now possess them. However startling this theory may at first sight appear, the more thoroughly it is canvassed the clearer the fact becomes.

To impute *Henry V.* in its present form, *in toto*, to Shakespeare at this period, or indeed at any period, argues a very nebulous sense of his style and stylistic development. Though the overwriting of this play has obscured both Peele's and Chapman's more obvious peculiarities of style, and at the same time greatly complicated a ready recognition of Shakespeare's mind and style, recognisable

PEMBROKE'S COMPANY

substrata of both Peele's and Chapman's hands undoubtedly remain; and even with the overwriting are distinguishable from each other, through the retention of a number of Chapman's characteristic neologisms and phrases, nearly all of which are to be found in the utterances, in the verse lines, of King Henry and his followers and of the Duke of Burgundy, as well as in some of the prologues to the acts. Some of these lines have apparently been overwritten by Shakespeare, and some of them completely rewritten. Most of the utterances of the French king and his followers in the verse lines of *Henry V.* were apparently written by Peele, but over an older base. These lines appear to be much less overwritten than Chapman's and show little evidence of Shakespeare's hand. The larger proportion of the play would then appear to have been originally written by Chapman, but also over an older base. Even in its present form the vocabularies of Chapman and Peele are more clearly discernible than Shakespeare's.

A very definite demonstration of either Chapman's or Peele's hands, overwritten as both are by Shakespeare, and probably to some extent by Dekker, is further complicated by the very evident fact that neither the work of Chapman nor Peele in the Admiral's *Henry V.* was original composition, nor even based directly upon *The Famous Victories*, but upon a play re-written from *The Famous Victories* by Greene and Lodge in collaboration, who, it will be shown, collaborated in the *Three Parts of Henry VI.* in their earliest forms, and also in a *Richard III.* in a form intervening between *The True Tragedie of Richard III.* and the work of Marlowe, revised by Shakespeare, as we now possess it. That a play upon Henry v., differing from its present form as well as from *The Famous Victories*, was acted in or before 1592, is indicated by Nashe in *Pierce Pennilesse*, where he says : " What a glorious thing it is to have Henry v. represented on the stage leading the French king prisoner, and forcing both him and the Dauphin to swear fealty." There being no scene in either *The Famous Victories* or Shakespeare's *Henry V.* where this incident is presented, and the old *Famous Victories* being, like *The True Tragedie of Richard III.*, an old Queen's company's play antedating Greene and Lodge, they were both evidently revised or re-written by these collaborators to link with their work in the originals of the *Three Parts of Henry VI.*, and the scene, described by Nashe, probably pertained to their collaborative revision of *The Famous Victories*.

As Shakespeare's *First Part of Henry IV.* contains no evidence whatever of Greene's nor Lodge's style, vocabulary, or influence, and is indubitably Shakespeare's composition, while both the *Second Part of Henry IV.* and *Henry V.* undoubtedly do, the idea suggests itself, that in the division of the old Queen's company's properties in 1591, between the Strange-Admiral's company and Pembroke's company, Alleyn or Henslowe in selling *The Famous Victories* to the Burbage's—whether by inadvertence or design it is difficult to tell—retained Greene's and Lodge's revision of it in their own hands. Their writers later finding it in their properties and knowing that they could not legally use it, lacking possession of the original, took means to secure possession of *The Famous Victories* from Creede after Shakespeare had authorised him to enter it upon the Stationers' Registers. It will later appear very probable that they used their youthful assistant, Thomas Dekker, as their go-between in this apparently dishonest transaction.

PEMBROKE'S COMPANY

If there was a third hand in the Admiral's company's *Henry V.*, and it appears very likely that there was, most of the comic prose passages were apparently delegated to him. In this event the evidence appears clearly to indicate that the third hand was that of Ben Jonson. At the present time we have no definite knowledge of Jonson's theatrical and dramatic career earlier than 1597, when we find him associated as a writer with Alleyn and Henslowe, and collaborating with George Chapman. The earliest record we possess regarding him is his borrowing four pounds from Henslowe, on July 28, 1597. In the following year Meres mentions him among other prominent poets and dramatists, as " our best for tragedy," which surely infers a dramatic standing of several years' duration. In *Satiromastix* (1601) Dekker alludes to him as at one time being an actor in *Jeronymo*, at a period during which his company was compelled to travel. This indicates a connection with Alleyn and Henslowe and Lord Strange's company in some capacity from 1591 to 1593, during which this play was revised and presented not only in London, but, during the plague months, also in the provinces. It is significant of the truth of Dekker's allusions in *Satiromastix* to Jonson's early career as an actor in *Jeronymo*, that Wood's and Aubrey's quite independent traditions concerning Jonson's early theatrical experiences connect him with " the Green Curtain at Shoreditch " at the same period. Seeing that the reciprocal arrangement between Burbage and Laneham regarding the use of their theatres by two companies did not end until 1592, it is apparent that Strange's men continued to play at the Curtain in the summer-time, when in London, until February 1592, when the Rose Theatre was made ready for their occupancy. This clearly was the period that Jonson was connected with the stage and played a part in *The Spanish Tragedy* indicated by Dekker, as well as by Wood and Aubrey. In this light a connection with Henslowe's stage as a collaborative writer in 1595 appears practically certain. Some time in 1597 or 1598, Jonson, who had now written in collaboration for some years with Chapman, was supplanted in this connection by Marston. It is evident that Jonson's first draft of *Every Man in his Humour*, which was presented by the Lord Chamberlain's company in 1598, was not written for this company, as Chapman's hand appears in it. When Jonson later revised this play, and changed the names of the characters from Italian to English, he also eliminated Chapman's purple passages. It appears probable that it was in process of composition when Jonson quarrelled with Marston and the Admiral's men, at this time, and that he finished it for the Lord Chamberlain's men.

As at present we know of nothing that Jonson wrote as early as 1595, and as *Henry V.*, as we know it, is so evidently a much overwritten play, it is difficult upon stylistic grounds to connect Jonson with its base, even though his history, and Shakespeare's satirical intention in revising the play, appear to indicate such a connection. The reason I so confidently suggest Jonson's as the third hand in the play, as it came from the Admiral's company, is my conviction that Shakespeare, in producing his play of the same title, intended to pillory to the eyes of the dramatic world the three Admiral's writers who had illegally appropriated *The Famous Victories* and revised it for the Admiral's men, and that in the caricatures he

PEMBROKE'S COMPANY

presents of them, Jonson's—from our knowledge of his appearance—is the most personally distinctive and easily recognisable of the three. Considering the presence of Shakespeare's arch-enemy Chapman among the collaborators in the Admiral's *Henry V.*, it appears not improbable that this play contained parody or caricature of Shakespeare. Much recriminatory matter between Chapman and Shakespeare and the dramatic and literary factions which formed about them must have perished. It is likely that the Admiral's *Henry V.* contained such matter, and that Shakespeare, having captured his enemies' battery, now turned their own guns upon them. Nym, Bardolph, and Pistol, under somewhat different characterisations from those they now present, may have appeared in the Admiral's play, in which the stealing of the Pax by Bardolph was evidently an incident.

I have never known Shakespeare to make an unprovoked attack upon any writer for the stage, though he appears not to have been backward in defending himself from such attacks, which were invariably caused by the envy of his scholastic competitors. In the dramatic characters of Nym, Bardolph, and Pistol we have in this order satirical reflections of the three scholars Chapman, Jonson, and Peele, and in the thieving propensities of these characters, allusions to the illegal appropriation of *The Famous Victories*, and its stage revision, by these writers. In the cases of Jonson and Peele the reflections are so obvious that certain past critics, who were quite unconscious of the theory here advanced, have recognised the intended caricatures, without being able to account for their underlying cause.

Pistol's utterances plainly parody Peele's early fustian

and grandiloquence, and some of them allude pointedly to his productions.

Of these three dramatic characters, Bardolph is the only one whose facial appearance is indicated, and Jonson is the only writer of the time whose recorded scorbutic complexion matches Bardolph's description.

As Nym's personal appearance is not in any way indicated, we must seek in his utterances the resemblance intended to his original. In May 1597 *The Comedy of Umers* appears in Henslowe's *Diary* as a new play. It is presented upon twelve other occasions by November 1597. This play was definitely identified by Fleay as Chapman's *A Humourous Day's Mirth*. It was evidently more popular than Chapman's usual productions, as Jonson at this time apparently tried to capitalise upon its vogue by producing two plays with the word " humour " in the title, *i.e. Every Man in his Humour* and *Every Man out of his Humour*. The indicative link between Chapman and Nym is, then, evidently the frequently repeated phrase of the latter, " that is the humour of it." Shakespeare also seems to reflect his knowledge that Chapman (who was a French scholar) had a hand in the French dialogue in the play by once altering the phrase to " that is the rendezvous of it."

Though Chapman apparently regarded himself as a rare humorist, no Elizabethan writer appears to have been so constitutionally destitute of all sense of that saving grace, his lumbering attempts at humour being quite as sad as those of his ironically humorous reflection, Corporal Nym, who is always presented as definitely labelling his stolid efforts in this direction with the words " that is the humour of it." To those who knew Chapman, his reflection in this character would probably have been equally

PEMBROKE'S COMPANY 87

obvious with those of Jonson and Peele as Bardolph and Pistol.

In the description of the personal appearance and characters of these three worthies, given by the boy who serves all three of them, the sentence I have italicised below evidently alludes to the dishonest manner of their acquisition of *The Famous Victories*. It appears very evident that Thomas Dekker had a hand in Shakespeare's re-writing of this play, and that the following description of Ensign Pistol, Lieutenant Bardolph, and Corporal Nym, as showing the relative standing of the company poet Peele, his chief assistant Jonson, and his second assistant Chapman, in the management of the Admiral's dramatic production, was written by Dekker, who, in 1595, and probably for a while before, evidently occupied exactly this status of " boy to all three of them " with the Admiral's company's writers. In 1595 Dekker was only eighteen years of age, and was then connected with the Admiral's company in a subordinate capacity, as his hand either as a transcriber, *or as an author*, and probably the latter, appears in a revision of *Sir Thomas More*, evidently attempted in that year.

At the time *Henry V*. was re-written, early in 1599, Dekker was closely allied with Shakespeare against his jealous rivals. It was at this exact time that Shakespeare made over his *Troilus and Cressida* to Dekker and Chettle. There is a sense of intimate personal knowledge in the following description that implies a close acquaintance between the writer and his models. The closing sentence :

> . . . I must leave them, and seek some better service; their villany goes against my weak stomach, and therefore I must cast it up—

is autobiographically significant, in view of Dekker's later association with Shakespeare.

> BOY. As young as I am, I have observed these three swashers. I am boy to them all three : but all they three, though they would serve me, could not be man to me ; for indeed three such antics do not amount to a man. For Bardolph, he is white-livered and red-faced ; by the means whereof a' faces it out, but fights not. For Pistol, he hath a killing tongue and a quiet sword ; by the means whereof a' breaks words, and keeps whole weapons. For Nym, he hath heard that men of few words are the best men ; and therefore he scorns to say his prayers, lest a' should be thought a coward : but his few bad words are matched with as few good deeds : for a' never broke any man's head but his own, and that was against a post when he was drunk. They will steal any thing, and call it purchase.[1] Bardolph stole a lute-case, bore it twelve leagues, and sold it for three halfpence. Nym and Bardolph are sworn brothers in filching, and in Calais they stole a fire-shovel : I knew by that piece of service the men would carry coals. *They would have me as familiar with men's pockets as their gloves or their handkerchers:* which makes much against my manhood, if I should take from another's pocket to put into mine ; for it is plain pocketing up of wrongs. I must leave them, and seek some better service : their villany goes against my weak stomach, and therefore I must cast it up.

This is Dekker or the devil. It certainly is not Shakespeare in 1599 : his weapon was irony, while Dekker invariably made frontal attacks—an effective method in cases of such bare-faced dishonesty.

It appears not unlikely that Dekker's arrest at the suit of the Lord Chamberlain's men, from which he was released by the payment of three pounds ten, which he

[1] The sinful old Adam, so acquisitively portrayed in the activities of Nym and Bardolph, is similarly manifested by certain of their New English academic congeners, who "' convey,' " as " the wise it call," important Shakespearean discoveries, and publish them as original.

borrowed from Henslowe on January 30, 1599, was in some manner connected with the affair of *The Famous Victories* and its revision by the Admiral's men, as well as with the recovery of one, or both, by the Lord Chamberlain's men at this period. *The Merry Wives of Windsor* and *Henry V.* were both produced shortly after this; as was also Dekker and Chettle's *Agamemnon*, which, as I have elsewhere shown, was evidently a revision of Shakespeare's *Troilus and Cressida*. This makes it probable that the latter play was given by Shakespeare to Dekker as a personal recompense for his arrest and involuntary aid in the recovery by the Lord Chamberlain's men of the former plays. Dekker, writing of himself as " boy to all three," intimates in the lines italicised above that Chapman, Jonson, and Peele had used him in aiding their dramatic peculations. Dekker's collaborative alliance with Chettle—a still earlier champion of Shakespeare against the attacks of the scholars —his evident hand in the present form of *Henry V.*, as well as his continued alliance for years afterwards with Shakespeare against the intermittent attacks of his scholastic competitors, probably reflect his appreciation of Shakespeare's generosity at this juncture.

While we have Henslowe's own record in the *Diary* that Dekker was arrested and imprisoned at this time " at the suit of the Lord Chamberlain's men," and that he was released in January 1599 upon the payment of money loaned to him by Henslowe for this purpose, his shortly subsequent co-operative relations with Shakespeare, as well as their continued and prolonged friendly relations, imply that there was no personal animus upon the part of the Chamberlain's men against Dekker, but that he was probably a hostage captured in the legal battle waged by the Chamberlain's men with Henslowe's writers to recover possession of *The Famous Victories* and its revision.

Returning to a consideration of Pembroke's company's plays between 1591 and 1594; in addition to the plays procured from the Queen's men, they also retained, amongst others from the Burbage-Alleyn stock before 1591, the old *Hamlet*, *The Taming of a Shrew* (old Kyd plays), and *Edward III.* (an old Marlowe play). It is unlikely that Shakespeare materially altered *Hamlet* at this time. *Edward III.* he revised after Marlowe's death, and at about the time that he wrote the third " book " of sonnets, and with the same admonitory intention regarding his patron, Southampton. His first revision of *The Taming of a Shrew* is clearly indicated early in 1594, and though Henslowe characteristically sticks to the old title in his *Diary*, it is plainly the revised play that was then in the hands of the Lord Chamberlain's company. Had they acted the old play, their name would have appeared with Pembroke's upon the title-page in this year. *Titus Andronicus*, which also appears in the Lord Chamberlain's list in Henslowe's *Diary* in June 1594, was first presented by Sussex's company, on January 3, in the same year when, as I have hitherto shown,[1] it had been re-written by George Peele from Kyd's older base, which he first re-wrote into *Titus and Vespasian*; which name is probably one of Henslowe's numerous misnomers, the correct title having probably been *Titus Vespasian*. It is significant that Henslowe at times names *Titus Andronicus*, *Titus and Andronicus*. The old German play in which Vespasian appears was evidently made from a MS. copy of *Titus*

---

[1] *Shakespeare's Sonnet Story*, pp. 98–100. Bernard Quaritch, London, 1922.

PEMBROKE'S COMPANY

Vespasian, taken to Germany by Robert Brown or Richard Jones at this period. The latter published several old Burbage-Alleyn plays, which he evidently bought from Edward Alleyn, with whom he had frequent similar dealings, and whom he joined as a Lord Admiral's man upon his return from Germany in 1594. As Pembroke's company is mentioned as presenting *Titus Andronicus* on the title-page of the Quarto, published in 1594, their possession of the play is clearly indicated after January 1594, when they procured it from Sussex's company, or men from that company, who now joined them in the general reorganisation of companies that took place in the summer of this year.

In Pembroke's stock at this period we may also include Marlowe's *Edward II.*, which was written for this company some time between the beginning of 1591 and May 1593. Its title-page reads : " As it was sundry times acted in the Honourable City of London by the Right Honourable the Earl of Pembroke his Servants," and evidently at the Crosse-Keys.

From the old Oxford's company's properties bought by the Alleyns in 1589 the Burbages retained, and Pembroke's company probably procured, *The Life and Death of Thomas Lord Cromwell* and a revision of *Fidele and Fortunio*, made by Chapman for Oxford's company in 1584, when the origina play was published. These went in 1594, with the majority of Pembroke's plays, into the hands of the Lord Chamberlain's men ; the former was apparently revised for the Lord Chamberlain's company by Dekker, and was later sold to Nottingham's men, who sent it to press in 1602. *Fidele and Fortunio*, or a revision of it made when the original was published in 1584, was altered into *The Two*

92 PEMBROKE'S COMPANY

Gentlemen of Verona by Shakespeare, in from 1593 to 1594; at the same time *Edward III*. was revised, and the third "book" of sonnets and *Lucrece* written, all of these poems and plays spiritually reflecting the peculiar phase of Shakepeare's relations with his patron, Southampton, that he passed through at that period. It will later be indicated that *Fidele and Fortunio* and *Thomas Lord Cromwell* were written before 1584 by Chapman and Munday in collaboration for Oxford's company. It will also be argued that at or about the time that Shakespeare's company inherited these two Oxford plays, they also probably inherited or later bought, amongst others, three plays dealing with the same subjects as *The Comedy of Errors, Timon of Athens,* and *Macbeth,* the latter two written for Oxford's company by Chapman and Munday, which Shakespeare transformed into the plays we now possess under these titles. *The Comedy of Errors* evidently came from the Admiral's company in 1591.

In addition to the plays already mentioned, Pembroke's company also possessed in the interval between the beginning of 1591 and the autumn of 1594 the following plays, written or revised specifically for them by Shakespeare during this period : *King John, The Comedy of Errors, Richard II., Love's Labour's Lost, Love's Labour's Won (All's Well that Ends Well* in an earlier form), *The Two Gentlemen of Verona, Midsummer Night's Dream,* the *First Part of Henry IV., Richard III.* (a revision of Marlowe's play of the same title), *Edward III.* (Marlowe's play revised). If these plays were not written or revised for, and presented by, Pembroke's men at this period, for whom were they written and by what company were they presented ? There would surely be some record of them in Henslowe's

PEMBROKE'S COMPANY

Diary had they been presented during the years 1591-4 upon his stage.

It is probable that all of Shakespeare's plays here mentioned, with the exception of the historical plays, were revised or written primarily with private or Court presentations in mind. The private presentations of plays by such a company as Shakespeare's were probably far more frequent than the comparatively few and chance records that remain of them would imply. It is significant of the standing and reputation of Pembroke's company that the first actual record we possess of it should be a mention in the Court records of its appearance before the Court on December 27, 1592. As it was the only company besides Henslowe's—which played at the Rose—that was used for " the service of her Majestie " between December 1592 and 1594, it will become obvious that it was using the Crosse-Keys as its winter quarters at this time, and that Lord Hunsdon's letter (quoted below) refers to Pembroke's company, under Burbage's recent management.

Pembroke's company is also mentioned in the Court records as presenting a play at Court on Twelfth Night (January 6) 1593. It is very probable that they appeared before the Court also on Twelfth Night 1594. Though no entry of a payment to any company for a Court performance upon this occasion is to be found in the Court records, Birch records that " on Twelfth Night, 1594, there was a play and dancing at court till one after midnight. The queen appeared on a high throne richly adorned, as beautiful," says Mr. Standen, " as ever I saw her, and next to her chair the Earl, with whom she often devised in sweet and favourable manner." A possible reason for no recorded Court payment may be that Essex upon this occasion provided the entertainment, and if so it is likely that Shakespeare's company was used, especially as they had appeared on Twelfth Night at Court in the preceding year; it is possible that Birch's record may refer to this occasion.

That Pembroke's company had performed publicly in London over six months before their first recorded Court appearance, upon December 27, 1592, is made evident by Robert Greene's allusion to Shakespeare as " Shakescene," in his posthumously published *A Groat's-worth of Wit* and his parody of a line from *The True Tragedy of the Duke of York*, which was a Pembroke property at this time.

As all of the London theatres were closed on account of the Plague on June 22, 1592, and not reopened until December, and as Greene died in September, his allusion to performances of this play *must necessarily have been to presentations preceding June 22*. At the same time, then, that Pembroke's men were presenting *The True Tragedy of the Duke of York* at the Crosse-Keys, Lord Strange's company, under Alleyn and Henslowe, were presenting *Henry VI.* at the Rose Theatre. A new revision of this play was presented by Strange's men fifteen times between March 3 and June 12, 1592. This revision was made by Peele, who had worked for Alleyn as company poet since 1589. Peele's revision, with the new Talbot scenes, and with Edward Alleyn probably in the heroic part of Talbot, proved very popular, as Peele's friend Nashe, who had been praising him as the " Atlas of Poetry," and complimenting Alleyn's histrionic ability for the past three years, triumphantly records its success, complimenting both the author and the actor as follows : " How would it have joyed brave Talbot (the terror of the french) to think that

PEMBROKE'S COMPANY

after he had lyne two hundred years in his tombe, he should triumph again on the stage, and have his bones new embalmed with the tears of ten thousand spectators at the least (at several times), who in the tragedian that represents his person, imagine they behold him fresh bleeding." In the same part of *Pierce Pennilesse*, dealing with plays and players, from which the above passage is taken, Nashe pays the direct compliment to Edward Alleyn previously quoted, whom he evidently had in mind in writing "the tragedian that represents his (Talbot's) person." Here he writes : " Not Æsope, nor those tragedians admired before Christ was borne, could ever perform more in action than famous Ned Alleyn."

The indefinite nature of past and current knowledge of Shakespeare's doings and whereabouts at this period is displayed by the fact that Greene's scurrilous allusion to Shakespeare as "Shakescene," indicating his connection with a presentation of *The True Tragedy* by Pembroke's company before June 22, 1592, and Nashe's highly complimentary reference to the reviser of the Talbot scenes in *Henry VI.*, which was being presented upon Henslowe's stage at the same time, are both recorded by his biographers as indicating the ubiquitous Shakespeare.

The facts that Shakespeare's hand has been recognised in the Temple Garden scene in the *First Part of Henry VI.*, and that this play was included in the First Folio, have led past critics nebulously to assume that Shakespeare was with Henslowe and Lord Strange's company from 1591 to 1594, and that it was *his* revision in this play, and *his* hand in the Talbot passages, that were so highly complimented by his late detractor, Nashe, in August 1592, at the same time that Nashe's recent anti-Shakespearean collaborator, Greene, so bitterly attacks and so definitely identifies Shakespeare as the object of his present, and their former, combined attacks. I have already indicated and will later develop evidence showing that Nashe collaborated with Greene in *The Old Wives' Tale* in this year.

Shakespeare's small revisionary touches in the *First Part of Henry VI.*, including the Temple Garden scene, were not added to this play until the new organisation of companies in the middle of 1594—which apparently involved also a redistribution of some of their properties—brought the *First Part of Henry VI.* into the hands of Shakespeare for the first time as a Burbage property. *Historical fact and textual criticism alike proclaim the Talbot scenes as unquestionably Peele's revisionary work.*

The untenable assumption that Shakespeare was with Henslowe and Alleyn from 1591 to 1594, and that Nashe compliments his work in the Talbot scenes of *Henry VI.*, imply on the part of the waspish Nashe—who in 1592 was still collaborating with Greene—a very drastic change from his former attitude towards Shakespeare, as well as the supposition that James Burbage, the most prominent and permanently established theatrical manager in London, was now out of business for three years.

No attempt has ever been made by the exponents or supporters of this baseless theory to account for James Burbage's activities between 1591 and 1594, though this is not surprising, as it has even been thought that Burbage had previously parted with the use and possession of his theatre for a period of ten years.

James Burbage was a pugnacious and persistent man and, as his history shows, not easily discouraged. Though

Alleyn, in 1590, took the majority of Burbage's players to Henslowe—probably under a three-year contract—Shakespeare and others, including Marlowe as a writer, still remained with him; and though the Theatre was now for a time in the hands of the Court, pending the settlement of litigation, performances there were not necessarily stopped; and he still had his winter stage at the Crosse-Keys, where it appears evident from a letter quoted below that many, if not all, of Shakespeare's plays composed between 1590 and 1594 were performed in the winter seasons, during this interval, when playing was permitted.

The reorganisation of companies that went on during the spring of 1594, and that was evidently completed in about the middle of the year, resulted in an independent Lord Admiral's company, under Alleyn and Henslowe; a reconstructed Lord Chamberlain's company, under Burbage; and a new Queen's company, which now absorbs Sussex's company, that had evidently been affiliated with it for the past three years. Pembroke's company apparently now submerges its identity and performs with some other company, possibly the Queen's or Worcester's, for a few years, when it reappears for a short time as a separate entity, most of its men later joining Henslowe and Alleyn as Admiral's men.

After leaving Alleyn and Henslowe and rejoining Shakespeare and Burbage in or about the end of June 1594, the Chamberlain's company made a short provincial tour, but had returned to London by the 8th October, upon which date Lord Hunsdon wrote to the Lord Mayor, requesting him to allow his players to perform at their old city headquarters, at the Crosse-Keys.

This portion of Lord Hunsdon's letter reads, " where my

nowe company of players have been accustomed for the better exercise of their quality, and for the service of her Majesty if need so require, to play this winter-time within the city, at the Crosse-Keys in Gratious Street." Lord Hunsdon's "nowe" company refers to his company as it was *now* reconstructed, with his old protégé Burbage as its theatrical backer. Burbage and that portion of his company *who had previously been Pembroke's men* had in the winter seasons played at Burbage's old winter quarters, the Crosse-Keys, from the time Alleyn and Strange's men left them in 1590, until they were rejoined by the Lord Chamberlain's men, and proposed now to do so again. As the portion of the new company that had been with Henslowe in this interval *played at the Rose Theatre in the two preceding winters*, it is clear that Lord Hunsdon does not refer to them, and equally clear that his reference is to the company as it is "nowe" reconstructed under Burbage, who had evidently used the Crosse-Keys as winter quarters long before we have the first record of it in this connection in a former Lord Mayor's letter, on November 6, 1589, which shows that Lord Strange's company, while then with Burbage, performed there the previous day.

The next stage record of Shakespeare and the Lord Chamberlain's company we possess — which leads us back to the point from which we started upon this investigation — is that it performed twice at Court in December 1594.

The records of the payment for these performances in the following March reveal Shakespeare as one of the sharers in what was now, and continued thereafter for forty years to be, the most important company of players in London.

CHAPTER V

SHAKESPEARE, CHAPMAN, AND SIR THOMAS MORE[1]

OVER fifty years have passed since Richard Simpson announced his unique critical and paleographical discovery of Shakespeare's composition, as well as of his actual autograph, in portions of the MS. play of *Sir Thomas More*, preserved at the British Museum as Harleian MS. 7368. Though a limited number of scholars have since acknowledged the probability of the truth of Simpson's conclusions, the majority appear to be still sceptical or at best timidly acquiescent.

To the layman, paleographical testimony, however authoritative, is not very convincing; knowing little or nothing of this study and noting the divergences between experts, he is apt to regard its conclusions as largely a matter of opinion. In this connection I must say, however, that while Sir Edmund Maunde Thompson's concurrence in the truth of Simpson's discovery has been no factor in leading me to my present belief in its authenticity, my own findings along a totally different line of research have given me a very high respect for his work. Sir Edmund's conclusions regarding the relative dates of both Munday's and Shake-

[1] Much of this chapter, with a preface by Professor Franck L. Schoell, was published in June and August 1926 in the *Revue Anglo-Americaine*. Paris.

speare's several autographs will be found to be automatically verified by the new critical, historical, and biographical light to be adduced.

Bibliographical efforts to support Simpson's discovery have not been so happy, but have tended rather to becloud than clarify the question, in needlessly departing from Simpson and proposing dates (1593-6) for Shakespeare's work, at which he had no connection with the theatrical interests then owning the MS., and at which the highly developed lyrical note and poetic excellence of his acknowledged dramatic verse—acquired in the composition of *Venus and Adonis* and *Lucrece*, and by several years' practice in sonnet-writing—do not bear the remotest time analogy to the laboured and argumentative verses attributed to him in *More*. Only in certain passages in *King John*, *The Comedy of Errors*, and *Love's Labour's Lost*, that pertain to these plays in their earliest forms, do we find anything approaching stylistic resemblance, and even in these instances the lines in *More* are plainly the earlier and more formative.

Simpson's brilliant discovery, which, so far as regards the 147 lines ascribed by Greg to hand D, I have no hesitancy in accepting *in toto*, and not merely as a fact of reliquian interest, but of unusual biographical and critical value, was not a fortunate guess, but was due to his possession of superior critical discrimination and a sound knowledge of social, literary, and political history. In the application of this knowledge to Shakespearean research, Simpson has blazed paths by which others, trusting his vision, may reach the truth, even in instances where his own pioneering deductions were at fault.

In dating the composition of *Sir Thomas More* late in 1586 or early in 1587, Simpson again was far from indulging in surmise; here also his guides were historical knowledge and critical acumen. He then knew nothing of Munday's authorship; as it is improbable we now would, without the literal aids of paleography and autographic subscription; as Munday's mind and style are so dull and commonplace as to have aroused little critical interest among scholars in the past; yet when the matter is carefully analysed, there cannot be any doubt that Simpson was sound in his conclusions. His fine critical sense and intimate knowledge of the Elizabethan drama seem to have taught him that such an inchoate play as *More* was unlikely to have been written during the last decade of the reign of Elizabeth, after Marlowe and Shakespeare had set such new and high standards for English historical drama. He appears to have recognised the fact that *More* was a hasty theatrical pot-boiler of a topical nature, and, looking for its probable inspiration, found it in what now appears to be the only possible occasion, historically and logically, consonant with Shakespeare's subsequent revision, which was the aborted apprentice rioting of 1586. Tilney's marginal notes on the MS. informed him that the play was altered soon after its composition, and he was one of the very few scholars who, then or since, appear to have been clearly aware of the facts that Shakespeare was indulging in such revisionary work as early as 1589, and that he was then being scurrilously alluded to and abused by Greene and Nashe, for his temerity as " serving man " to a theatrical manager, in thus encroaching upon the preserves of the " scholars."

Simpson also appears to have been unique, in possessing a sufficiently fine appreciation of the stylistic stages of the development of Shakespeare's verse, to realise the impossibility of linking the versified portions of the lines he attributed to him in *More* with any except the earliest possible period of his work, and, as will appear, judiciously placed his revision at the *only* period at which these lines could logically have been written by Shakespeare.

About a year after Simpson's announcement James Spedding acknowledged agreement with his conclusions, and also called attention to several other autographs in the MS. besides those of the original scribe, and of the lines attributed to Shakespeare. Later on, Mr. Furnival recognised six, and possibly seven, different autographs; and Professor C. F. Tucker Brooke, in *The Shakespeare Apocrypha*, either four or five. In 1911 Dr. W. W. Greg, in his edition of *Sir Thomas More*, made for the Malone Society, tentatively endorsed Furnival's findings by recognising seven different autographs, including the notations of Edmund Tilney, the Master of the Revels.

In 1923 five well-known scholars united, with the purpose of strengthening the evidence of Shakespeare's autograph and composition in the three pages of *Sir Thomas More*, by collaborating upon bibliographical, paleographical, and critical lines.[1] In the introduction to the interesting volume resulting from this effort, I learn that the addition of a critical essay was an afterthought, which proves to have been a very happy one. Mr. R. W. Chambers' contribution on "The Expression of Ideas in the Three Pages" is admirably presented and very convincing.

This excellent collaborative plan, however, lacked two things, which, if added, might have given its conclusions a

[1] *Shakespeare's Hand in Sir Thomas More*, by Alfred W. Pollard, W. W. Greg, E. Maunde Thompson, J. Dover Wilson, and R. W. Chambers. Cambridge University Press, 1923.

SIR THOMAS MORE   103

finality at present lacking: which were, a critical examination of the whole MS., following similar methods to those applied by Mr. Chambers to the three pages; as well as a careful biographical and historical survey of extant knowledge concerning the persons and companies involved in the writing, revisions, and attempted presentations of the play. In preceding chapters I have partially supplied these needs, and will now endeavour still further to do so.

The *More* MS. consists of twenty sheets, of which thirteen have been recognised as the autograph of the original scribe, whose identity, however, was unknown until 1912. The other seven sheets are now known to be in the autographs of at least four, and possibly five, different scribes. In 1912, the late J. S. Farmer published a facsimile of a MS. play, then in possession of Lord Mostyn, entitled *John-a-Kent and John-a-Cumber*, which is written and subscribed in the autograph of Anthony Munday. A comparison of this hand with that of the original thirteen leaves of the MS. of *Sir Thomas More* enabled Dr. Greg, in 1912, to identify Munday as their scribe, and possibly also as their author.

A critical analysis of the subject-matter and diction of the original thirteen leaves of the *More* MS. has now convinced me, that although they are written in the hand of Munday, he undoubtedly had at least one collaborator in the original composition of the play, and that this collaborator was none other than Shakespeare's "old sweet enemy," George Chapman; the idiosyncrasies of whose style are, I believe—to those who know him well—more easily recognisable and distinguishable from others than those of any writer of his period.

Assuming, then, for the present that I am correct in my

ascription of a portion of the original thirteen leaves to Chapman, and tentatively acknowledging also the correctness of Mr. Furnival's and Dr. Greg's conclusions, that there are five other hands paleographically recognisable in the remainder of the MS.—one of which, however, Dr. Greg plausibly ascribes to a playhouse director—we have in all at least six authors or revisers for one play, certainly a very unusual number. The most logical inference, then, is that the thirteen leaves in Munday's hand, and containing his and—as I affirm—Chapman's compositions—which are generally recognised as older than the seven remaining leaves—are portions of the play as it was first composed, and that the newer leaves displaying five other hands pertain to a later period or periods of revision, and evidently to more than one revision.

Dr. Greg classified and ascribed the autographs in the MS. as follows: hand S to Munday; C to a playhouse director; D, following Simpson, to Shakespeare; E to Dekker—with whose extant autographs he has compared it—leaving A and B as yet unidentified.

Though Dr. Greg refrains from making a definite ascription of hand B, he notices and mentions its resemblance to the writing of the MS. of *The Captives*, "presumably" by Thomas Heywood, preserved in the British Museum as MS. Egerton 1994 (fol. 92–95).

Following this suggestion of Dr. Greg's, Dr. Samuel A. Tannenbaum, in a privately printed volume issued in 1927, described as "a Bibliotic Study" and entitled *The Booke of Sir Thomas Moore*, advanced sufficiently convincing paleographical arguments for Heywood's identity as the writer of hand B to lead me to make a careful comparison of the two writings. This scrutiny, combined with

Heywood's history and my critical deductions concerning his freedom of style in his clownish parts, has convinced me that hand B is Heywood's writing and composition. While I also agree with Dr. Greg's conclusions that the clownish part alone is original matter by hand B in Scene iv. (fol. 7a), and that Scene ix.a (fol. 16a) is also B's original work, and an addition to, rather than a revision of, the original matter, I am forced to differ with him regarding any stylistic resemblance between the original scene in hand S and the addition by B on folio 16a.[1] In the former we have a large proportion of exactly the same doggerel Alexandrines used by Chapman and Munday in *Fidele and Fortunio*, and in the latter not the slightest attempt at rhyme, rhythm, or form; the former being as archaically typical of Munday's and Chapman's early work as the formlessness of the latter is of Heywood's.

Dr. Tannenbaum, by a similar comparison of hand A with Henry Chettle's writing in Henslowe's *Diary*, in turn identifies hand A as Chettle's. This identification, which my own historical and critical conclusions corroborate, I also freely accept, despite the fact that I find his still further identification of Kyd as the writer of hand C quite as wide of the mark paleographically as it is critically and historically. Hand C is clearly that of the company poet, George Peele.

My examination of the one hundred and seventy lines in the *More* MS. attributed to Shakespeare has convinced me that the verse lines are not Shakespeare's original composition, but a full and free revision of a portion of the play originally written by George Chapman; in which Shakespeare has retained distinct traces of Chapman's

[1] *The Booke of Sir Thomas More.* The Malone Society's reprints, 1911.

phraseology and diction, using a number of words peculiar to Chapman, which he himself seldom or never again uses in any of his acknowledged poems or plays. If this inference is correct, Shakespeare's revision must necessarily postdate Chapman's composition.

In extant knowledge of the Elizabethan stage and drama we have no record, hint, or suggestion from which we may infer that Munday and Chapman at any time in their known career would be likely to collaborate in a play for a company with which Shakespeare was connected. Following the history of the MS., we are again led to an impasse; nothing is known of it before it came into possession of the British Museum with the Harleian Collection. By a comparison of the autograph in the MS., which he classifies as hand C, with other contemporary autographs, Dr. Greg has shown the practical certainty that the *More* MS. was in possession of theatrical interests connected with Alleyn and Henslowe between about 1592 and 1598. Here, however, all present evidence ends; so that whatever further light we may hope for must necessarily come from new critical discoveries, or from deduction or inference to be drawn from such knowledge as we may possess concerning the participants in the composition and revisions of the play, *which are now*: Munday, Chapman, Shakespeare, Dekker, Heywood, Chettle, and Peele.

I place these names in the order given for the reason that I propose to show that Munday and Chapman were the original authors of the play in or about 1586; that Shakespeare revised it in or about 1589-90, after it had become a Burbage-Alleyn property through the purchase, by Alleyn and his brother, of Oxford's properties in 1589, and before Alleyn left Burbage for Henslowe at the end of 1590, when the play became a Strange-Admiral's property. It is logically impossible that Shakespeare should have revised the play after this date, or that he should have collaborated with the Admiral's writers in their revision, which, it will appear, must have been made in or about 1595, in an evidently abortive endeavour to capitalise the public interest in the apprentice rioting in that year. While we have hitherto been aware that Chapman held dramatic relations with the Admiral's men as early as 1596, and Heywood as early as 1595, we have had no definite evidence of Chettle's relations with them earlier than the end of 1597, nor of Dekker's earlier than the beginning of 1598. The forty lines of his composition, and written in his own hand by Dekker at the end of Addition IV., in which all of the Faulkner lines are as evidently his work as the More, Surrey, and Erasmus passages are Chapman's, afford strong evidence that the play was revised in or about 1595, and while Dekker was still a bonded serving man in the company and working with Peele, Chapman, and Jonson as their assistant.

The presence in this Addition of Chapman's revision of his own earlier hand in the play reveals him also as one of the several revisers of this period, and as using his young and Cockney-bred assistant, Dekker, to give the Faulkner dialogue a vernacular flavour suitable to the character, which is entirely lacking in his own stilted lines in the original version. The transcription of his and Dekker's hands by Peele gives added evidence, were it needed, of the validity of Dr. Greg's conclusion that hand C was that of an editor and director and not of a writer or reviser.

While it is possible that Chettle also may have been

connected with the Admiral's men at the time *Sir Thomas More* was revised for them in 1595, it appears unlikely that his revision pertains to this date, and much more probable that it was made in or about 1598 to 1599. I will give my reasons for this opinion in detail.

In 1595 Chapman was himself undoubtedly one of the revisers, all of the lines in Addition IV.—except the Faulkner lines, for which he used his assistant Dekker—being his own revision of his own lines. It appears most unlikely then that he would allow Chettle to take the liberties which he did in so completely changing the spiritual characterisation of More and presenting the kindly, gentle, and philosophic More of Addition I.

In the original scene in hand S Chapman's More—characteristically of Chapman—exhibits towards his wife the attitude of a domineering barnyard cock to a mildly clucking hen, while Chettle's More treats his wife with tenderness, respect, and admiration, and his children—to whom he refers as " my little ones "—with a fatherly regard lacking in the original.

The facts that Addition I. is not fitted to its contexts, as are all of the other Additions, and that it alone of the Additions shows no trace of Peele's regulative pen, seem also clearly to infer a later period of revision.

I will now indicate the probability that Chettle revised *Sir Thomas More* at the same period that he and Porter produced *The Spencers* for the Admiral's company in March 1599, and after the death of Peele. Chettle's play was based upon Marlowe's *Edward II*.

Peele's *Edward I.*, Marlowe's *Edward II.*, and Marlowe's and Shakespeare's *Edward III.*, which were, all three, Pembroke's properties between the beginning of 1591 and

SIR THOMAS MORE

from 1593 to 1594, when a new allignment of companies and properties began, appear at or about this time to have been transferred to Alleyn and Henslowe. *Edward I.*, in a revised form and under a new name—*Longshanks*—appeared on the Admiral's boards as a new play a few months later; *Edward III.*, which was made use of by Chapman and Peele in their composition of the Admiral's *Henry V.*—presented by them as a new play on November 28, 1595—was evidently now sent to press by them, being entered upon the Stationers' Registers three days later, *i.e.* on December 1, 1595. *Edward II.* was revised into *The Spencers* in March 1599 for the Admiral's company by Chettle and Porter, the old play at this time passing into the hands of the Worcester-Oxford's men — afterwards known as Queen Anne's company—by whom or their successors it was sent to press in 1622.

In his presentation of More in Addition I. Chettle shows distinct evidence of his recent acquaintance with Marlowe's *Edward II.*, appears to endeavour to endow More with something of that king's philosophic resignation to the loss of his kingship, and uses a characteristic phrase of Marlowe's, and in lines plainly re-echoing somewhat similar lines in *Edward II.*

Edward II., Act IV. Scene vi. :

> Stately and proud, in riches and in train,
> Whilom I was, powerful, and full of pomp:
> But what is he whom rule and empery
> Have not in life or death made miserable ?
> Come, Spencer ; come, Baldock ; come, sit down by me;
> Make trial now of that philosophy,
> That in our famous nurseries of arts
> Thou suck'dst from Plato and from Aristotle.
> Father, *this life comtemplative is heaven.*
> *O that I might this life in quiet lead !*

Sir Thomas More, Addition I. :
>   Perchance the king
> seeing the Court is full of vanitie
> has pittie least our soules shuld be misled
> and sends us to *a life contemplative.*
> *O happy banishment from worldly pride*
> *when soules by private life are sanctifide.*

The lines italicised in Chettle's verses evidently reflect those italicised in Marlowe's *Edward II.*, and the phrase " a life contemplative " is not to be found elsewhere than in *Edward II.*, Chettle's Addition to *More*, and, curiously, only in one other place, where J. P. Collier attributed it to Peele, in one of his clumsiest, yet most elaborate inventions, exposed in a later chapter.

From Dekker's history, coupled with the presence of his autograph in the MS., we gain some new light, though nothing has hitherto been known of his whereabouts or doings until his name appears in Henslowe's *Diary* in 1597-8. Fleay's ascription of dramatic work to him in the late 'eighties and early 'nineties of the sixteenth century has absolutely no basis, but from a statement made by Dekker in 1637, in the Preface to his *English Villanies*, that he was then threescore, which would make him eighteen years old in 1595, coupled with his evident connection with the affair of *The Famous Victories*, we may now judge that he worked for Henslowe and Alleyn in 1595 in the capacity of a bonded serving man. Whatever faults Dekker may have had, he was essentially frank and honest, and not likely to lie about his age, as his vainer and less reliable contemporary, Florio, undoubtedly did.

Coming now to Shakespeare's suggested connection with the play between 1592 and 1598, unless we are prepared to believe that he, as a Burbage employee and a

SIR THOMAS MORE

member of Pembroke's company between 1591 and 1594, or as a sharer in and the principal writer for the Lord Chamberlain's company from 1594 onwards, would be likely to collaborate with a number of Henslowe's writers in revising an old play—and especially a play of this dangerous nature—*for his employer's foremost theatrical competitor*, this late date is entirely out of the question, as Shakespeare was certainly with Burbage during these years.

The present writer has elsewhere[1] given irrefutable evidence for Shakespeare's connection with Burbage and Pembroke's company from 1591 to 1594, while no particle of evidence exists for the now age-old but utterly untenable assumption still followed by a number of prominent scholars and reputed critics, that Shakespeare worked at the Rose Theatre, under Alleyn and Henslowe, during these years.

If, then, it is logically impossible that Shakespeare should have revised the *More* MS. at any time after the beginning of 1591, when, and under what circumstances, could he be likely to have done so, and how does it come about that his autographic revision appears in a MS. play, apparently owned by Alleyn and Henslowe's organisation, between about 1591 and 1598 ? Again, seeing that no record nor grounds for inference exist for Munday or Chapman, singly or in collaboration, ever having written for the Burbages, nor for any company of which Shakespeare was a member, how does it happen that he came to revise a play of their composition ? I will allow the developing historical facts and deductions to answer all of these questions.

A comparison of Chapman's composition in *Sir Thomas*

[1] *Shakespeare's Lost Years in London.* Bernard Quaritch, 1920.

More with his known work will show those competent to judge that his work in *Sir Thomas More* pertains to a very early, though, as will appear, not the earliest period of his dramatic work. We have hitherto known so little about Chapman's career before 1594 that it has been generally assumed he came to London in or shortly before that year. In 1594 his first at present known publication, *The Shadow of Night*, appeared. *The Blind Beggar of Alexandria*, his first known play previous to Professor Schoell's discovery of *Charlemagne*, appeared upon Henslowe's boards in February 1596. At this time Chapman was thirty-seven years old. I will now make it evident that he had then been producing for the stage, as a collaborator, for at least twelve to thirteen years, and that his advent in London may be dated, not in from 1593 to 1594, but as early as from about 1581 to 1582.

Students conversant with recent continental research are already aware that Professor Franck L. Schoell, in 1920, by demonstrating Chapman's authorship of the old anonymous play of *Charlemagne*,[1] referred to by Peele in his *A Farewell* in 1589, has conclusively proved that Chapman had already entered upon his London dramatic career at least as early as from 1588 to 1589. I have now no hesitancy in affirming that Chapman was engaged in dramatic work in collaboration with Anthony Munday as early as from 1581 to 1582, and possibly still earlier; and yet—despite the fact that the work of both Chapman and Munday are recognisable in *Sir Thomas More*—that neither he nor Munday, either singly or in collaboration, ever produced an accepted play directly for a company with

[1] *Charlemagne*, Franck L. Schoell. Princeton University Press, Princeton; Oxford University Press, London, 1920.

which Shakespeare was connected. A consideration of Munday's literary and dramatic beginnings will serve to resolve this seeming riddle.

Anthony Munday was born in London in 1553, five years before the birth of Chapman. He was apprenticed to John Alde, the stationer, in 1576, at the age of twenty-three—an unusually mature age to begin an apprenticeship. Two years later, and while still in his alleged apprenticeship, he went abroad accompanied by a companion, who, he informs us, was named Thomas Nowell, of whom we know nothing further; but as Munday admits that he himself travelled at this time under an assumed name,[1] we may infer that the name of his companion was also assumed. There can be little doubt, however, that Munday and his companion were spies in the pay of some member of the Council, or of some of its secret agents. Munday's later patronage by Burghley's son-in-law, the Earl of Oxford; his long-held office as Queen's Messenger and as official pagenter for the city; as well as his association with Topcliffe, the anti-recusant agent, in the arrest and conviction of Campion and other Jesuits, coupled with his evident zeal in the work—all imply that his continental travels, as well as his prolonged sojourn as the Pope's Scholar at the English College in Rome, were undertaken in other than purely personal interests.

Shortly after reaching France, and upon leaving Boulogne for Amiens, Munday and his companion Nowell were set upon and robbed by disbanded soldiers. At Amiens they were relieved by an English Catholic priest named Woodword, who sent them on with introductions to Dr. Allen at Rheims. Instead of proceeding to Rheims,

[1] *The English Romayne Life*, Antony Munday, 1582.

however, they went to Paris and reported to the English Ambassador, who—Munday informs us—advised them to return to England. Instead of doing so, he and his companion stayed some time in Paris, making the acquaintance and worming themselves into the confidence of certain self-exiled English Catholics living there, through whom they secured introductions to the authorities of the English College in Rome. It appears likely that in this procedure they followed instructions given them in England, and amplified by the English Ambassador at Paris. The strongly anti-Catholic bias of Munday's account of his Roman experience, and his active co-operation with Topcliffe in the prosecution of the Jesuits after his return, belie his statement that the sole purpose of his travels was " the desire to see strange countries and affection to learn the languages."

While the exact dates of Munday's departure for the Continent and of his return are not known, he spent part or most of the year 1578 in Rome, and was back in England some time in or before 1579. In the latter year he formed a new company of boy actors, under the patronage of the Earl of Oxford, and continued as its manager and poet until 1584, when he secured a Court appointment as Queen's Messenger. The title-pages of most of Munday's publications issued between 1579 and 1584 mention him as servant to the Earl of Oxford ; and from that date onwards until 1592 as Queen's Messenger. Though the latter office precluded his further actual theatrical management of Oxford's boys, it did not put an end to his dramatic work for the company, with which he was evidently connected as poet, until the time of its disappearance from theatrical records late in 1588 or early in 1589. It was precisely at this

SIR THOMAS MORE 115

time that Burbage's old company—Leicester's—his later company, the Lord Chamberlain's (Hunsdon's), and Lord Strange's company of boy actors disappear also from the records, and that Lord Strange's new company was formed. This latter company, which, between 1589 and the end of 1590, included Richard Burbage, Shakespeare, and no doubt others from the Lord Chamberlain's company, and Kemp, Pope, and Bryan from Leicester's company, continued to work under the management of Burbage and Alleyn until the end of 1590, when Burbage and Alleyn parted, and Strange's men, with the exception of Shakespeare and probably a few others, went with Alleyn to Henslowe ; Burbage and Shakespeare at the same time forming Lord Pembroke's company.

At the time of the first general reorganisation of companies mentioned above, in 1588-9, when Oxford's company disappears into thin air for fifteen years, while remnants of the other companies disappearing are found reunited as Strange's company, I have shown that Edward and John Alleyn bought all of the plays previously owned and presented by Oxford's company ; this may imply also that some of their men were absorbed by Burbage and Alleyn at this time.

Two years later, *i.e.* at the end of 1590, when Burbage and Alleyn ended their theatrical association, which had now lasted since 1585, they again divided their properties ; and in doing so some of the old Oxford properties, including *John-a-Kent* and *Sir Thomas More*, were taken by Alleyn with Lord Strange's men to Henslowe ; and others, already mentioned, retained by Burbage. It becomes apparent then that Shakespeare's revisionary work in *Sir Thomas More* must have been written between the end of 1588 and the end of 1590, and while *Sir Thomas More* was still in the possession of Burbage's company.

A further consideration of Munday's early career, and of—as I affirm—his collaboration with Chapman, will demonstrate these facts, and also solve other riddles that have long puzzled scholars; as, for instance, the questions of the authorship and date of composition of *The Life and Death of Thomas Lord Cromwell*, and of the manner in which Shakespeare's company became possessed of it; and why Bodenham, in *England's Helicon*, ascribes to Shepherd Tony (Anthony Munday) verses ascribed to George Chapman by Allot in *England's Parnassus*.

During Munday's connection with Oxford's company as manager, between 1579 and 1584, and during his later connection as writer for it from 1584 to 1589—a period of ten years—he must have produced for its use, either alone or in collaboration, a much larger number of plays than the meagre three of which we have hitherto had record: namely, *Fidele and Fortunio, The Weakest Goeth to the Wall,* and *John-a-Kent*, all three of which, though the latter two were revised later, plainly pertain to a very early period of Munday's dramatic work. To this same decade I now ascribe also the composition—in collaboration with George Chapman—of *The Life and Death of Thomas Lord Cromwell* and of *Sir Thomas More*, and to a period earlier than either, the composition of *Fidele and Fortunio*, as a collaborative effort of the same two men.

In this light, and from the evidences I also find of Chapman's and Munday's hands as substrata in *The Comedy of Errors, Timon of Athens,* and *Macbeth*, and a number of other plays, it appears very probable that other MS. plays of Chapman's and Munday's became Burbage properties also in 1589, as in all these plays I recognise Chapman's hand, and in some also slight traces of Munday's work. A number of passages in *Timon of Athens* and *Macbeth* have long been recognised as non-Shakespearean, and though some of them have been shown to be due to later-time revision, I regard it as demonstrable that both plays were based upon early originals by Chapman and Munday. A number of Chapman's passages still remain practically unchanged. This matter will be examined in a later chapter.

In dating the other five plays mentioned above some time between 1579 and the end of 1588, and in ascribing three of them to collaboration between Munday and Chapman, it becomes pertinent to endeavour to ascertain their relative order of composition. As two of these plays, *More* and *John-a-Kent*, remained unpublished until the nineteenth century, and as *Fidele and Fortunio* was published in 1584, *The Weakest Goeth to the Wall* in 1600, and *Cromwell* in 1602—while all five were written, as I affirm, in or before the 'eighties of the sixteenth century—it becomes apparent that bibliographical data can be of no aid in this endeavour, and that we must rely upon new biographical and historical facts and inferences, combined with internal and stylistic evidence.

A careful examination of all such available evidence has led me to date these five plays in approximately the following order : *John-a-Kent*, in 1579 ; *The Weakest Goeth to the Wall*, in about 1580–1 ; *Fidele and Fortunio*, 1581–2 ; *Cromwell*, 1582–3 ; and *More*—following Simpson's suggestion—in 1586–7.

In neither *John-a-Kent* nor in *The Weakest Goeth to the Wall* do I find any trace of Chapman's style ; for this reason, as well as their dramatic and stylistic immaturity when compared with *Cromwell* and *More*, I place them anterior to the period at which Munday and Chapman began to collaborate. The MS. of *John-a-Kent* bears the date of 1596, but written in a hand quite dissimilar to that of its author, Anthony Munday. It is clear that whatever this date may mean, it cannot be the date of composition, as the play was then obsolete, having been replaced as a company property two years before (1594) by the *Wise Man of Westchester*, which is now recognised to have been the same play in a revised form.

On August 13, 1579—the year Munday started Oxford's company—the ballad of *British Sidanen* was entered on the Stationers' Registers. The subject of this ballad is the same as that of *John-a-Kent*, and it is very probable that its publication at this date either reflected extant knowledge of the play, or else that the ballad suggested the composition of the play. I believe the former to be the case, not only in this instance, but in nearly every instance when plays and ballads appeared on the same subject. This was due either to independent financial ventures upon the part of ballad-writers, who synchronised the publication of ballads to popular plays; or, as is more probable, was an advertising device of theatrical managers of the type of Munday—who were also ballad-writers[1]—to arouse public interest in their presentations. It occurred too frequently to be mere chance. It is altogether unlikely, too, that an ephemeral ballad-sheet published in 1579 would suggest the composition of a play to Munday seventeen years later. For these reasons I date the composition of *John-a-Kent* in 1579, the first year of Munday's new theatrical venture with Oxford's company.

[1] Munday was a prolific ballad-writer.

SIR THOMAS MORE 119

As in the case of *John-a-Kent*, *The Weakest Goeth to the Wall* shows no trace of Chapman's composition. While it probably was revised in later years, before its publication, it was evidently first presented while Oxford's boys were still young, as the members of the caste presenting it are referred to in the text as "pigmies." Fleay tentatively dates its composition in 1584. A company of boys of from thirteen to fifteen years of age in 1579 would be stalwart youths and men by 1584, and could scarcely be described as "pigmies" at that date. I therefore date it shortly after the composition of *John-a-Kent*, and in about 1580 to 1581, and about a year before Munday's next play, *Fidele and Fortunio*, in which Chapman's inceptive hand appears.

Of the three Munday plays in which I recognise Chapman's mind and style, *Fidele and Fortunio* is plainly the earliest. Chapman is here at his most primitive stage. If it be possible to speak of any of Chapman's work as lyric, his verse lines in *Fidele and Fortunio* may be said to represent his lyric period. In fact, though over thirty years of intimate acquaintance with Chapman's work has rendered his middle and later styles readily recognisable to me, I doubt that I would have recognised his earlier and formative style in this play, had I not first found his hand in *Sir Thomas More* and *Cromwell*, and been led to a critical consideration of *Fidele and Fortunio* in this connection, by Collier's ascription of the play to Munday. In the new light here being thrown upon collaborative relations between Munday and Chapman in those early years, it is significant that Bodenham, the compiler of *England's Helicon* (1600), attributes to "Shepherd Tony"—whom Mr. Bullen has identified as Anthony Munday—certain verses from *Fidele and Fortunio* which I very confidently affirm are correctly ascribed to Chapman by Allot in *England's Parnassus*, published in the same year. The editor of the latter publication apparently possessed information regarding Chapman's early collaboration with Munday which the editor of the former lacked. It is not unlikely, as suggested by Mr. Charles Crawford in his excellent edition of *England's Parnassus*, that Allot, its compiler, procured his knowledge of Chapman's authorship of these lines directly from Chapman himself, especially as Allot does not once mention Munday; while the latter, as "Shepherd Tony," is mentioned a number of times in *England's Helicon*, published in the same year, and Chapman not once.

Following *Fidele and Fortunio*, the next extant play in which Munday and Chapman collaborated was, I suggest, *The Life and Death of Thomas Lord Cromwell*, which I date in or about 1582–3, following the publication of Munday's *Romayne Life*, some phases of which appear to be reflected in the play. *The Romayne Life* was a defensive pamphlet, issued by Munday in an attempt to justify his late proceedings against the Jesuits, and to combat their claim that he had never been to Rome. The anti-Catholic spirit of *Thomas Lord Cromwell* was probably intended to cater to the public interest excited by the recent Jesuit trials and executions.

In the vicissitudes of Cromwell and his servant Hodge, penniless and begging at Florence after being robbed by the "bandetti," Munday seems to reflect similar conditions in his own and his friend Nowell's experience, described in his recently published *Romayne Life*.

The spirit in which Cromwell undertakes his travels is also reminiscent of Munday's avowed motives in wishing to travel.

Cromwell:
> But, Cromwell, this same plodding fits not thee:
> Thy minde is altogether set on travell,
>
> . . . .
>
> Experience is the jewell of thy hart.

Romayne Life:
> When as desire to see strange countries, and also affection to learn the languages had persuaded me to leave my native country, etc.

When Burbage and Alleyn parted and divided their properties at the end of 1590, Alleyn and Strange's men taking *John-a-Kent* and *Sir Thomas More*, Burbage evidently retained *Thomas Lord Cromwell*, which apparently remained among their properties until some time before its publication in 1602, its title-page reading: " As it hath beene sundrie times publikely Acted by the Right Honorable the Lord Chamberlaine his servants." It was evidently sold to Henslowe and Alleyn, who employed Chettle, Drayton, Munday, and Smith to write *Cardinal Wolsey*, between June 1601 and May 1602, when they sent *Cromwell* to press.[1] Shakespeare had no hand in its revision for the Chamberlain's men, but it appears likely that he employed that " dresser of plays," Thomas Dekker, for this purpose. Dekker was closely in touch with Shakespeare at this period, being affiliated with him in defensive measures against the attacks of Jonson, Marston, and Chapman. All of the choruses to the acts and scenes, as well as improvements in the comic passages introducing Cromwell's servant Hodge, appear to have been written by Dekker. Hodge's portions are very suggestive of

[1] This play was published by William Jones, who appears to have published only for Henslowe and Alleyn and never for Burbage.

Dekker. It is significant also that Dekker at this period should have introduced a character named Orlando Friscobaldi, into *The Honest Whore*, seeing that Dekker's play owes nothing except this name to Foxe's *Book of Martyrs*, upon which *Thomas Lord Cromwell*—in which a character of the same name appears—is largely founded.

No scholar with a modicum of critical sense can read *Thomas Lord Cromwell* and *Sir Thomas More* with the theory here advanced in view, without becoming aware of the fact that in their original forms these two plays were the products of the same stilted, literal, and uncreative minds, even though in both instances revision has marred the evidence.

If the introductory portions of each play be eliminated, that is, the insurrection scenes from *More* and the continental travels of *Cromwell*, the successive stages of the rise and fall of *More* and *Cromwell* will be seen to be an obvious repetition, one of the other. Both are promoted rapidly to high and higher places, both expatiate upon the tickleness of climbing and apprehend a fall, both stalk to their doom with the same portentous and unctuous gravity, while Foxe's *Book of Martyrs* is their common source. It is very apparent, however, that *More* is the later and maturer composition, and that some years must have intervened between them. In both plays, also, the utterances of the protagonists distinctly reveal Chapman's mind and style, which are easily to be differentiated from Munday's.

The logical conclusion, then, is that Anthony Munday, who—whatever his other merits or demerits—appears to have been an alert business man, desiring to capitalise the public interest in the apprentice rioting of 1586, before it had died down, took from the company's properties his and Chapman's old play of *Thomas Lord Cromwell*, which had long since served its original topical purposes, and, again in collaboration with Chapman, hastily rehashed it into *Sir Thomas More*.

Two years later Oxford's company disappears, and their properties are absorbed by Burbage and Alleyn's organisation, which quasi-partnership or business connection was first formed in 1585, and apparently renewed in some form upon the reorganisation of companies late in 1588 or early in 1589, Alleyn now taking a larger and more prominent part in the direction of affairs.

Some time before Burbage and Alleyn parted, late in 1590, Shakespeare revised *Sir Thomas More* for Lord Strange's company, which took *More* and *John-a-Kent* with them as properties when they left Burbage; while Burbage, who then formed Pembroke's men, retained *Thomas Lord Cromwell* and *Fidele and Fortunio*, or, more probably, a revision of the latter made by Chapman upon the publication of the original play in 1584.

About three years later—in 1594—Strange's men, now known as the Lord Chamberlain's men, returned to Burbage, the Admiral's men in the company remaining with Alleyn and Henslowe, as the Lord Admiral's men. At this time another division of properties took place; Alleyn and Henslowe's organisation still retaining *John-a-Kent* and *Sir Thomas More*, and other properties which had belonged to the Burbage-Alleyn combination before 1591, as well as most of the properties owned and used by Strange's men and their successors, the Lord Chamberlain's men, from 1591 to 1594. Burbage's men also retained plays from both periods, such as *Thomas Lord Cromwell* from the earlier, and the *First Part of Henry VI.* and *Titus Andronicus* from the latter ; as well as nearly all of the plays used by Pembroke's company, or acquired by them between 1591 and 1594, which necessarily include all of the plays written by Shakespeare or revised by Marlowe in this interval. *Queen Dido*, which was left unfinished at Marlowe's death, was finished by Nashe for the Children of the Chapel. Marlowe's *Edward III.* went to Alleyn and Henslowe at this time, and *Edward II.* a year or two earlier.

It has already been made evident that neither Dekker's, Heywood's, nor Chettle's Additions to *Sir Thomas More* can possibly pertain to the same period as Shakespeare's, yet these Additions evidence the fact that it was revised at least once, and probably twice, after it became, and remained, an Alleyn and Henslowe property.

Sir Thomas More ceased to be a Burbage property and became a property of the Alleyn and Henslowe interests at the end of 1590. The most probable date for its next revision is 1595, as a reflection of the intermittent rioting in June and July of that year. The cruel and tragic end of this rioting, in the hanging, drawing, and quartering of five " lads " for alleged treason, probably precluded its presentation at that time.

The reference to the scouring of Moreditch by the long-haired servitor Faulkner, as suggested by Dr. Percy Simpson, appears in the concluding forty lines of Addition IV., which are written in hand E—attributed by Dr. Greg to Dekker—while the remainder of the Addition is in hand C. Recognising in hand C merely a playhouse transcriber, Dr. Greg ascribes the composition of the whole of Addition IV. to Dekker. It is very evident that the concluding forty lines of this Addition are the composition of the same author as all the other Faulkner passages in this

SIR THOMAS MORE 125

Addition; but it is equally evident that the More, Surrey, and Erasmus lines are the product of an entirely different method, mind, and style. All of the lines spoken by these latter persons are manifestly by George Chapman, being his own revision of passages in the older portion of the play, also of his composition.

In the preceding chapter I have shown the possibility that Dekker worked with Shakespeare in the revision of the Admiral's *Henry V.* for the Lord Chamberlain's men in 1599, and indicated the probably autobiographical character of his description of himself as "boy" to Nym, Bardolph, and Pistol, as representing Chapman, Jonson, and Peele; and in a former publication[1] have given conclusive evidence that Dekker, from this period onwards for several years, continued in a defensive alliance with Shakespeare against his scholastic enemies, including Jonson, Marston, and Chapman.

Shakespeare's revision in *Sir Thomas More* being impossible after the end of 1590, we are driven back upon the only period at which it could logically have been made, that is, between the end of 1588—when Oxford's company came to an end as a separate entity—and the beginning of 1591, when the inheritors of their properties, Burbage and Alleyn, parted.

None of the scholars who have endeavoured to ascertain the date of Shakespeare's work in *More* has noticed the rather threatening tone of Tilney's notations in the MS. as being unusual or peculiar. We find none of this spirit exhibited in the records of Henslowe's relations with Tilney in the *Diary*. There we find Tilney's fees collected with apparent regularity, and his agents at times even

[1] *Shakespeare's Sonnet Story.* Bernard Quaritch, London, 1923.

borrowing money from Henslowe. It must have been to Tilney's interest to preserve cordial relations with the players and to encourage, rather than discourage, performances. The closure of the London theatres, and the dispersal of the companies into the provinces, must have been quite as distasteful to Tilney as to the players, as it resulted in pecuniary loss to both. In adopting the threatening tone he uses in the notations to *Sir Thomas More*, it appears likely that Tilney was acting under orders, and at a period of unusual perturbation on the part of the authorities.

All of the evidence so far advanced points to a date between the beginning of 1589 and the end of 1590 for Shakespeare's revision of *More*. The Martin Marprelate controversy, in which the Burbage interests were involved, as I have shown, reached a climax in 1589. At this time, Burghley ordered Tilney to command all of the London players and playmakers to appear before him, bringing the plays they were presenting or proposed to present, in order that he might correct and reform in them anything that he considered immoral or seditious. While it is possible, though unlikely, that Tilney may again have censored *More* at some still later period of revision, the sternly official tone of his injunctions makes it practically certain that Shakespeare's alterations of the insurrection scene and of *More's* speech were made at the time of the official censoring ordered by Burghley in 1589, shortly after the MS. of *Sir Thomas More* came into the possession of Burbage and Alleyn; certainly before they severed theatrical relations at the end of 1590.

In view of the attacks made by Greene and Nashe upon Shakespeare, in their publications issued in 1589, for daring to revise the work of " scholars," it appears evident that his revision of *Sir Thomas More* was not an isolated instance of such work upon his part in that year.

Burbage and Alleyn, through the recent consolidation of companies, had become the largest owners of theatrical properties in London. The plays they were now forced to submit to Tilney's censorship probably outnumbered those of all other London theatrical interests combined. It appears likely, then, that Tilney would order similar emendations to those ordered in *More*, in a number of the other plays, and that the task of emendation would fall largely upon Burbage's *Johannes Factotum*, William Shakespeare, whose fitness for the work—Nashe sneeringly suggests in his *Epistle to the Gentlemen-Scholars of both Universities*, prefixed to Greene's *Menaphon* in 1589— "was nourished in a serving man's idleness."

It was doubtless, then, the large amount of revisionary work in their current plays, forced upon Burbage and Alleyn by Tilney in 1589, and delegated by them to Shakespeare, that now brought him prominently into the limelight and aroused the resentment of the "scholars." Had Shakespeare made a failure of his revisions, without doubt we would never have known that he made them. The success that they must have proved is evidenced by the superiority of his work in *Sir Thomas More* to that of Chapman and Munday, as well as to that of all the later revisers.

Abusive allusions to Shakespeare, of the same nature as those made by Greene and Nashe in 1589, were continued by Greene in nearly all of his publications until his death in 1592; and also appear in one posthumous publication —*A Groat's-worth of Wit*—in that year. Though I have as yet found no evidence that Munday or Chapman in

1589 resented the revision of their work by Shakespeare, there can be little doubt that his revision of *Sir Thomas More*, and other plays by Chapman and Munday among the Oxford properties, marks the beginning of the spiteful and envious hostility with which, as I have hitherto indicated,[1] Chapman pursued him from, at least, 1593, until he retired to Stratford in 1609.

In tracing the literary evidence of the collusive hostility of a scholastic clique to Shakespeare from the end of his servitorship to Burbage, in about 1589, until he retired to Stratford twenty years later, as well as Shakespeare's dramatic reprisals to their attacks, I have not yet found an instance in which Shakespeare makes an unprovoked reflection of a humorous or satirical nature upon any contemporary writer. When, then, we find Anthony Munday mildly caricatured in *Love's Labour's Lost*, and in passages that manifestly pertain to the play in its earliest form (1591–2), it is reasonable to assume that such reflections are, in this instance also, Shakespeare's answer to previous expressions of Munday's resentment at his revision of *Sir Thomas More* and other old Oxford's company's plays among the Burbage properties.

Shakespeare's caricature of Anthony Munday, the Queen's Messenger, as Anthony Dull, the King of Navarre's messenger, however it may have been developed in the original form of *Love's Labour's Lost*, is now very mild. Anthony Dull is introduced in Act I. Scene i. as bearing a letter from Armado to the King of Navarre, under the stage direction of " Enter Dull, bearing a letter." Dull describes himself as " his grace's tharborough," and Armado, in his letter to the King, describes him as " thy

---

[1] *Shakespeare's Sonnet Story.* Bernard Quaritch, London, 1924.

sweet grace's officer, a man of good repute, carriage, bearing, and estimation." He next appears in Act i. Scene ii. as the bearer of a message from the King to Armado. These two appearances are apparently all of his action in the play that pertain to its early form.

He appears twice later on in the play, but accompanied by Holofernes and the curate Nathaniel, who are caricatures of Chapman and Royden, introduced into the play in 1595 as Shakespeare's reprisal for the attacks made upon him at this time by the publication of Royden's *Willobie his Avisa* and Chapman's *Hymns to the Shadow of Night* and *Ovid's Banquet of Sense*, in the dedications of which, to Royden, Shakespeare is scurrilously indicated.

As I find no further trace of hostilities between Shakespeare and Munday, it appears probable that the latter soon cut adrift from, and ceased to be influenced by, Chapman, who from this time onwards appears to have been the centre and inspirer of the continuous scholastic opposition to Shakespeare.

The earliest evidence I had hitherto found of Chapman's hostility to Shakespeare is in the old anonymous play of *Histriomastix, or the Player Whipt*, which, though revised by Chapman in collaboration with Marston in 1599 as a later attack upon Shakespeare, was first composed by Chapman in the autumn of 1593, after the return of Shakespeare and Lord Pembroke's company from their unprofitable provincial tour upon which they were compelled—as Henslowe informs Alleyn—" to pawn their apparel for their charges," an incident which is reflected in the play.

Richard Simpson, who was unaware of Chapman's authorship, and who tentatively attributes the play in its early form to Peele, placed its original composition at the time that Raleigh, Northumberland, Harriot, Warner, and others attempted to set up an academy in London. The references to this movement in Peele's *Honour of the Garter*, published in June 1593, and in Chapman's dedication to Royden of the *Hymns to the Shadow of Night*, published in 1594, indicate its date in 1593. The inceptive meetings of the academy were held at Raleigh's house, and were referred to at the time by a Jesuit as a " School of Atheism." It probably came to an end in 1593, because of the investigations into atheistic charges against certain of its members instituted by Cecil after the murder of Marlowe. In a forthcoming publication it will appear that these investigations were merely a smoke screen to divert attention from the shockingly criminal facts in Marlowe's case, as no prosecutions followed.

Kyd, in his letter to Sir John Puckering already quoted, mentions three members of the academy as friends of Marlowe, *i.e.* Harriot, Warner, and Royden. He also mentions Raleigh as Harriot's patron. In another letter of the same period (Harleian MS. 6848 f. 154),[1] Kyd informs Puckering that " Marlowe would persuade with men of quality to go unto the King of Scots, whither I hear Royden is gone, and where, if he had lived, he told me when I saw him last, he meant to be." The report that Royden had fled to Scotland—though untrue—indicates that Marlowe's murder, and the subsequent investigations into the alleged atheistic leanings of his academic acquaintances, had put an end to the meeting of the academy. We hear nothing further concerning its activities after 1593.

[1] This document was discovered in 1921 by Mr. Ford K. Brown, an American Rhodes scholar at Oxford, and announced in the *Times Literary Supplement* on June 2.

SIR THOMAS MORE

It appears, from the letter mentioning Royden here quoted, that this saintly soul had not yet entered holy orders, but that the atheistic charges against the "academy," of which he was a member, decided him upon taking this protective step; and that he now fled to Oxford and the horns of the altar, and when danger had passed indited his pious exercise, *Willobie his Avisa*, from "My chamber at Oxford," publishing it in the following year. It is not at all improbable that Royden was tacitly instigated to this by Cecilian agents.

The interested reader who wishes to convince himself of Chapman's authorship of the early *Histriomastix* may do so by analytically comparing the majority of the Chrysoganus passages of the play with Chapman's *Hymns to the Shadow of Night* (1594), his poem to Harriot (1598), and his *Tears of Peace*, which, though not published until 1609, was obviously written years earlier, as it displays all of the stylistic idiosyncrasies of his middle period. The few Chrysoganus passages in the play that were re-written by Marston in 1599 are easily to be distinguished from the unrevised work of Chapman.

In the original *Histriomastix*, Chapman endeavoured to dramatise the academic projects of Harriot and his noble patrons in 1593; Harriot, who was an astronomer and mathematician, is represented as Chrysoganus, an astronomer and mathematician who has set up an academy to expound the seven liberal sciences—Grammar, Logic, Rhetoric, Arithmetic, Geometry, Music, and Astronomy. The name Chrysoganus is a reflection of Harriot's unpublished *Ephemeris Chrisometra*, a MS. copy of which is preserved at Sion College. Chapman evidently presents himself in the character of Peace, whose utterances and mental attitude are identical with those of Peace and an interlocutor in *The Tears of Peace*; in the induction to which Chapman intimates that Peace is the spirit of Homer—who appears to him—and that he is himself the interlocutor. Shakespeare is caricatured as Postehaste, the stage poet for Sir Oliver Owlet's players, who, as in the case of Pembroke's men at the same period, are forced " to pawn their apparel for their charges."

When Marston, in 1599, revised *Histriomastix* as a later attack upon Shakespeare, he introduced the following lines referring to *Troilus and Cressida*, which had been presented in the preceding year by Shakespeare's company, and to make his satirical purposes unmistakable named Shakespeare in the words which I have italicised :

> Enter Troilus and Cressida
> Come, Cressida, my cressit light,
> Thy face doth shine both day and night.
> Behold, behold, thy garter blue . . .
> Thy knight his valiant elbow wears,
> That when he *shakes* his furious *speare*
> The foe in shivering fearful sort
> May lay him down in death to snort.

In a former publication, by the collation of passages in *Histriomastix* with Chapman's acknowledged work and other evidence, I have indicated his collaborative authorship to the satisfaction of the most authoritative students of Chapman.

Certain scholars already mentioned, who apparently still hold to the theory that Shakespeare was connected with Alleyn and Henslowe and Lord Strange's company between 1591 and 1594, have suggested the composition of *Sir Thomas More* as well as Shakespeare's Addition, in 1593, supposing the play to reflect riotous conditions incident to the alleged promulgation of libels against the foreigners in April and early in May in that year. The untenable nature of this surmise appears in the facts that there were no public performances in London for from ten to twelve weeks before this time, nor for seven months afterwards, the theatrical companies being absent in the provinces during this period, owing to the prevalence of the plague in London. Lord Pembroke's company, with which Shakespeare was then connected, and which never possessed *Sir Thomas More* as a property, returned to London late in August 1593, after an unprofitable spring and summer in the provinces, as Henslowe, in a letter to Alleyn dated September 28, 1593, reports : " As for my lord a Pembrokes which you desire to know where they be, they are all at home and hausse ben this five or six weakes, for they cane not save their charges with travell as I heare, and were fayne to pane their parell for their charges."

During this same period Strange's and the Admiral's men, who were combined into one company between 1591 and 1594, and who owned the MS. of *Sir Thomas More* at this time, were continuously in the provinces from early in the spring until late in December. In the provincial records they are recorded as acting as far away from London as York, in April 1593. By May 2 they had returned as near to London as Chelmsford, where they evidently refrained from coming to London, and awaited the receipt of a warrant from the Privy Council to enable them to continue playing in the provinces. A letter written by Alleyn to his wife from Chelmsford, upon May 2, 1593, shows clearly that he and his company had not recently left London, but that they had then been in the provinces for a prolonged period. Their return to a point near

London was apparently to secure a new warrant from the Privy Council, specifying the plague as the reason for their travelling. This warrant was issued on May 6.

A company coming from a plague-infested centre without such a specific and highly authoritative warrant would at times be refused permission to play by the provincial authorities, as knowledge of the severe plague conditions in such a centre spread abroad. It is probable that the ill-success of Shakespeare and Lord Pembroke's men in their travels during this spring and summer was due largely to this cause. It is now apparent that Lord Strange's and the Admiral's men and their writers could not have prepared, cast, or presented a play upon the subject of *Sir Thomas More* during the prevalence of the alleged agitation it is supposed to reflect, in April and first few days of May 1593. In a forthcoming publication it shall be made equally evident that after these events the Privy Council was in no mood to allow the reflection of such affairs upon the stage, and that theatrical managers and writers were not so unwise as to attempt them.

CHAPTER VI

GREENE'S COLLABORATION WITH LODGE AND NASHE

IN his epistle prefixed to Greene's *Menaphon*, in 1589, Nashe informs us that *The Arraignment of Paris* was Peele's earliest dramatic effort, by referring to it as his "first increase." On the title-page of the first issue of this play, published in 1584, we learn that it was "presented before the Queen's Majestie, by the Children of the Chapel"; as Peele took his B.A. degree at Oxford in 1579, it appears unlikely that it was presented before that date. That it was not presented in 1579 is evident in the fact that the Children of the Chapel appeared twice before the Queen in this year, presenting two plays, the names of which are recorded, i.e. *Loyalty and Beauty* and *Alcius*. They appeared also on February 5, 1581, and on February 27, 1582, no mention being made of the plays presented upon these occasions.

Upon December 26, 1582, they appeared again, presenting a play entitled *Game of Cards*. This being their last appearance at Court until 1601, it becomes evident, as Mr. Fleay suggested, that *The Arraignment of Paris* was presented upon one of the two occasions when no plays are recorded.

Sir Clyamon and Sir Clamydes, written by Greene at

about the same period and in fourteeners, in which most of *The Arraignment* is written, was played by the Queen's company; as this company was organised in 1583, this is clearly the earliest possible date for its production. Chapman's *Fidele and Fortunio*, written for Oxford's men, also in fourteeners, I find pertains also to about this period. These writers for competitive stages were evidently following the lead set by Peele in *The Arraignment of Paris*, the pronounced success of which led Nashe, in 1589, to proclaim Peele " The Atlas of Poetry and *primus verborum artifex*, whose first increase, *The Arraignment of Paris* . . goeth a steppe beyond all that write."

The sole reason given by Dyce for attributing *Sir Clyamon* to Peele is that " on the title-page of a copy of this play, a MS. note in a very old hand attributes it to Peele": not a very valid reason if, as appears to be the case, it is entirely unsupported by other evidence. The tradition that Peele wrote *Sir Clyamon* probably had its inception in its metrical similarity to most of *The Arraignment*, combined with the facts that it was for several years a property of the Admiral's men, during the period that Peele was the company poet, and that he or some of his collaborators in 1598, prior to sending this play to press, re-wrote it for Henslowe into *The Four Kings*, which was licensed for presentation in March 1599, the outworn version being published in this year.

As Mr. Fleay acutely noticed, this is the only known play of the period having four kings among its characters. Critics who have challenged Fleay's conclusion in this instance have, like Fleay himself, been apparently unaware of the corroborative value of concurrent publication, licence, or the entry of a play upon the Stationers' Registers, in indicating the approximate date of its revision, in instances where records of stage presentation are not available. As in numerous other instances of re-written plays already noticed, the old play here survives, while the revision is lost, a fact not at all surprising, the reason no doubt being that such revisions were probably as a rule so near in substance to the old plays that their publication would have been regarded as infringement of the copyright of the published plays. I have already made it clear that Peele's *Arraignment* antedates the production of *Sir Clyamon*. With the later history of the play now also clarified, a critical comparison of the poetical merits, the graceful diction, and the pleasing pastoral spirit of *The Arraignment* with the archaic, stilted, and prosy *Sir Clyamon*, should suffice to convince the critical reader of the practical impossibility of their common authorship. I will now indicate my reasons for attributing the latter play to Greene in his formative years.

When *The Arraignment of Paris* was written and presented before the Queen, Peele was from twenty-three to twenty-four years of age, and Greene about the same age when he produced *Sir Clyamon* a year or two later. Neither of them at that period had developed the characteristic floridity of style displayed for a period in some of their later plays, and each then still possessed and naturally used, in a large measure, the simpler vocabularies of their youthful environments. That of the London-bred, Oxford-schooled, untravelled, and essentially English Peele would naturally differ somewhat from the Norwich-bred, Cambridge-schooled, widely travelled, and more cosmopolitan Greene; though certain academic shibboleths acquired from their classical studies—and in Greene's case mostly from John Studley's Senecan translations—which were rather overworked by both Greene and Peele in their dramatic productions, would be common to both. Their acquisition of new ideas and forms of expression would accord with their differing degrees of receptivity and taste, and especially with their divergent experiences with life, at this receptive and formative period, and some slight habits of thought, phraseology, and diction, now acquired, be likely to persist in their future work as stylistic idiosyncrasies, the style being the man.

The Arraignment of Paris, while dealing with a classical subject, has its setting in a distinctively English landscape, and is redolent of English pastoral life. It requires no stretch of the imagination to fancy Peele, while still at Oxford, composing much of its matter in the open air in the late spring or early summer, in sight of green fields and grazing flocks. *Sir Clyamon*, on the other hand, suggests the labour of a study. Its folklore scenes and characters partake of the distorted perspectives of a mediæval tapestry, and savour more of earlier black-letter plays than of out of doors. Such sources of inspiration are indeed suggested in its John Gilpin-like prologue,

> As lately lifting up the leaves of worthy writers' works,
> Wherein the noble acts and deeds of many hidden lurks,
> Our Author he hath found the glass of glory shining bright;
> Whereas their lives are to be seen which honour did delight—

one at least of such " worthy writers' works " being " English Seneca." Greene and Nashe, in 1589, inferentially accuse Kyd of bleeding " English Seneca " " line by line " and " page by page," until " at length it must die to our stage," suggesting his lack of scholarship and that he based his work upon these translations. While Kyd was undoubtedly an ardent disciple of Seneca's, there is now no evidence in his phraseology or vocabulary that he was indebted to these translations; while in Greene's case very plain evidence exists for his free use of John Studley's translations of Seneca's *Agamemnon, Medea, Hercules Œtæus,* and *Hyppolytus.*

Though *Seneca his Tenne Tragedies* was not issued as a whole until 1581, when Thomas Newton translated the *Thebais* to make the tenth play in the collection then published, the other nine had been published separately from fourteen to twenty-two years earlier. Greene was apparently impressed at an earlier and formative period by Studley's translations, which were published in 1566 and 1567; as all of the Senecan elements and much of the vocabulary and phraseology of his earliest two plays, *Sir Clyamon and Sir Clamydes* and *Alphonsus of Arragon,* distinctly reflect, and, at times, parallel Studley.

The striking analogy between the diction alone of these two plays, though one is written in fourteeners, and the other—evidently a revision—in blank verse, should be enough to convince any critic that *Sir Clyamon* is a work of Greene's.

To quote one parallel between Studley and Greene: When Phædra, in Studley's translation of *Hyppolytus,* prepares to kill herself, she invocates the ghost of Hyppolytus as follows:

Have thou my life, give me thy death, that more deserveth it.
Cannot my proffer purchase place? Yet vengeance shalt thou have.
Hell shall not hold me from thy side, nor death of dompest grave.
Sith fates will not permit thee life, though I behest thee mine,
Myself I shall in spite of fate my fatal twist untwine.

Greene makes Sir Clamydes pledge his troth to Juliana in somewhat similar words:

Take here my hand of life and limb the living gods do lend,
To purchase thee the dearest drop of blood my heart shall spend;
And therefore, lady, link with me thy loyal heart for aye,
For I am thine till fates untwine of vital life the stay.

Other of Studley's characteristic words and phrases used by Greene, revealed by a casual examination of *Sir Clyamon* and Studley's translations, are: spoused, spousall, maugre, glittering (Peele in *The Arraignment* always uses glistering), wight, hight, grisly ghosts, grisly grief, stern cerberus (all of the Senecan allusions in *Sir Clyamon* are Studley's), dint, withouten, hughy, trudge, grudge, bale, baleful, accursed fate, greater griefs, hungry paunch, glittering gold, flickering fame, noble state, brunt of blows, dire distress, dire destruction, bruit of fame, winding waves, waltering waves. In the unusual and excessive alliteration Greene uses in *Sir Clyamon*, he seems to have modelled himself upon Studley's translation; he also appears to have taken his idea for the flying serpent from Studley's *Medea*.

While Greene's natural vocabulary at this period was simple and commonplace, he apparently endeavoured to impart an old-world flavour to his lines by the use of such odd words as: perstand (for understand), needly, needsly, valure (value), to sack (to heap), certis (certes), ensample, glazing; some of which he never afterwards uses. In his later plays, Greene occasionally coins words such as squeltering, nutrimented, contentation, which he afterwards abandons.

Were we unaware of the authorship of *The Arraignment of Paris*, the characteristic expression " the house of fame," used here by the London-bred Peele for the first time, when he evidently had Westminster Abbey in mind, but used frequently afterwards in his later works, and even in his revision of *Titus Andronicus*, where it signifies a similar imaginary Roman Valhalla, or the frequent use of such a simple word as " lovely "—always a great favourite with Peele—would tell us to look further for his hand; while the entire absence of this latter word from a long poem like *Sir Clyamon*, containing, as it does, over two thousand lines, would be enough to cast suspicion upon its attribution to Peele, and lead us to seek further evidences of wrong ascription.

In affirming my conclusion that *Sir Clyamon* is not by Peele, I will ask the interested reader who may wish for further evidence to read both plays carefully, and, having done so, to examine the first three hundred lines in each play, and to select from each three hundred all the words he does not find in the other play. If he does so, he will compile two lists, the volume and nature of which will convince him that the two plays were written by two men possessing at that time two comparatively simple, yet widely differing, native vocabularies, and differing also in their selective acquisition of new words.

In choosing such words from *Sir Clyamon*, he will find the now common word " pensive " used a number of times, but never in *The Arraignment*. This appears to have been acquired by Greene from Studley, and to have been an uncommon word at this period, as it is used only once by Shakespeare, though it appears also in Greene's *Third Part of Henry VI.*, and occasionally in Greene's other plays.

In *Sir Clyamon* we also have the following words,

which are not to be found in *The Arraignment*, but are used a number of times in Greene's known productions: environ, environed, ure, latitude, longitude, beck, amates (daunts), shift, shifts (Peele in *The Arraignment* uses wiles, policy, cunning, trick, in this sense, but never shift or shifts, while Greene frequently uses the latter in all of his plays), valliancy or valiance, foltering or faltering, waltering or weltering, propound, maugre, shrouds, paunch, veriest, gladsome, gladsomeness, darksome, darksomeness, bale, baleful, froward, cosenage, arrogancy, oblivion, contention. Most of these words are common also, in *Mucidorus Locrine* and *Selimus*, and are mostly acquisitions from Studley.

The coined word "clubbish," used in *Sir Clyamon*, while not to be found again in Greene's work, he also acquired from Studley, as well as his use of similar words ending in ish, such as hardish, blackish, greenish, lakish (like a lake). In *Mucidorus* I find darkish, and in *Selimus*, bookish. This characteristic of Greene's I do not find elsewhere at this early period except in Studley, who indulges in it freely.

In dealing with *Sir Clyamon*, and endeavouring to trace evidences of Greene's style, we are presumably working upon his earliest dramatic attempt, written at an inceptive period and before his matured style had formed. It is very significant, then, that we should also find in this play one other phrase peculiar to Greene, and never to be found elsewhere, that would definitely indicate his hand in the play, even though no other positive evidence existed. This phrase, "King and Kaiser" or "King or Kaiser," was evidently acquired by Greene in his early continental travels. He uses it also four times in one of his most

GREENE, LODGE, AND NASHE 143

characteristic plays—*Alphonsus of Arragon*—and once in *George-a-Greene*.

The fact that no play written by Peele is known to have been presented by the Queen's company, and that Peele's history indicates no connection at any time with that company, while all of Greene's known, and some hitherto unknown plays, are shown to have been presented by the Queen's men, or their affiliated company, Sussex's men, combined with the significant internal evidence already adduced, as well as the entire absence of negative evidence, appears to warrant the conclusion that in the old Queen's company's play of *Sir Clyamon and Sir Clamydes* we have Greene's "first increase," as in *The Arraignment of Paris*, written for the Children of the Chapel at the same period, we have Peele's.

Greene having been connected with the Queen's company from 1583 to 1591, and with the new Queen's and Sussex's men from 1591 to 1592, it becomes evident that he must have produced a much larger number of plays during these nine years than the six at present attributed to him in nearly all editions of his works.

In *The Repentance of Robert Greene*, published shortly after his death in 1592, Greene writes: "After I had proceded Maister of Arts, I left the university and away to London, where (after I had continued a short time . . .) I became an author of plays." As Greene took his M.A. degree in 1583, this clearly refers to that year, and evidently to the beginning of his connection with the Queen's men, who were organized at the same date. Nashe's report, that Greene produced "more than four others for the company," his undoubted connection with the Queen's company, and the entire absence of any indication that he ever wrote for other companies until 1591—when he wrote two plays in collaboration with Nashe for the new Queen's company and its affiliated company, Sussex's men —give good grounds for the inference that he produced a number of other plays for the old Queen's company between 1583 and 1591. This latter company, as I have shown, disbanded late in 1590 or early in 1591, when a large number, if not all, of its old plays were absorbed by Strange's and Pembroke's companies.

Of the six plays generally attributed to Greene by his editors, *Orlando Furioso*, *Friar Bacon and Friar Bungay*, and *A Looking Glass for London* went into the hands of Strange's company, and *James IV.* to Pembroke's men, in 1591. *Alphonsus King of Arragon* was never entered upon the Stationers' Registers, but was published in 1599. It also was evidently a property of the Strange-Admiral's men from 1591 to 1599, as Fleay's suggestion that Jonson, in the prologue to *Every Man in his Humour*, referred critically to this play in the phrase "descending throne"— alluding to the fact that in its stage directions Venus is "let down from the top of the stage"—appears very plausible, as no other known play then being presented exhibited the same characteristic.

There is no evidence that *George-a-Greene* was ever owned by the old Queen's company. The first we know of this play is its presentation upon Henslowe's boards by Sussex's company on December 29, 1593, as an old play. While Greene's hand is undoubtedly present in the play, it appears to have been somewhat overwritten by a later hand, and even much of the original matter appears to have been the work of a collaborator. There being no trace of Lodge's hand, which is clearly present in *A Look-*

GREENE, LODGE, AND NASHE 145

ing Glass for London and the *Three Parts of Henry VI.*, all produced before the beginning of 1591 for the old Queen's company—and being also a Sussex play, produced after this date, it is probably, like *The Old Wives' Tale*, a joint production of Greene and Nashe, for Sussex's company, between 1591 and 1592. Nashe and Lodge were the only writers that are known to have collaborated with Greene at this period ; and it will be shown that all three wrote for the Queen's and Sussex's men, between 1591 and 1592. *George-a-Greene* was enterd on the Stationers' Registers in 1595 but not published until 1599. It evidently underwent some changes in these four years, during which it was probably played by a provincial company. As there is nothing satirical in the play, and Greene alludes to his " last " collaborative effort with Nashe as of a satirical nature, I place *George-a-Greene* anterior to the production of *The Old Wives' Tale*, which was evidently produced late in 1591 or early in 1592, as Harvey's *Lamb of God*, in answer to it, appeared in 1592, and Greene's *Quip for an Upstart Courtier*, in answer to Harvey, appeared also in this year. It will be noticed that both *The Old Wives' Tale* and *George-a-Greene* are very short plays, the latter being entered on the Stationers' Registers as an interlude. This was evidently due to the fact that they were written primarily for provincial performances, the Queen's and Sussex's men being continuously in the provinces from 1591 till 1594, except for six or eight weeks at the end of this period, when a new reorganisation of companies was under way.

The elimination of *George-a-Greene* leaving only five plays as Greene's production for the old Queen's company between 1583 and 1591, it becomes evident, in view of Nashe's mention of the prolific nature of his work for this company, that he must have produced for it a number of other plays. I have already shown that Pembroke's men, in addition to *James IV.*, secured from the Queen's companies' properties, in 1591, *The True Tragedy of Richard III.*, *The Famous Victories of Henry V.*, *The Troublesome Raigne of King John*, the originals of the *Three Parts of Henry VI.*, and *Locrine*; and, as I recognise Greene's and Lodge's hands in the earlier form of *Mucidorus*, which was published in a revised form in 1610, with a title-page reading, "amplified with new additions, as it was acted before the King's Majestie at Whitehall on Shrove Sunday night. By his Highness Servants usually playing at the Globe"—if I am correct in my ascription of the play to Greene and Lodge, it is evident that this play also became a Burbage property in or about 1598, when the earlier form was sent to press along with Chapman's *The Blind Beggar of Alexandria* by the Admiral's company, and published by William Jones, who is mentioned only three times in the Stationers' Registers, and each time as issuing Admiral's plays.

I have now no hesitancy in ascribing to Greene the following plays written for the Queen's company before 1591, and in their original state, in approximately the order given.

    1583 . *Sir Clyamon and Sir Clamydes.*
    1584 . *Alphonsus of Arragon* (revised in 1587).
    1584–5 . *Mucidorus* (revised in 1587, and later).
    1585–6 . *Locrine* (revised in 1588–9).
    1586–7 . *Friar Bacon and Friar Bungay.*
    1587–8 . *Selimus.*
    1588–9 . *Orlando Furioso.*
    1589–90 . *James IV.*

GREENE, LODGE, AND NASHE

To Greene and Lodge, in collaboration, I ascribe the following plays at about the dates given :

1588 . *The Troublesome Raigne of King John.*

This play is mostly by Lodge ; Scene xi., evidently introduced as comic relief, is definitely recognisable as Greene's ; the short-lined verses, interspersed with Latin phrases, in this scene plainly reproducing similar verses spoken by Miles in *Friar Bacon and Friar Bungay*, produced in the preceding year.

1588 . *The First Part of Henry VI.*, in its original form.

In collaborating in this play in its original form in about 1588-9, the division of the work appears to have been arranged by Greene taking the French and Lodge the English scenes; and though both hands at times appear in scenes where the two nationals are presented, Greene, being the company poet, evidently linked their dual efforts. While this distinction has been somewhat complicated by the introduction of new matter, or the alteration of lines or scenes in both Lodge's and Greene's work by Peele or his collaborators in revising the play for Strange's men in 1592, Lodge's monotonous rhythm, prosy diction, and preponderance of evenly measured and end-stopped lines are readily distinguishable in the English scenes from Greene's greater freedom of rhythm and more heightened and animated style, with its larger proportion of run-on lines in the French scenes.

Yet, notwithstanding Peele's revision, a few scenes still remain in which no material alterations seem to have been made. Act v. Scene iii., from line 45 onwards, as well as all of Act v. Scene v., are still as definitely recognisable as

Lodge's work, as Act I. Scenes iii. and vi. are as Greene's.

Shakespeare's sole contribution to *Henry VI. Part I.* is the Temple Garden scene, and possibly a few lines linking with this scene in later parts of the play. These additions, or revisions, cannot have been made before about the middle of 1594, when the play became a Burbage property for the first time.

In revising this play in 1592 Peele, as the company poet for the Strange–Admiral's men, devoted his efforts largely to enhancing the part taken by Talbot, making him practically the protagonist of the action; and in doing so was evidently suiting himself to the desires of his chief, Edward Alleyn, to whom Nashe alludes as the company's " Cæsar," and who evidently had a penchant for dominant star rôles.

The rhymed Talbot passages in Act IV. Scenes v. vi. and vii., though apparently a drastic revision of less spirited and unrhymed lines written by Lodge, are in their present form entirely Peele's verses, though he may have retained a few words and phrases from Lodge's vocabulary, such as misbegotten, sapless, bastard, warlike sword, warlike rage, leaden, well I wot, lither, mickle, Icarus, smeared, brandished.

In the latter part of Act IV. Scene vii., which is devoted to French characters and consequently—if my deduction is correct—written by Greene, we have the word " giglot " which I have not found elsewhere earlier than in Greene. In *Orlando Furioso* we have :

> Whose choice is like that Greekist giglots love.

Lodge also uses the word in *Rosalynde,* but probably

borrowed it from Greene. Marlowe, to whom it has been attributed, never uses it. Peele's revisionary hand is also to be found in every scene in the remainder of the play in which Talbot appears in the action. As these appearances are generally in scenes originally written by Lodge, *i.e.* the English scenes, it is not difficult to distinguish the two hands. Peele's and Greene's hands, however, are not so readily distinguishable. The expression, " the terror of the French," which Nashe uses in commending the revival of the play in 1592, was evidently a phrase of Peele's. It is used for the first time in Act I. Scene iv., originally a Lodge scene, and now largely and typically Peele's. A few lines below this phrase we have the lines :

> And with my nails digged stones out of the ground
> To hurl at the beholders of my shame."

A similar expression of hardihood is used by Peele in *Edward I.*, Act I. Scene ii. :

LORDS. These are they will enter brazen gates
And tear down lime and mortar with their nails.

The fact that Greene, as the company poet, would be likely in his collaboration with Lodge to write the portions of the plays which linked their work, and the likelihood that each might unconsciously copy the other's vocabulary, render it difficult at times clearly to distinguish one hand from the other. Greene, being the more exuberant dramaturgist and ardent neologist, exercised a much more pronounced influence upon Lodge's vocabulary than did Lodge upon Greene, yet Lodge's qualifying influence upon Greene is noticeable as their work progresses,

Greene's diction losing much of its former excessive floridity and overworked classicism. A comparison of *Locrine* and *Orlando* with Greene's hand in the *Henry VI.* plays, *James IV.*, and *A Looking Glass for London*, reveals a much less flamboyant Greene in the later plays.

As Greene's simpler and more restrained style dates from about 1589, when we find him, with Nashe, resenting the dramatic theories of a certain "idiot art-master," whom they accuse of "contemning arts as unprofitable," it is not improbable that Shakespeare's dramatic judgment, though scurrilously resented, had borne fruit. Even Marlowe appears to have seen a new light at this time. *Edward II.*, written for Shakespeare's company after the end of 1590, when compared with *Tamburlaine*, reveals in an enhanced degree the same distinction noticed in the case of Greene's plays. We might never have had a play of Marlowe's differing so distinctly in style from *Tamburlaine* as *Edward II.* had Shakespeare's critical influence upon Marlowe been lacking.

Much has been written by past critics concerning Marlowe's stylistic influence upon Shakespeare. Such opinions were originally formed almost entirely upon the erroneous supposition that Shakespeare wrote the *Three Parts of Henry VI.* and *Richard III.* in their entirety, and that the traces of the hand that we now recognise as Marlowe's in three of these plays were written by the youthful Shakespeare while under the spell of Marlowe's style. It is not long since these opinions were generally held by scholars, and though in recent years critical students have recognised that Shakespeare's was merely one of several hands in these plays, the nature and the dates of his work and of the work of the others are still very nebulously and divergently considered, and even latter-day writers still continue to repeat the fiction of Marlowe's stylistic influence. The actual fact seems to have been that in 1588-9 a new authority appeared in the dramatic world, who was tacitly recognised as such by the scholars, who yet opposed and belittled him by terming him an " upstart reformer of arts." He was an authority in a double sense : in the teeth of the schoolmen, he advocated a naturalistic drama, portraying and expressing life and nature, and he fortunately occupied also an authoritative position as a reader and critic for the most important theatrical organisation in England, a position in which he was enabled to make his ideas operative in spite of the opposition of his critics. They attacked him in print and, no doubt, in other ways. Their attacks, while veiled, were vicious and bitter. Yet within a year of the time that these attacks first begin we have evidence, in the productions of his rivals, that they had recognised the practical common sense of his views and were endeavouring to conform to the naturalness he advocated.

Lodge's collaborative work with Greene for the old Queen's company seems to have had its inception early in 1588, as his hand is recognisable only in Greene's and Queen's plays produced from this date onwards, except in the case of a few passages in *Mucidorus* in the Bremo and Amadine scenes, which, however, are evidently due to a revision of this much-revised play in about 1588.

Though Lodge appears to have been connected with theatrical and dramatic affairs as early as about 1580, when he wrote *A Reply to Stephen Gosson's School of Abuse, in Defense of Poetry, Music, and Stage Plays*, we have no record of dramatic work by him until about 1587, when *The Wounds of Civil War*, as " Publicly plaid in London " by the Admiral's servants, was published. It was probably produced some time between 1585 and 1587, during which interval it will appear that Lodge worked with Kyd for the Burbage-Alleyn interests. As the Admiral's men had their inception in 1585, this play cannot have been presented by them before that date; and as Lodge was continuously connected with Greene and the Queen's company from about the beginning of 1588 until the end of 1590, it cannot have been produced later than 1587, when it was published. This infers that Lodge had written for the Burbage-Alleyn interests earlier, and that he collaborated with Kyd for some time during his régime as company poet preceding the advent of Marlowe. Evidence will later be adduced that he worked with Kyd or revised Kyd's work in an earlier form of *The Comedy of Errors*, which was evidently an old Burbage property. Both Lodge's and Greene's hands, though much overwritten by Marlowe, and slightly by Shakespeare, are still clearly recognisable in the *Second* and *Third Parts of Henry VI.*, written in about 1589-90.

Though Marlowe's, and in a lesser degree Shakespeare's, revisions of the *Second* and *Third Parts of Henry VI.* have greatly obscured both Lodge's and Greene's hands, there are still sufficient remains of both the older hands to enable us to judge that they divided their labours in these two plays in much the same manner as in *Part I.*, Lodge apparently writing the Lancastrian, and Greene the

GREENE, LODGE, AND NASHE

Yorkist scenes, as well as most of the dialogues uniting the action of the two parts.

All of Marlowe's revisions in these two plays were necessarily made between the beginning of 1591 and his death in 1593; and most, if indeed not all, of Shakespeare's after this date, with the possible exception of an early retouching of the Jack Cade scenes in *Part II*.

As all of these plays remained in MS. until the issue of the Folio in 1623, and were probably acted at intervals as late as, if not later than, 1599 to 1600, when Shakespeare's *Henry V.* was first presented, it appears likely that some slight changes were made years after the early revisions of 1591-2.

The Temple Garden scene in *Part I.*, which is generally accepted as Shakespeare's work, cannot at the earliest have been written before the last part of 1594, while comparative metrical considerations point to from 1595 to 1596.

The first twenty lines of Young Clifford's declamation in *Part II.*, Act v. Scene ii., which, in their present form, seem surely to be Shakespeare's verses, whoever may have written the original matter which he revised, indicate a still later period. Neither Marlowe, Greene, nor Lodge at any time, nor Shakespeare before about 1598-9, ever produced any lines exhibiting the dramatic exaltation and passion, combined with the rhythmic and metrical freedom, here displayed. The word " particularities " which Shakespeare uses here he probably found, for the first time, in the Admiral's company's *Henry V.*, which he revised into its present form in 1599. It is not to be found elsewhere in Shakespeare, and I have not found it in either

Greene or Lodge. It sounds like a coinage of Chapman's. Young Clifford's declamation in these twenty lines reads :

> Y. CLIFF. Shame and confusion! all is on the rout ;
> Fear frames disorder, and disorder wounds
> Where it should guard. O war, thou son of hell,
> Whom angry heavens do make their minister,
> Throw in the frozen bosoms of our part
> Hot coals of vengeance ! Let no soldier fly.
> He that is truly dedicate to war
> Hath no self-love, nor he that loves himself
> Hath not essentially but by circumstance
> The name of valour. (*Seeing his dead father.*) O, let
>   the vile world end,
> And the premised flames of the last day
> Knit earth and heaven together !
> Now let the general trumpet blow his blast,
> Particularities and petty sounds
> To cease ! Wast thou ordain'd, dear father,
> To lose thy youth in peace, and to achieve
> The silver livery of advised age,
> And, in thy reverence and thy chair-days, thus
> To die in ruffian battle ?

The original, as it appears in *The Contention*, and apparently Lodge's work overwritten by Greene, containing as it does Greene's characteristic phrase, " Lukewarm blood," reads :

> YOUNG CLIFFORD.   Father of Comberland,
> Where may I seeke my aged father forth?
> O ! dismall sight, see where he breathlesse
>   lies,
> All smeard and weltred in his luke-warme
>   blood.
> Ah, aged pillar of all Comberlands true house,
> Sweete father, to thy murthred ghoast I
>   sweare
> Immortall hate unto the house of Yorke,
> Nor never shall I sleepe secure one night,
> Till I have furiously revengde thy death,
> And left not one of them to breathe on
>   earth.

GREENE, LODGE, AND NASHE

It is very clear that the above passage afforded little inspiration for Shakespeare's revision, and equally clear that the presence of the word "particularities" in his revision, as well as the distinct dramatic analogy between Shakespeare's version of Young Clifford's speech and Northumberland's speech in *Henry IV., Part II.,* Act I. Scene i., denotes Shakespeare's revision of, at least, this passage in *Henry VI., Part II.,* in about 1598-9, at the same period that he revised the Admiral's *Henry V.* into *Henry IV., Part II.,* and the present *Henry V.* Northumberland's reaction to the news of his son Hotspur's death produces the same dramatic expression, and in lines exhibiting similar metrical freedom, as Young Clifford's to the sight of his dead father.

> NORTH. Now bind my brows with iron ; and approach
> The ragged'st hour that time and spite dare bring
> To frown upon the enraged Northumberland !
> Let heaven kiss earth ! now let not Nature's hand
> Keep the wild flood confined ! let order die !
> And let this world no longer be a stage
> To feed contention in a lingering act ;
> But let one spirit of the first-born Cain
> Reign in all bosoms, that, each heart being set
> On bloody courses, the rude scene may end,
> And darkness be the burier of the dead !

Morton's lines in this same Act and Scene of *Henry IV., Part II.*:

> .... for their spirits and souls,
> This word, rebellion, it had froze them up,
> As fish are in a pond—

also appear to have suggested the phrase "frozen bosoms" in the following lines in Young Clifford's speech :

> ... O war, thou son of hell,
> Whom angry heavens do make their minister,
> Throw in the frozen bosoms of our part
> Hot coals of vengeance !

156   GREENE, LODGE, AND NASHE

In passing, I will here propose an emendation of lines 34 to 41, Act I. Scene iii. of *Henry IV., Part II.*, which in their present state have always puzzled critics—an emendation so simple and obvious it seems strange that it has never before been suggested. These lines read :

> HAST. But, by your leave, it never yet did hurt
> To lay down likelihoods and forms of hope.
>
> L. BARD. Yes, if this present quality of war
> Indeed the instant action : a cause on foot,
> Lives so in hope, as in an early spring
> We see the appearing buds ; which to prove fruit,
> Hope gives not so much warrant as despair
> That frosts will bite them.

The only change needed here to give the passage clear Shakespearean meaning is the alteration of the first *e* in the word " indeed " into a *u*, making it *indued*. Shakespeare uses this word five times elsewhere in his plays, and in four out of the five spells it " indued," and only once " endued." " Indeed " is obviously a misprint for " indued."

As the above instances indicate late but slight revisions by Shakespeare, so the following example clearly displays an early revision by Marlowe, and probably a later change by Shakespeare.

A comparison of lines 214 to 235 in *Henry VI., Part II.*, Act I. Scene i. with lines 236 to 259 plainly reveals the latter as a revision of the former lines, which appear followed by their revision in *Henry VI., Part II.*, while only the revised lines appear in *The Contention*. I formerly regarded lines 236 to 259 as Shakespeare's early revision of Greene's lines immediately preceding them. A more careful consideration now leads me to the conclusion that these lines are Marlowe's, written in 1591–2 and slightly altered by Shakespeare in 1594-5, when he probably added or altered the last six lines in conformity with his purpose, recently indicated in his writing or revision of the Temple Garden scene, of making the Wars of the Roses the connecting theme in the *Three Parts of Henry VI.* and *Richard III.* All but one of the references to red and white roses as factional emblems appear to have been introduced into these four plays by Shakespeare. Such references in the Temple Garden scene, which initiates this theme, outnumber those in all of the other plays. The one exception is in characteristic lines of Greene's in *Part III.*, Act I. Scene ii. :

> I cannot rest until the white rose that I wear
> Be dyed even in the lukewarm blood of Henry's heart.

Shakespeare's revisionary work in the *Three Parts of Henry VI.* is very subsidiary to that of Peele in the *First Part*, and of Marlowe in the *Second* and *Third Parts*. Had Shakespeare revised these three plays in the thorough manner in which he appears to have revised *Richard III.*, he would not have left in them an average of from thirty to forty classical allusions, but would, no doubt, have reduced the proportion to about the minimum of from three to four, at present to be found in his own historical plays of this period, as well as in his revisions of *Edward III.* and *Richard III.*

The last collaborative work by Lodge and Greene for the old Queen's company was produced before the end of 1590, when the bulk of their properties were absorbed by Strange's and Pembroke's men. I assign to the year

1590 . *A Looking Glass for London.*

That this play was one of Greene's latest productions

for the old Queen's men is indicated by the fact that it was still a current play in the spring of 1592, when Henslowe's records of Strange's performances first began. That the *First Part of Henry VI.* was older is suggested by the fact that it was re-written by Peele and his collaborators at the same time that the former play was still current.

To Greene and Nashe, in collaboration, for the new Queen's and Sussex's companies, which performed together between 1591 and 1594, I ascribe in

    1591 . *George-a-Greene* and *The Virgin Martyr* (under an older title and in an earlier form);

and in

    1592 . *The Old Wives' Tale.*

To Lodge's hand, written for the new Queen's and Sussex's men, I ascribe in

    1591 . the old *King Leir.*

Though nothing is known of Greene's *Alphonsus of Arragon* until 1587–8, when it was evidently re-written in emulation of Marlowe's *Tamburlaine*, a critical examination of Greene's vocabulary and construction reveals it as a very early play, dating shortly after his *Sir Clyamon*, and, like this play, lacking in the comic element so prominent in *Mucidorus, Locrine, Friar Bacon, Selimus,* and *Orlando.* Its plot and action are also, as in *Sir Clyamon*, simpler and less developed than in the later plays mentioned, the scenes being given over largely in *Sir Clyamon*, and probably in *Alphonsus* in its early form, to long-winded Senecan declamation. When these two plays were first written Greene still held closely to Studley's translations in "English Seneca" as his model. It is evident that *Locrine*, another comparatively early play, was also re-written in about 1588 to 1589.

If the first appearance of Strumbo in *Locrine*, Act I. Scene ii., in which he is depicted as inditing a love note to Dorothie, be compared with his characterisation in the remainder of the play, this scene, as well as a few lines in Act II. Scene ii. and Act II. Scene iii. mentioning Dorothie, will plainly be recognised as interpolations at a later period of revision; and that this later period was from 1589 to 1590 is indicated by the close resemblance of the themes of Strumbo's love letter to Dorothie and Mullidor's love letter to Mirimida in the *Second Part of Never Too Late*, which was published in 1590. Both Strumbo's and Mullidor's letters caricature Shakespeare's 153rd and 154th Sonnets, which were written at a very early date, probably as early as 1588, and certainly not later than 1590, to Anne Sackfielde, while she still lived at Hotwells, near Bristol. Both letters satirically reproduce the torridity of love expressed in these two sonnets; both represent the writer as a simple country clown attempting literature; and Strumbo's letter, in addition, alludes very pointedly to the "fountain" of the 153rd Sonnet. Strumbo's letter is as follows :

> "So it is, mistresse Dorothie, and the sole essence of my soule, that the little sparkles of affection kindled in me towards your sweet selfe hath now increased to a great flame, and will ere it be long consume my poore heart, *except you, with the pleasant water of your secret fountaine, quench the furious heate of the same.*"

There is nothing remotely suggestive of any literary endeavour in the Strumbo of the later scenes. Strumbo's first appearance in the earlier form of the play was evidently in Act II. Scene ii., where he appears as a master cobbler. Dorothie is brought into the round sung by the cobblers in this scene in order to link with the preceding scene, but is disposed of by being burnt to death in Scene iii., and is dismissed by Strumbo in the lines :

> And that which grieves me most
> My loving wife
> (O cruel strife)
> The wretched flames did roast.

The Strumbo of the early form of the play, exhibiting the type of love-making more grossly natural to Greene's yokels and clowns, appears in Act III. Scene iii. Here also appear the countryman, Oliver, and his son, William—the father and brother of his wife, Margerie—*for the first and last time*, evidently a vestige of the older play, where the countryman's part was, no doubt, more largely developed ; and probably reproducing Corin, the countryman in *Sir Clyamon and Sir Clamydes*, who talks in exactly the same manner.

In a preceding chapter I have argued that *Locrine* was a property of Pembroke's company sent to press by Shakespeare in 1594. It was published in the following year with a title-page reading :

> Newly set foorth, overseene and corrected,
> By W. S.

It will probably be thought by some who may not be inclined to agree with my conclusion, that Shakespeare would not be likely to send to press a play containing personal caricature upon himself. Until I recognised the fact that Scene ii. of Act I., displaying Strumbo as a lover and a writer of ardent and fiery love epistles, and also as a replica of Mullidor, must have been introduced into the revised *Locrine* at or about the date of the publication of

Never Too Late in 1590, and intended, like Mullidor in the latter, as an attack upon Shakespeare, I had given the phrase upon the title-page and Shakespeare's initials no particular attention, and had dismissed it as a liberty taken by the publisher.

In the light of Greene's attack upon Shakespeare in *Locrine*, a careful consideration of the phrase on its title-page, the unusualness of the word " overseene " in such a connection, the fact that Greene was dead, and that friends of his, such as Nashe, Roydon, and Chapman, were now arrayed against Shakespeare, and, doubtless, cognizant of Greene's intention, lead me to conclude that in this instance Creede took no liberties, but was instructed and authorised by Shakespeare to use this phrase and his initials, as the best means, under the circumstances, of showing his unconcern of the implied attack. I now regard it as a mildly ironical gesture very typical of his usual attitude towards his jealous critics. It is probable that the only correction made by Shakespeare in this play was in the fourth line from the end, where the words " eight and thirty years," which coincide with the date of publication in 1595, took the place of a number indicating either its date of composition or of its previous presentation. *Locrine*, in its earliest form, pertains to a period near to that of the early *Mucidorus* and *Sir Clyamon and Sir Clamydes*, and was certainly not later than from 1585 to 1586.

Greene, conceiving his failure with the re-vamped *Alphonsus*—which he admits in *Perimedes the Blacksmith* in 1588—to be due to the lack of blasphemy in his lines, shortly afterwards produced *Selimus*, which still more plainly attempts to imitate Marlowe's style and subject.

Here he endeavours to make up for his deficiency in *Alphonsus* by making Selimus voice all of the atheistic views currently imputed to Marlowe, to whom he had recently alluded as " that atheist Tamburlaine ":

> Then first the sacred name of King began:
> And things that were as common as the day
> Did then to set possessors first obey;
> Then they establisht laws and holy rites
> To maintain peace and govern bloodie fights,
> Then some sage man above the vulgar wise,
> Knowing that lawes could not in quiet dwell
> Unless they were observed: did first devise
> The names of God, religion, heaven, and hell,
> And gan of pains and fained rewards to tell;
> Pains for those men which did neglect the law,
> Rewards for those that lived in quiet awe;
> Whereas indeed they were mere fictions,
> And if they were not Selim thinks they were:
> And these religious observations,
> Only bugbears to keep the world in fear,
> And make men quietly a yoke to bear.
> So that religion of itself a fable,
> Was only found to make us peaceable.

Towards the close of the play, as a sop to orthodoxy, he presents Selimus's brother, Corcut, as dying in the Christian faith :

> Selimus I have convert with Christians,
> And learned of them the way to save my soul,
> And please the anger of the highest God:
> Tis he that made this pure christalline vault,
> Which hangeth over our unhappy heads;
> From thence he doth behold each sinner's fault,
> And though our sinnes under his feet he treads
> And for a while seeme for to winke at us,
> But is to recall us from our ways,
> But if we do like headstrong sons neglect
> To hearken to our loving father's voice,
> Then in his anger will he us reject
> And give us over to our wicked choice:

Selim before this dreadful majestie,
There lies a book written with bloodie lines,
Where our offences all are registered,
Which if we do not hastily repent,
We are reserved to lasting punishment.

In the epilogue to *Selimus* Greene promises a *Second Part*, of which we have no record. The *First Part*, in its present form, was published in 1594, without entry upon the Stationers' Registers. A comparison of the plot of *Tamber Cam*, in *Alleyn's Papers*, with *Selimus* suggests the probability that Greene produced a *Second Part*, and that the *Two Parts* were elaborated, and transformed by Peele into the *Two Parts of Tamber Cam*. Both plays deal with the conquests of a powerful nomadic chieftain of the type of *Tamburlaine*. Peele took similar liberties in the case of *Titus Andronicus*, even to the changing of the name of the play.

The first knowledge we possess of the old *King Leir* is its presentation upon Henslowe's boards as an old play upon April 6, 1594, by the Queen's and Sussex's men performing together. The Queen's company mentioned here was the new Queen's company organised in 1591. It was evidently not a large company, as in nearly all of its provincial appearances between 1591 and 1594 it performs in company with Sussex's men.

Among the properties of these united companies during this period were *George-a-Greene* and *The Old Wives' Tale*, written for them by Greene and Nashe in 1591-2, and the old *King Leir*, written for them by Lodge. As Lodge left England in August 1591, with Thomas Cavendish, on a voyage to the Straits of Magellan, and did not return until 1593, it is evident that he produced *King Leir* before

August 1591. There being no extant plays attributed to Lodge after this date, it appears probable that *King Leir* was his last dramatic effort. In this play he shows less of Greene's influence upon his vocabulary and phraseology than in any of his dramatic work, most of which was produced in collaboration with Greene. *King Leir* has usually been regarded as a very early play, dating somewhere in the early 'eighties of the sixteenth century. In its present form, it shows no evidence of revision or re-writing, nor of more than one period. The extensive use made by its author of Warner's *Albion's England,* published in 1586, evidences its production after that year, while his still more palpable debt to Spenser's *Fairie Queen,* published in 1590, as well as the fact that it was a property of the new Queen's company, definitely indicates its production between about the end of 1590 and August 1591, when Lodge left England. An analytical comparison of Lodge's hand in *King Leir, The Troublesome Raigne of King John,* and *A Looking Glass for London* with the *Three Parts of Henry VI.*—making allowances for Peele's revision in the *First Part* and Marlowe's and Shakespeare's in the others—sheds much light upon the large share he undoubtedly had in these three plays; while a similar comparison with Shakespeare's *Richard III.* suggests the strong probability that a play by Lodge, or by Lodge and Greene, based upon *The True Tragedie of Richard III.,* intervened between that play and Marlowe's work, and that it was Lodge's and Greene's revision or re-writing of *The True Tragedie of Richard III.,* rather than the old play itself, that Marlowe and Shakespeare in turn worked upon in producing *Richard III.* as we now know it. The substratum in this play that is not recognisable either as Marlowe's or Shakespeare's shows no stylistic analogy to *The True Tragedie of Richard III.*, but reveals an unmistakable resemblance to Lodge's hand. Lodge's revisionary hand is here and there recognisable even in the old *True Tragedie of Richard III.*, though the play as a whole is not his nor Greene's composition.

The old *King Leir* was evidently written by the same author as *The Troublesome Raigne of King John*, which it strongly resembles, though the latter play is clearly the earlier composition. It contains the characteristic phrases attributed by Fleay to Lodge, " razors of Palermo " and " a cooling card," and *The Troublesome Raigne of King John* also contains the latter. While these phrases were undoubtedly characteristic of Lodge, who uses them also in his acknowledged work, they were not both peculiar to him. " A cooling card " appears to have been first adopted as a metaphor by Lyly, and to have been borrowed from him by Greene and Lodge. Fleay, aware of its original medical significance, and knowing Lodge to have become a physician, supposed it to have been his invention as a metaphor.

There is no evidence that Lodge took up the study of medicine until about 1596, and he never uses the phrase in a therapeutic sense; while Greene, who describes himself upon the title-page of *Planetomachia*, in 1585, as a student in physics, nearly always does.

In *Never Too Late* (1590) he writes: " This news was such a cooling card to the curtesan that the extreme heat of her love was already grown to be lukewarm." [1]

Ten years earlier, in *Mamillia*, he uses it in a similar sense, " a cooling card to quench the fire of fancie," and

[1] Greene's dramatic use of the word "lukewarm" will be noticed later.

three years later, in *Mucidorus*, " Oh lord ! nay, and you are so lustie I'll call a cooling card." Greene uses this phrase fifteen times in his prose works between 1580 and 1590, and frequently in the same semi-medical sense. I find only one instance of the use of the phrase as a metaphor earlier than in Greene's *Mamillia* in 1580 : Lyly uses it in his *Euphues* as early as 1579.

Lodge always uses the phrase in a more general sense. It is used in *The True Tragedie of Richard III.*, but in a passage that is clearly Lodge's revisionary work. Its use in *The Troublesome Raigne of King John*, and in the *First Part of Henry VI.*, in both instances indicate Lodge's rather than Greene's hand.

In *The Troublesome Raigne*, when Meloun, having betrayed the traitorous purposes of the French King, dies with the words:

> Farewell my Lords, witness my faith when we are met in heaven, and for my kindness give me grave room here, my soul doth fleet ; world's vanities farewell,

Salisbury, referring to the nature of his confession, says :

> How now my Lords, what cooling card is this,
> A greater grief grows now than erst hath been,
> What counsel give you, shall we stay and die
> Or shall we home and kneel unto the King ?

Again, in the *First Part of Henry VI.*, in the one-sided dialogue between Margaret and Suffolk, where the latter, instead of answering her questions, communes with himself, in the same manner as Falconbridge, in *The Troublesome Raigne*, when questioned by King John regarding his parentage, the phrase is again used in the sense of restraint. In passing, I wish to call the student's attention to the characteristic use Lodge makes of self-communion in dialogue. We have it in *King John* and *Henry VI.*, and also in *Mucidorus*, in the case of Amadine and Bremo. Other writers of the period indulge in brief "asides," but Lodge carries his through long dialogues.

Henry VI., Part I., Act v. Scene iii. :

MARGARET. Say Earle of Suffolk—If thy name be so—
  What ransom must I pay before I pass?
  For I perceive I am thy prisoner.
SUFFOLK. How canst thou tell she will deny my suit,
  Before thou make a trial of her love?
MARGARET. Why speak'st thou not? What ransom must I pay
SUFFOLK. She's beautiful and therefore to be woo'd;
  She is a woman, therefore to be won.
MARGARET. Wilt thou accept of ransoms? Yes or no.
SUFFOLK. Fond man, remember that thou hast a wife;
  Then how can Margaret be thy paramour?
MARGARET. I were best to leave him, for he will not hear.
SUFFOLK. There all is marred; there lies the cooling card.
  And yet a dispensation may be had.

In both instances here quoted, the accompanying contexts display the same sedately measured, monotonous, and unemotional style exhibited in *King Leir*, where the phrase is also used in the general sense shown in the above quotations.

King Leir, Act III. Scene iv. :

> My eldest sister lives in royal state,
> And wanting nothing fitting her degree :
> Yet hath she such a cooling card withal,[1]
> As that her honey savoureth much of gall.
>
> . . . . . .
>
> My father with her is quarter-master still,
> And many times restrains her of her will :

---

[1] In *Rosalynde*, Lodge has similar lines to these :
  Who brings thee wealth and many faults withal,
  Presents thee honey mixed with bitter gall.

In the instances quoted from Greene, it is used twice by him in person, and once by one of his very typical clowns; and in each case, with the original and literal meaning of the words still tacitly in mind.

All available historical and bibliographical evidence, as I have shown, points directly to Greene's authorship of the Queen's company's plays here ascribed to him, as well as to collaborative relations with Lodge, and for a shorter period with Nashe. As a detailed collation of the numerous analogies in diction, phrase, and sentiment, between these and Greene's known plays, would lead too far afield from the purpose of the present volume, for the guidance of interested students I will briefly indicate the broader lines of internal evidence which, in conjunction with their and Greene's histories, have led me to attribute them to his hand. I will also quote a few suggestive parallels.

The most plainly recognisable evidence of Greene's authorship of *Sir Clyamon, Mucidorus, Locrine,* and *Selimus,* and of his revisionary hand in *The Troublesome Raigne,* is in the basic likeness of their clowns and comic characters to those of his known plays. Except in *The Old Wives' Tale* and *George-a-Greene,* where portions of the comic elements are supplied by Nashe, Greene always wrote the clownish and comic parts in his plays, including those in which Lodge collaborated. Lodge's one independent attempt at humour, in the comic portions of *King Leir,* is very dismal. In *Sir Clyamon* there is no clown, though Subtle Shift, who is made to refer to himself as "the ambodexter"—an allusion to Ambidixter, the vice, in *Cambyses*—is a very inceptive sketch of Mouse, in *Mucidorus*; Strumbo, in *Locrine*; Bullethrumble, in *Selimus*; Miles, in *Friar Bacon*; Ralph, in *Orlando*; Adam, in *A*

Looking Glass for London; Slipper, in *James IV.*; and Jenkin, in *George-a-Greene*. All of these characters are built upon the same model, and frequently repeat each other's buffoonery and at times each other's phrases. From Mouse on they are all valiant trencher-men and great consumers of ale, their desires and capacities in these respects seeming to increase in each succeeding play; probably reflecting the developing experience in their creator's life, which ended in September 1592, after "that fatal banquet of Rhenish wine and pickled herrings" recorded by Nashe, who was then a guest. The broadly humorous and at times daring realism of the speeches and action of Greene's clowns probably did more to popularise his plays with the masses than any poetic or dramatic merit they possess.

In *Alphonsus of Arragon* there are no comic characters, which doubtless accounts for its stage failure, complained of by Greene in *Perimedes*.

Other noticeable characteristics of Greene's are the repetition of his plots, and, in his earlier plays, the manner in which he reflects his continental travels, in placing his scenes in the countries he had visited, as well as in the wide land and sea peregrinations of his protagonists, who are constantly encountering the winds and waves of "the greedie gulf of ocean," or "crossing the bounds" or "frontiers" of this or that foreign country. In *A Notable Discovery of Cosenage*, in 1591, he writes regarding his earlier travels: "I have smiled with the Italian, . . . I have eaten Spanish mirabolanes, and yet am nothing the more metamorphosed; France, Germanie, Poland, Denmark, I know them all yet not affected to any in the forme of my life; onlie I am English borne, and have English thoughts, not a devil incarnate because I am Italianate, but hating the pride of Italie because I know their peevishness; yet in all these countries where I have travelled, I have not seen more excesse of vanity than we English men practise through vain glorie."

In his first play, the scene of which he casts in Denmark, Clamydes, the son of the King of Suavia, crosses tempestuous seas to Denmark, where he learns from Juliana, the King's daughter, that her hand is to be won by the knight who kills and brings her the head of the Flying Serpent. Having retained Subtle Shift as his man, with the words, "*Well I see thou art a merrie companion. I shall better like thy company. . . .* Come away," he seeks, kills, and takes the head of the Flying Serpent, when his retainer, Subtle Shift, for no apparent reason than to live up to the conventional vice, reports Clamydes' success to the cowardly Sans-foy, who is engaged in the same quest. Sans-foy, possessing magical powers in his own demesne, in which these events take place, exercises them upon Clamydes, imprisons him, appropriates the serpent's head, and hies him to the court of Denmark, where he personates Clamydes so successfully that Juliana is temporarily deceived. Subtle Shift, again living up to the Ambodexter, now releases Clamydes, who hastens to the court, challenges Sans-foy, who refuses to fight, admits his deception, and surrenders the lady to Clamydes. The same plot and similar characters, with minor changes, such as a bear instead of a flying serpent, and slightly less infantile dramatic verisimilitude, is used in his next play, *Mucidorus*, where the King of Valentia's son, Mucidorus, having heard of the beauty and virtue of Amadine, the daughter of the King of Arragon, disguises himself as a shepherd and journeys to Arragon, arriving in a wood, where the cowardly Sagasto and beautiful Amadine are taking a walk, when a bear appears and rushes upon them, Sagasto taking to his heels, whereupon Mucidorus appears, clothed as a shepherd, but fortunately carrying a sword, and cuts off the bear's head. Later on Sagasto is shown up, surrenders the girl, and accepts his defeat in the same philosophical spirit as Sansfoy. In *Mucidorus* the villain, instead of the hero, retains the services of the clown, but in similar words :

> SAGASTO. *This seems to be a merrie fellow,*
> *I care not if I take him home with me,*
> . . . .
> *How saist thou sirrah, wilt thou dwell with me ?*

When Sagasto retains Mouse, the clown, as his man, Mouse says :

> Then heare's my hand, I'll dwell with you. And harke you sir, now you have entertained me I will tell you what I can do. I can keep my tongue from picking and stealing and my hands from lying and slandering I warrant you.

In *Selimus*, when Bullithrumble, the clown, engages Corcut and his page as his helpers, Bullithrumble says :

> A good *well nutrimented* lad, well if you keep my sheep truly and honestly, *keeping your hands from lying and slandering and your tongue from picking and stealing*, you shall be Master Bullithrumble's servitures.

The phrase " well nutrimented " used here is a coinage of Greene's, and is not to be found elsewhere. It is repeated in *Orlando Furioso* :

> ORGALIO. God save your majestie Sacripant. My majestie ; come here my *well nutrimented* knave, whom takest thou me to be ?

Bullithrumble in *Selimus*, in turn, in his speeches

repeats phrases of Strumbo's in *Locrine*, and has exactly the same experience with his wife :

Locrine, Act IV. Scene ii. :

> STRUMBO. My wife and I are in great love and charitie now, I thank my manhood and my strength. For I will tell you masters : upon a certain day at night I came home . . . with my stomach full of wine . . . when she saw me come with my nose foremost, she snatchet up a faggot stick in her hand . . . and as she began to play *knaves trumpes* . . . I trembled, fearing she sould set her *ten commandments in my face*, etc.

Selimus, Scene xix. :

> BULLITHRUMBLE. Ha, ha, ha. Married quoth you ? Marry and Bullithrumble were to begin the world again, would set a tap abroad and not live in daily feare of *my wife's ten commandments*. I'll tell you what, I thought I was as proper a fellow at wasters as any in all our village, and yet when my wife begins to play *clubbes, trumpes*, with me I am fain to sing, etc.

In the *Second Part of Henry VI.*, Act I. Scene iii., Greene again uses "ten commandments" in the same sense :

> I'll set my ten commandments in your face.

Allusions to and the dramatic use of ferocious animals, natural and mythological, such as flying serpents, triple-headed Cerberus, hydras, crocodiles, tigers, bears, and lions are very characteristic of Greene, and are used by him with greater frequency than by any writer of the period. The flying serpents of *Sir Clyamon* are referred to again in *Selimus*.

Line 2524 :

> Those swarming armies of swift winged snakes.

Line 2528 :

> The generation of those flying snakes.

In *Mamillia* (Grosart, vol. ii. p. 259) the crocodile is described as follows: "The nature of the crocodile, madam, is with grevious groans and trickling tears to crave help as one in distress, but whoso cometh to succour him is presently devoured." In *Venus' Tragedie*, one of the tales in *Planetomachia* (1585), it is again mentioned: "And with the crocodile, to weep rosewater at me first and spit venom at me last."

In the *Second Part of Henry VI.*, Act III. Scene i., the crocodile is again mentioned in the same manner:

> As the mournful crocodile with sorrow
> Snares relenting passengers.

In *Never Too Late* we have a number of Greene's favourite animals mentioned in one short passage, including the tiger and crocodile: "O, Francisco, she hides her clawes but looks for her prey with the tiger, she weeps with the crocodile, smiles with the hyena, and flatters with the panther."

The crocodile is referred to in similar terms in *Locrine* and *Selimus*:

Scene iii. :

> Even as the great *Egyptian crocodile*
> Wanting his prey, with artificial tears
> And fained plaints his subtle tongue doth file,
> To entrap the *silly*, wandering traveller.

Locrine, Act III. :

> High on a bank by Nilus boisterous streames
> Fearfully sat the *Egyptian crocodile*,
> Dreadfully grinding in his sharpe long teeth
> The broken bowels of a *silly* fish.
> . . . .
> And as he stretched forth his cruel pawes
> A subtle adder creeping closely near,
> Thrusting his forked sting into his clawes
> Privily *shed his poison thro his bones.*

The reference in the last line to poison entering the bones links again with *Selimus*.

> Scene xix. :
>
> Now know old lords that you have drunk your last.
> That was a potion that I did prepare
> To poison you by Selimus' instigation
> And now *it is dispersed through my bones*.

In drinking the poison himself, before giving it to his victims, Abraham says :

> Here's to you lordings with a *full carouse*.

The phrase, "full carouse," is used several times by Greene in *A Looking Glass for London* :

> Now Alvida begins her quaff and drinks a *full carouse* under her King
> And no man drink but quaff a *whole carouse*
> Unto the health of beautiful Alvida.

> That will he swear it to my lord the King
> And in a *full carouse* of Greekish wine.

Greene's very typical references to tigers serve to indicate that in alluding to Shakespeare, in *A Groat's-worth of Wit*, in 1592, he parodied one of his own lines from *Henry VI., Part III.* :

> O tygers heart wrapt in a woman's hide

Locrine :

> What, is the tygre started from the cage,
> Is Guendoline come from Cornubia ?

Mucidorus :

> Vaunt bloodie curre, nurst up with tygres sap.

Selimus :

    And the Hyrcanian Tygre gave thee suck.

Sir Clyamon :

    Both tygre fell and monster fierce by dint for to
    drive down.

Henry VI., Part III. :

    . . . more inexorable
Or ten times more than tygres of Hyrcania.

I have referred above to Greene's use of the word "lukewarm." This word is to be found only once in Shakespeare's acknowledged plays. It is used in *Timon of Athens*, but in lines that are evidently Chapman's, overwritten by Shakespeare. The phrase "lukewarm blood," used by Greene in *Mucidorus, Locrine,* and *Selimus,* indicates Greene's hand also in the *Third Part of Henry VI.* :

    I cannot rest until the white rose that I wear be dyed
    Even in the lukewarm blood of Henry's heart.

Mucidorus :

    Now glut thy greedie guts in lukewarm blood.

Locrine :

    passing the frontiers of brave Graecia
    were bathed in our enemies' lukewarm blood.

Selimus :

    Go wash thy guiltie hands in lukewarm blood.

Such parallels as these may be continued indefinitely by any student who wishes to take the time to do so.

The Old Wives' Tale is so plainly the satirical play referred to by Greene as "lastly" written by him and Nashe, that a demonstration of his hand seems unnecessary.

Greene so frequently repeated himself that his repetitions in this play will be apparent to those who know his work and who have already recognised *Locrine* and *Selimus* as his productions. The name Sacrapant in this play is borrowed from *Orlando Furioso*, in which we find the following lines:

> I'll pass the Alps and up to Meroe
> (I know he knows that watery lakish hill)
> And pull the harp out of the minstrel's hands
> And pawn it unto lovely Prosperine,
> That he may fetch the fair Angelica;

and in *Locrine*:

> Curst be her charms, damned be her cursed charms
> That doth delude the wayward hearts of men—
> Of men that trust unto her fickle wheel
> Which never leaveth turning upside down.
> O God! O heavens! allot me but the place
> Where I may find her hateful mansion,
> I'll pass the Alps to watery Meroe,
> Where firie Phoebus in his chariot, etc.

The Old Wives' Tale:

> In Thessaly was I born and brought up
> My mother Meroe hight, a famous witch,
> And by her cunning I of her did learn
> To change and alter shapes of mortal men.
> There I did turn myself into a dragon,
> And stole away the daughter of a King,
> Fair Delia, the mistress of my heart.

Again, in *Orlando* we have:

> Northeast as far as is the frozen Rhene;
> Leaving fair Voya, crossed up Danuby,
> As high as Saba, whose enhancing streams
> Cut twixt the Tartars and the Russians:
> There did I act as many brave attempts, etc.

Old Wives' Tale:

> For thy sweet sake I've crossed the frozen Rhine ;
> Leaving fair Po, I sailed up Danuby,
> As far as Saba, whose enhancing streams
> Cut twixt the Tartars and the Russians :
> These have I crossed for thee, fair Delia.

Nearly all the verse in *The Old Wives' Tale* was written by Greene, and the majority of the prose passages by Nashe. The parts in the play bearing Greene's stamp are those taken by the Two Brothers, Sacrapant, Euminides, Lampriscus, Delia, Venelia, Zantippa, and Celanta. The remainder of the play, including the Huanebango passages in which Harvey is satirised, are by Nashe, who here quotes typical verses from the works of Harvey's metrical disciple, Richard Stanyhurst, as well as from Harvey himself ; and in the same satirical vein in which a couple of years before, in his *Epistle* prefixed to Greene's *Menaphon*, he parodied Stanyhurst's hexameters. This verse form was used by Stanyhurst in his translation of Virgil to demonstrate the practical application to English verse of Harvey's classical theory of metre.

In *The Old Wives' Tale* Nashe not only indulges in parody, but also makes Huanebango, who personifies Harvey, quote both Harvey's and Stanyhurst's actual verses, which, however, when compared with his parody, make it difficult to distinguish one from the other.

HUANEBANGO.

> Philada, philideros, pamphilia, florida, flortos :
> *Dub dub a dub, bounce, quoth the guns,*
> *With a sulphurous huffe snuffe :*
> waked with a wench, pretty peat, pretty love,
> and my sweet pretty pigsnie ;

Just at thy side shall sit, surnamed
great Huanebango :
Safe in my arms, I will keep thee, threat Mars
or thunder Olympus.

ZANTIPPO (*aside*).

Foh, what greasy groom have we here ? He looks as though he crept out of the backside of a well, and speaks like a drum perished at the west end.

HUANEBANGO.

O that I might, but I may not,
Woe to my destiny therefore,
Kiss that I clasp! but I cannot :
Tell me, my destiny, wherefore.

The first line italicised above is taken literally from Stanyhurst's *The Description of Liparen*, and the second from Harvey's *Encomium Lauri*. Both of these parallels, as well as one of the Greene parallels already quoted, were recognised by Dyce, to whom, notwithstanding, it apparently never occurred to question the publisher Danter's ascription of the play to G. P.

In his *Epistle* to Greene's *Menaphon*, in 1589, Nashe parodies Harvey as follows :

Then did he make heavens vault to rebounde, with rounce, robble, hobble, of ruffe, raffe roaring, with thwick, thwack, thurley bouncing [1];

---

[1] The presence of these same lines in *The Virgin Martyr*, published in 1622 as by Massinger and Dekker, indicates this play as a revision of an old play produced by Nashe, or Nashe and Greene, during their quarrel with Harvey in from 1589 to 1592. It was the obvious connection of these lines with the attacks upon Harvey's hexameters in from 1589 to 1592, coupled with Dekker's name upon the title-page of this volume, that led Fleay so far astray in attributing dramatic work to Dekker in these years. This again illustrates the misleading possibilities of bibliography unaided by literary history and biographical data.

having in mind such lines as the following from Harvey's *Encomium Lauri*:

> Of ruffe raffe roaring, men's harts with terror agrising.

In his *Strange News from Purgatory*, in 1593, Nashe writes of Harvey: "He goes twitching and hopping in our language, like a man running up quagmires, up the hill in one syllable and down the dale in another," and again parodies him as follows:

> But eh! what news do you hear of that
> Good Gabriel huffe snuffe
> Known to the world for a fool
> And clapt in the fleet for a runner.

In the opening scene of *The Old Wives' Tale*, Frolic says: "What resteth, then, but we commit him to his wench, and each of us take his stand up in a tree, and sing out our ill fortune to the tune of 'O man in desperation.'" In Nashe's only known surviving play, *Summer's Last Will and Testament*, we have: "by this straw and thred, I swear you are no gentleman, no proper man, no honest man, to make me sing 'O man in desperation.'" Again, in the same scene we have a significant parallel with Nashe's *Martin's Month's Mind* (1589).

Old Wives' Tale. Clunch: "Well, masters, if you will eat nothing, take away. Come, what do we to pass away the time? . . . What, shall we have a game at trumpe or ruffe to drive away the time? How say you?" In the epistle to the reader prefixed to *Martin's Month's Mind*: "And to confounde all, to amende their bad game, having never a good carde in their hands, and leaving the ancient game of England (trumpe) where every coate and suite are sorted in their degree, are running to Ruffe," etc.

The foregoing parallels between Greene's and Nashe's known work and *The Old Wives' Tale*, taken in conjunction with their histories and the history of the play, make it clear that the play is a collaborative effort of these two men. This perfectly obvious, yet hitherto unrecognised and apparently unsuspected fact illustrates the misleading possibilities, as well as the limitations of bibliography as a factor in Elizabethan and Shakespearean criticism, when unco-ordinated with literary history and stylistic evidence.

All of Lodge's collaborative work with Greene that is now traceable appears to have been produced between about the end of 1587 and the end of 1590. The slight traces of Lodge's hand in *Mucidorus*, which are comprised in Act IV. Scene iii. and a few linking passages, appear much more like a later addition than an integral portion of the earliest form of the play. Yet it appears likely that Lodge had written for the stage before 1587, at about which time he wrote *The Wounds of Civil War* for the Admiral's men. In both the Stationers' Registers and Henslowe's *Diary* there are several old plays mentioned which have not survived, that were probably also either Oxford's, Admiral's, or old Queen's company's properties, before 1591. Upon May 14, 1594, Lodge's *King Leir* was entered upon the Stationers' Registers by Edward White. As no copy of a publication following this entry is known to exist, and as the same play was entered again by Simon Stafford in 1605, it is probable that White, or those who sold him the publication rights, first sold the stage reversion, not only of this play, but also of other plays entered by him at this date, which were afterwards re-written for the stage and never published; such as *The Famous History of John of Gaunte*, and also *A Pastoral Comedy of Robin Hood and Little John*.

Both of these plays were afterwards re-written for Henslowe's stage ; as we know, *King Leir* was re-written for Burbage's. *John of Gaunte* was re-written by William Rankin and Richard Hathaway, though Henslowe treats it as a new play, and makes no mention of an older play, of which we would have had no knowledge but for its entry, in 1594, on the Stationers' Registers. Rankin, two years before, also wrote a play for Henslowe entitled *Malmutius Donwallow*, which, like *John of Gaunte*, was probably also an old Queen's, or Admiral's, play re-written. *John of Gaunte* has to do with the same phase of English history as *The True Tragedie of Richard III.* and the *Three Parts of Henry VI.* ; and *Malmutius Donwallow* with the same phase of British mythological history as *Locrine, King Leir,* and *Cymbeline.* It appears not unlikely, then, that all three were originally by Lodge, or by Lodge and Greene in collaboration, and that still other old Queen's, Oxford's, and Admiral's plays, of which we have no record as such, were among both Pembroke's and Strange's companies' properties after 1591, and passed from them to the later Chamberlain's and Admiral's men.

I will later on endeavour to indicate the fact that a large number, probably the majority, of Shakespeare's plays were re-written from older plays procured or inherited by the Burbages from the old Queen's, Oxford's, or Admiral's companies' properties. In this light it will become probable that *Cymbeline*, like *Locrine* and *Malmutius*, was originally an old Queen's play written by Lodge, or Lodge and Greene, before the end of 1590, and re-written by Shakespeare in about 1609. It is significant that Malmutius is mentioned in *Cymbeline*, and the ownership by Shakespeare's company of an older play on the subject of *Cymbeline* as early as 1599, is suggested by the fact that Shakespeare mentions Innogen in *Much Ado About Nothing* in that year as " the wife of Leonato."

We have now definite evidence of Nashe's collaboration and close personal relations with Greene from 1589, when he returned to England from a two years' absence on the Continent, and wrote his *Epistle to the Gentlemen-Scholars of both Universities*, prefixed to Greene's *Menaphon*, and the time of Greene's death, in September 1592. From this year onwards until his death in about 1601, we have hitherto known little of Nashe's connection with dramatic affairs. We have merely a mention of his play, *The Isle of Dogs*, produced for the Admiral's men, his only surviving drama being *Summer's Last Will and Testament*. It appears probable, however, that he collaborated for a short period after the death of Marlowe, in 1593, with George Chapman. My reason for this suggestion is that he and Chapman appear to have constituted themselves Marlowe's literary executors, Chapman completing Marlowe's *Hero and Leander* and Nashe his *Queen Dido* ; I also find slight traces of Nashe's hand in the early form of *Histriomastix*, which Chapman wrote after the death of Marlowe in 1593. It is probable also that the much re-written play, *Jack Drum's Entertainment*, which was revised by Marston in about 1598, is an old play of Chapman's, in which Nashe collaborated with him. There are still slight traces of Chapman's hand in the play, the original title of which was evidently *Pasquil and Katherine*. It appears to have been first written at about the same time as *Romeo and Juliet*, which it attempts to parody in one scene. *Histriomastix* repeats anti-Shakespearean phrases used by Nashe and Greene between 1589 and 1592. It is unlikely that

Chapman and Nashe would both have worked upon Marlowe's literary remains unless they were co-operating in some manner at that period. It will later be indicated that Nashe and Chapman collaborated at this period also in earlier forms of *Julius Cæzar* and of *The Tempest*.

CHAPTER VII

STAGE HISTORY OF KYD AND HIS PLAYS

THOUGH *The Spanish Tragedie* is the only play for which we possess definite external evidence of Kyd's authorship, the numerous links between the diction, and more especially the construction and plot of this play and a number of other plays owned by theatrical interests with which I will show that Kyd was connected before and after the period at which *The Spanish Tragedie* may reasonably be dated, enables us to trace his original revisionary or collaborative hand in these plays, and also to indicate the strong probability of his authorship of still earlier recorded plays that are now lost or re-written into extant plays under other titles.

The evidence of this nature that I find for Kyd's connection as stage poet with Burbage and Alleyn preceding the advent of Marlowe in 1587, indicates that he joined Burbage and Lord Hunsdon's men early in 1583, following the disruption of the Earl of Derby's men, for whom he had evidently written for the past three to four years.

In 1582 Burbage's theatrical patron, the Earl of Leicester, left England for a prolonged stay upon the Continent. This compelled Burbage, for the protection of his theatrical interests, to seek a resident patron. In this

KYD AND HIS PLAYS 185

year he first secured the patronage of Lord Hunsdon. A few months later, *i.e.* early in 1583, the Earl of Leicester's company, which had been his most permanent customer at the Theatre from the time it was erected in 1576, was temporarily disrupted, owing to the selection of five of their most competent men for membership in the new Queen's company, which Tilney, the Master of the Revels, under orders from Sir Francis Walsingham, formed in this year. Stowe's *Chronicle* informs us that in 1583 " twelve of the best " men were " chosen " from the companies of " divers great lords " for this purpose. Five of these men were chosen from Leicester's company, as follows : John Laneham, John Perkyn, William Johnson, Robert Wilson, and Richard Tarleton. Two, at least, and possibly three or four, came from the Earl of Warwick's company, which disappears from the records in 1582. We have evidence that Laurence and John Dutton, who were both members of the new Queen's company, were previously with Warwick's company. Where the remainder of the Queen's membership came from is not at present known. An analysis of the records of the dramatic companies at this period makes it practically certain, however, that some, if not all, of the number necessary to make up the twelve, came from the Earl of Derby's company, which also disappears from all theatrical records at this time, its last appearance being in a presentation before the Court on December 30, 1582. These men were John Singer, William Slaughter, —— Bentley, and probably —— Knell. My reason for including Knell is that " Bentley and Knell " are linked as recent actors of note, connected with a company rivalling Lord Strange's and the Admiral's companies, in a letter written to Edward Alleyn in about 1589, which has already been quoted. Including Knell, we have here eleven players; there is no means of knowing who was the twelfth.

That the Earl of Derby's company was, like Leicester's, an important London company and likely to be drawn upon in the formation of a new Court company, is evidenced by the facts that it presented plays before the Court during the Christmas seasons of 1580, 1581, and 1582; its last recorded appearance at Court, or elsewhere, being on December 30, 1582, and then presenting a play in which Kyd's diction, construction, and plot are very apparent, entitled, *A History of Love and Fortune*. It is probably significant that Lord Hunsdon's company made its first appearance before the Court only three days previously, *i.e.* on December 27, 1582. As the Merchant Taylors' company, with which it will be shown that Kyd was connected a few years earlier, made its last recorded appearance in February 1583, it is possible that the Burbages, through Kyd's influence, became possessed of some of their properties at this time, and that it was their *Ariodante and Genevora*, presented at Court on February 12, 1583, or a later revision of this play by Kyd, that Shakespeare re-wrote into *Much Ado about Nothing*, in 1599; though there is nothing now in the vocabulary, diction, nor characterisation of this play suggestive of Kyd's hand. There is a greater probability that some of the Merchant Taylors' company and its properties were now absorbed by Anthony Munday and Oxford's boys, and that *Ariodante and Genevora*, or a revision of it by Chapman and Munday, came to Burbage's hands through this channel upon Alleyn's purchase of their properties in 1589. Dogberry's " comparisons are odorous: palabras, neighbour Verges," in

Act III. Scene v. line 18, appears to be a vestige of Munday's work repeated from Chapman's *Sir Giles Goosecap*, in which I find that Munday also collaborated.

It has already been made evident that Robert Greene commenced to write for the new Queen's company, as company poet, at about the time of its inception in 1583; and as there is nothing remotely suggestive of Kyd's hand in any of the Queen's company's plays, it is apparent that Kyd did not accompany Derby's leading men in their departure to the Queen's company at this time; and fairly evident, from the available literary history of his known and traceable plays, that he became affiliated with Burbage in about 1583. It will also appear that in similar future reorganisations of companies for the use of the Court, in which Burbage and his men were involved, that Burbage restored the personnel of his company, or of companies affiliated with him, largely from the men that were left of the companies disrupted. As both Warwick's and Derby's men now disappear from the records for many years, while the depleted Leicester's company carries on; and as Lord Hunsdon's company begins to appear both in Court records and in the provinces at this period, it appears that the same procedure was followed at this time, and that Leicester's and Hunsdon's men absorbed part, or all, of the remaining men of Warwick's and Derby's companies, including the stage poet for Derby's company, Thomas Kyd.

All of Kyd's known and traceable work for the stage was produced between about 1579 to 1580, when he was twenty-one to twenty-two years of age, and 1587, when he was twenty-nine. He was only thirty-five at the time of his death in 1594. No evidence exists indicating his connection with any dramatic interests other than with the Merchant Taylors' Boys before 1580; with Derby's company from 1580 to the end of 1582; with Burbage and Hunsdon's company from 1583 to 1585; and with Burbage and Alleyn and the Lord Chamberlain's and Admiral's companies from 1585 to 1587, when, being supplanted by Marlowe, he ended his connection with the stage and entered Lord Hunsdon's service in a private capacity.

Thomas Kyd was born in London in 1558, six years before the birth of Marlowe and Shakespeare, who succeeded him as writers for Burbage's stage. He was the son of Francis Kyd,[1] " Citizen and Writer of the Courte Letter," which is synonymous with scrivener or noverint. Upon October 26, 1565, at the age of seven, Kyd was entered at the Merchant Taylors' School, the headmaster at that time being Richard Mulcaster, who appears to have been unusually interested in dramatic composition and presentation, as he trained and established a company of boy actors among his pupils, known as " The Children of the Merchant Taylors' School "; and who are also mentioned in the Court records as " Richard Mulcaster's Children." Though they were probably in existence at an earlier date, the first record we possess of them is of an appearance at Court early in 1573. They appeared at Court upon four later occasions between this date and 1583, when they made their last recorded appearance. It is probable that both Kyd and Lodge were led to choose the drama as their vocations through their training under Mulcaster, as boys in his company. They were of about the same age, and Kyd was evidently still at the Merchant Taylors' School

[1] See *Notes and Queries*, vol. v. pp. 305–6. By Mr. Gordon Goodwin.

KYD AND HIS PLAYS

when Lodge was entered there, early in 1571. I have found that some time between 1585 and 1587 Lodge for a time became associated with Kyd as a writer for Burbage and Alleyn ; this was probably due to their early school acquaintance. Though we have record that Lodge was entered at Trinity College, Oxford, in 1573, we have no specific facts concerning Kyd's future studies. It has been plausibly suggested by Sarrazin, from significantly pedagogic allusions in Kyd's plays, that he may have taught school for a time. If so, where would he have been as likely to do so as at the Merchant Taylors' School, by continuing postgraduate studies, in the capacity of pupil teacher or assistant master, after he had finished his elementary course, which I find, for boys entered at the age of seven to eight, was then a period of about seven years?

While what Nashe calls " the home-bred mediocritie " of Kyd's classical attainments fell short of those of his university-bred critics, he appears to have possessed a far better working knowledge of Latin, French, and Italian than he would have been likely to acquire in seven years' general study at a day school. He must have continued his study of languages after this date, and also have devoted himself particularly to a study of the dramas of Seneca. It appears very probable, then, that Kyd's superior dramatic and theatrical technique was the result of prolonged technical training, and actual practice, under Mulcaster ; and also that his earliest essays at dramatic composition were made while he was still working with Mulcaster and his troupe of boy actors, either as a pupil, or later in a monitorial capacity.

Between the date that Kyd severed his connection with

the Merchant Taylors' School—which is at present unknown—and 1582, when I find him writing for the Earl of Derby's company, and his play, *The Rare Triumphs of Love and Fortune*, presented at Court, all the knowledge we possess concerning him is gained from satirical but indicative allusions made by Nashe in his veiled attacks upon the Burbage-Alleyn stages and their writers, in his *Epistle* to Greene's *Menaphon*, published in 1589. Nashe was primed for these attacks by his colleague, Greene, who came up to London from Cambridge in 1583, and Nashe in 1589. Neither of them can then have possessed any intimate personal knowledge of Kyd's life previous to 1582, at which time we are now enabled definitely to place him as a writer for the Earl of Derby's company. It becomes evident, then, that Nashe's allusion to Kyd as follows: " It is a common practice now a daies, amongst a sort of shifting companions, that runne through every art and thrive by none, to leave the trade of *Noverint*, whereto they were borne, and busie themselves with the indevors of art, that could scarcelie latinise their neck-verse if they should have neede," merely indicates Kyd's identity as the son of a scrivener, and as lacking the advantages of a collegiate education. Nashe's words, " whereto they were borne," display no personal knowledge on his part that Kyd, after leaving school, had followed his father's profession. The few legal phrases used by Kyd in his plays would naturally have become part of the vocabulary of the son of a scrivener.

Nashe's *Epistle*, being written in a spirit of academic conceit, is addressed to " The Gentlemen-Scholars of both Universities," whose erudite efforts he exalts over the " home-bred mediocritie " of the " indevors of art " of such

KYD AND HIS PLAYS

stage poets as Kyd and Shakespeare; the relative success of whose work, however, when compared with that of their learned critics, appears to have more than compensated for their lack of learning by the technical training they gained in the school of practical experience.

It will appear fairly evident that Kyd continued either scholastic or dramatic relations, if not both, with Richard Mulcaster as late as from 1578 to 1579, *i.e.* until his twentieth or twenty-first year; and also very probable that he became connected with the Earl of Derby's company as early as from 1579 to 1580.

The indicative relevance of Nashe's further allusions to Kyd, which concern matters within his own personal knowledge, is now fully substantiated by facts and cumulative inferences. Nashe alludes to Kyd as a follower of and borrower from Seneca; as the author of, or as having had some hand in the authorship of an early play upon *Hamlet*; of an earlier form of *The Taming of a Shrew* and of *The Spanish Tragedie*; and as later on forsaking play-making and taking to Italian translation, the latter an evident reference to Kyd's translation from Tasso, entitled *The Householder's Philosophie*, published in 1588, about a year after he was supplanted by Marlowe as stage poet for Burbage and Alleyn.

As *The Taming of a Shrew* and *Hamlet* are both found to have been Burbage properties after 1590, when Burbage and Alleyn parted, and *The Spanish Tragedie* in Henslowe's and Alleyn's hands at the same period, it becomes evident that all three were still Burbage-Alleyn properties in, or shortly before, 1589, when Greene and Nashe made their allusions in *Menaphon*, published in that year. Other plays in which evidences of Kyd's diction, construction, plot, or all three combined, are in a greater or less degree still discernible, are as follows:

> *The Rare Triumphs of Love and Fortune.*
> *Soliman and Perseda.*
> *The First Part of Jeronimo.*
> *Titus Andronicus.*

Including the three plays mentioned above, we have here seven plays, all of them produced between about 1582 and 1587, in which Kyd's dramatic methods of plot and construction, or—in a greatly varying degree—his original diction and vocabulary, are still discernible. All seven of these plays were the properties of companies with which Kyd was connected as a writer, and probably as stage poet, during this period. All of them were owned by these or later companies inheriting or purchasing them, *for from two to nineteen years after Kyd had ceased to write for the stage, before being published in the earliest forms in which we now possess them;* and during these varying periods were subjected, as company properties were at that time, to revisions or re-writings by later hands employed by the owners of these properties for this purpose. The shorter the period between 1587—when Kyd ceased to write for the stage—and the publication of these plays, the more plainly recognisable as a general rule are the evidences of Kyd's diction, though his very typical and practically standardised technique, construction, and plot are apparent even where his diction and vocabulary are now only dimly, if at all, discernible as substrata, the former being the case with

> *The Rare Triumphs of Love and Fortune.*
> Published 1589.

Soliman and Perseda.
    Entered on Stationers' Registers, 1592.
The Spanish Tragedie.
    Entered on Stationers' Registers, 1592.
And the latter with
    The Taming of a Shrew. Published 1594.
    Titus Andronicus. Published 1594.
    Hamlet. Published 1603.
    The First Part of Jeronimo. Published 1605.

For the present I have here placed these plays merely in the order of their publication, which has very little to do with their order of composition. Though any attempt to indicate the latter, in the extremely involved nature of the case, must necessarily be largely inferential, it may yet serve to clarify and broaden our present very uncertain and limited knowledge, and suggest lines of research for future students.

In *The Rare Triumphs of Love and Fortune*, presented at Court on December 30, 1582, by the Earl of Derby's company, we have, though evidently not the earliest, yet a very early, and what is more important, *a largely unaltered play* of Kyd's, which, still retaining the archaic verse forms in which it was originally written, allows a more definite point of contact than has hitherto been realised, from which to trace the previous and future development of his dramatic work. The long passages of recitative declamation in this play, the presence of fourteeners, and its numerous Senecan reflections, would indicate its production in the late 'seventies or early 'eighties of the sixteenth century, had we no more definite evidence to guide us. Its production was the result of the same stylistic and metrical influences under which Chapman and Munday produced *Fidele and Fortunio,* and Greene his *Sir Clyamon and Sir Clamydes.* Both Kyd and his competing dramatic contemporaries were influenced in the use of fourteeners at this period by the publication, for about two decades past, of single plays of Seneca's, translated into this verse form, and their collection and publication as a whole in 1581, as *Seneca his Tenne Tragedies.* The vogue of the fourteener for dramatic use rapidly declines at this period, completely disappearing before the middle 'eighties. It was doubtless the virulence of Gabriel Harvey's critical strictures upon " barbarous and balductum rhymes," in his ardent but unsuccessful efforts to introduce Latin quantitative rules into English verse, which brought about the quick realisation of the unsuitability and ineffectiveness of such bastard hexameters as the fourteener, Alexandrine, and doggerel for English drama, that so accelerated their decline and elimination, and the substitution of rhymed pentameters and blank verse at this period, Marlowe being one of the brilliant effects rather than—as is usually supposed—the moving cause of this reformation.

Much of the revisionary work upon plays as stage properties, from about 1585–6 onwards for several years, consisted in altering old fourteener and doggerel plays into other verse forms. The presence of fourteeners, Alexandrines, or doggerel in certain of Shakespeare's early comedies, almost invariably indicates their retention from older dramatic bases among his company's properties from which he worked, rather than his own early use of these obsolescent verse forms.

It now becomes fairly evident that if any plays written by Kyd before 1582 are still extant, they were originally

KYD AND HIS PLAYS

written, as was *The Rare Triumphs of Love and Fortune*, largely in fourteeners and doggerel, and were later revised into other verse forms, and probably presented under new titles, either by Kyd himself or his successors, as stage poets for the company, or companies, owning his plays as company properties. Kyd's plays being presented at Court by Derby's men in or before 1582, it is a reasonable inference that he was then their chief writer or company poet. I now find that Greene, Marlowe, and Peele, in producing such plays as *Alphonsus of Arragon, Tamburlaine, Selimus*, and *The Battle of Alcazar*, in from 1585 to 1589, probably followed a lead in the dramatic development of Eastern, Turkish, and Mahometan subjects, first attempted by Kyd, at the latest as early as 1580. Upon February 1, 1580, the Earl of Derby's company presented a play before the Court entitled, *The Historie of the Soldan and the Duke of* ——; and on January 1, 1581, a play entitled *A Storie of* ——. While it is quite likely that both of these Court plays were written for them by the same writer (Kyd) that produced their Court play in the following year, the extreme indefiniteness of the latter title offers little or no suggestion of its identity as a work of Kyd's. *The Historie of the Soldan and the Duke of* ——, however, strongly suggests its identity as an early form of Kyd's *Soliman and Perseda*, which other correlative evidence implies to have been—in an inceptive form—a very early, if not indeed his earliest, dramatic effort. In its present form *Soliman and Perseda* is evidently a very late revision of an older fourteener play of his own early composition, made by Kyd shortly before he severed his relations with Burbage and Alleyn, in 1587. Its present verse forms plainly postdate all of the dramatic verse we possess of

Kyd's, with the exception of his *Cornelia*, written shortly before his death in 1594. To this it bears a stronger stylistic time analogy than to any other of his verses.

The two lines from *The Spanish Tragedie* quoted below have frequently been noticed by critics as possibly, or probably, bearing an autobiographical significance. Certain critics, who apparently had their own personal experience rather than Kyd's in mind, have suggested that the lines—

> When in *Tolledo* there I studied
> It was my chance to write a Tragedie

may have indicated an unknown period of residence by Kyd at Oxford or Cambridge, where, as a student, he had taken part in the production of university plays, and so naturally represents his protagonist, when called upon to furnish a performance for the Court, as providing one of his own student-day compositions. If for " Tolledo " we read London, instead of Oxford or Cambridge, and link the suggestions in the passage quoted below with Kyd's school-days, and their probable aftermath under Richard Mulcaster, as well as with the date and circumstances of the publication of Henry Wotton's *Courtlie Controversie of Cupids Cautels*, upon which Kyd's *Soliman and Perseda* is undoubtedly based, the autobiographical importance of Hieronimo's allusion is very greatly enhanced, and appears definitely to indicate that *Soliman and Perseda*, in its earliest form, was written shortly after 1578, while Kyd was still connected in some capacity with Mulcaster and his boy players, and shortly before 1580, when *The History of the Soldan and the Duke of* —— was presented by Derby's men before the Court.

The apparent anomaly that a grammar-school youth, lacking the prestige of a university course, should at the age

of twenty-two, and probably at twenty or before, have
secured Court presentation for his plays, seems reasonably
explainable only in the light of his previous Court experience
with Mulcaster's Boys, who are recorded in Court presentations—once in 1573, twice in 1574, and once in 1576—during which years and later it now appears likely that Kyd
was still associated with them.

In Act IV. Scene i. of *The Spanish Tragedie*, Lorenzo
approaches Hieronimo, requesting his help in the prepara-
tion of a play to entertain the Court, as follows :

LOR. But now, *Hieronimo*, or never, wee
    Are to entreate your helpe.
HIER.   My helpe ?
    Why, my good Lords, assure your selves of me ;
    For you have given me cause ; I, by my faith, have you.
BAL. It pleasd you, at the entertainment of the Embassadour,
    To grace the King so much as with a shew :
    Now, were your studie so well furnished,
    As for the passing of the first nights sport
    To entertaine my father with the like,
    Or any such like pleasing motion,
    Assure your selfe, it would content them well.
HIER. Is this all ?
BAL. I, this is all.
HIER. Why then, ile fit you ; say no more.
    When I was yong, I gave my minde
    And plide my selfe to fruitles Poetrie ;
    Which though it profite the professor naught,
    Yet is it pleasing to the world.
LOR. And how for that ?
HIER.   Marrie, my good Lord, thus :
    (And yet me thinks you are too quicke with us):
    When in *Tolledo* there I studied
    It was my chance to write a Tragedie,
    See heere, my Lords.   [*He shewes them a booke.*
    Which, long forgot, I found the other day.
    Now would your Lordships favour me so much
    As but to grace me with your acting it—
    I meane, each one of you to play a part.

The old play he produces, which was originally written in his student days, is *Soliman and Perseda*, now to become the play within the play of *The Spanish Tragedie*.

Kyd's *Soliman and Perseda* is palpably based upon the story of Soliman and Perseda in Henry Wotton's *Courtlie Controversie of Cupids Cautels*, which was published in 1578, being printed by Francis Coldocke, an intimate friend of Kyd's father, to whom he left a legacy in his will. Wotton's book is a translation of *Printemps d'Iver*, by Jacques Yver, published in 1572. It is unlikely that Kyd worked from the French version at a still earlier date, and more probable that he worked upon the translation printed in 1578 by his father's friend, Coldocke, who probably presented him with a copy soon after its publication.

In this light there can be little doubt that *Soliman and Perseda* in its original form preceded the composition of *The Spanish Trgaedie*, and very probable, in view of the date, that the original form was a play written in fourteeners, entitled *The Historie of the Soldan and the Duke of* ——, presented before the Court by Derby's men upon February 1, 1580. In a greatly abbreviated form it was incorporated some time later in *The Spanish Tragedie*, and very probably in an earlier version of that play than the earliest one we now possess, judging by a number of differences between our present play and the version presented in Jacob Ayrer's German translation, in which Balthasar, who takes the part of Soliman in the play within the play, is mentioned in the stage directions as the "Soldan," a term that does not now appear in either *The Spanish Tragedie* or *Soliman and Perseda*.

It is inherently and logically much more likely that the numerous, and apparently unnecessary, divergences between the present English versions of such plays as *The Spanish Tragedie, Titus Andronicus, Hamlet*, and the originals of *The Two Gentlemen of Verona* and of *Much Ado about Nothing* and other plays—all Burbage-Alleyn properties before the end of 1590—and the early Dutch and German versions of the same plays, were due to the fact that the latter were translated from *early, unrevised, and, for the purposes of the English stage, obsolete versions*, sold cheaply by Edward Alleyn to his impecunious Worcester associates, Richard Jones and Robert Browne, and their fellows when they left England to play in Holland and Germany in 1590, and again in 1592, than to surmised changes made in the plot and action by the German translators, who would have been most unlikely in all five cases mentioned deliberately to have created such extra work for themselves.

Soliman and Perseda was evidently the last play worked upon by Kyd for the stage, and shortly before he left Burbage in 1587. Between this date and early in 1589 it remained a Chamberlain-Admiral's property. As I find no trace of Marlowe's revisionary hand in the play, it probably remained unaltered during this period.

At the beginning of 1589, when Lord Strange's new company of adult actors was formed, the old Burbage-Alleyn properties, as well as the newly acquired Oxford's properties, were divided between Strange's men at the Curtain, with Marlowe as the company poet and Shakespeare as his assistant, and the Admiral's men at the Theatre, with Peele as the company poet, and Munday and Chapman, and possibly others, as his collaborators. At this time *Soliman and Perseda* evidently became a property of the Admiral's company, who apparently retained it until

Burbage and Alleyn parted at the end of 1590, when a new division of properties took place — *Soliman and Perseda* now becoming a Pembroke's property, and by them probably being sent to press in 1592. Between the beginning of 1589 and the end of 1590 it was materially altered by Peele and his collaborators, his principal collaborator in these revisions being Anthony Munday, whose hand is plainly recognisable in most of the lines spoken by Piston and Basilisco. It may appear not at all improbable, however, that several passages in these portions of the play were slightly overwritten by Shakespeare between 1590 and 1592.

When Peele, upon the departure of Sir John Norris and Sir Francis Drake with the English forces upon their Portuguese adventure in 1589, wrote his *A Farewell*, and mentioned "theatres," "tragedians," and a number of plays being presented at that period upon a London stage, he was not advertising the London theatres in general, but definitely referring to the Burbage-Alleyn stage, for which he himself was then writing. He mentions only plays which at that immediate period were being presented upon the Admiral's company's boards, for which company he had recently become stage poet :

> Bid theatres and proud tragedians,
> Bid Mahomet's Poo, and mighty Tamburlaine,
> King Charlemagne, Tom Stukeley, and the rest
> Adieu.

Mahomet's Poo evidently refers to his own lost play, *The Turkish Mahomet and Hiren the Fair Greek*; *Tamburlaine*, Marlowe's play of 1587; *King Charlemagne*, Chapman's play, *The Distracted Emperor*; *Tom Stukeley*, the original form of Peele's *Battle of Alcazar*.

KYD AND HIS PLAYS

Charlemagne was either written for the Admiral's company by Chapman at this time, or recently bought for them by Alleyn with the remainder of Oxford's properties. As I find Munday's revisionary, but overwritten, hand in *Soliman and Perseda*, I regard it as more likely that *Charlemagne* was written for the Admiral's men at this time, and that Chapman and Munday were now among their writers, having been taken over from Oxford's company by Alleyn a few months before, when he purchased their properties.

The allusion to "Charleman" in Act II. Scene i. lines 227-30 of *Soliman and Perseda*, which has hitherto been such an enigma to critics, was evidently not a part of the play in the form in which it was left by Kyd, in 1587, but plainly an interpolation, made by Peele or his collaborators, in 1589, their revision evidently being made late in this year, and after the return of the Portuguese expedition, and also after Chapman's *Charlemagne* had frequently appeared upon the Admiral's company's boards. In this same act and scene of *Soliman and Perseda*, Erastus, in order to procure from Lucina the chain given to her by Fernando, arranges a masquerading party to call upon her and challenge her to play with dice ; Lucina, thinking that her lover, Fernando, is the masked player, freely enters into the spirit of the supposed jest, plays with Erastus, and loses the chain.

ERAST. Desire *Guelpio* and signior Julio come speake with me,
and bid them bring some store of crownes with them ;
and, sirra, provide me foure Visards, foure gownes, a
boxe, and a Drumme ; for I intend to go in mummery.
. . . . . .
Sound up the Drum to Lucinaes *doore.*
LUC. I, marrie, this showes that *Charleman* is come.

This expression of Lucina's refers to the similarly

animated and loudly heralded first entry of Charlemagne and his Court upon the scene in Act I. line 156 of Chapman's *Charlemagne*, which, as appears from Peele's reference to it, was being presented in this year upon the Admiral's boards.

> *Hoboyes. Loud Musique. Enter* CHARLIMAYNE, *Bishop* TURPIN, GANELON, RICHARD, THEODORA, GABRIELLA *and attendants.*
> CHARL. Thys musyque is to dull to mixe it selfe with the full joy
>   I tast, o Ganelon.

A casual comparison of *Soliman and Perseda* with *The Rare Triumphs of Love and Fortune*, reveals the fact that Kyd, in making his last revision of the former play, incorporated in it a number of elements from *The Rare Triumphs*, and also modelled his new play largely upon its general structure. The dialogue between the dramatic persons of Love and Fortune, that runs as a chorus through *The Rare Triumphs*, he incorporates as an induction and chorus to *Soliman and Perseda*, though adding the figure of Death. Penulo and Lentulo, the knave and the fool in the old play, match Piston and Basilisco in the new; while the Shows of *Alexander, Queen Dido, Pompey and Cæzar*, and *Hero and Leander*, parallel Act I. Scene ii. of *Soliman and Perseda*, in which the knights of several nations are introduced. This latter scene in its present form shows little of Kyd's diction, and was evidently materially overwritten by Peele, or his collaborators, in 1589.

A critical comparison of the character, action, and vocabulary of Munday's Captain Crackstone, in *Fidele and Fortunio*, with the braggart Basilisco in *Soliman and Perseda*, reveals so close a stylistic and dramatic analogy as to make it practically certain that Munday revised the Piston and Basilisco scenes some time in 1589. This conclusion also provides a logical solution of the presence in this play of a number of words and phrases that are quite incongruous and out of accord with the remainder of Kyd's known work, while approximating closely to Munday's early manner *and to that of no other known writer of the period.* In making such a comparison due allowance should be made for the facts, that about seven years intervened between Munday's work in *Fidele and Fortunio* and his revision of the Piston and Basilisco scenes in *Soliman and Perseda*; that in the former we have his original composition, and in the latter an overwriting and transposition of Kyd's lines; and that his revision was probably improved by a later hand, some time between the end of 1590, when *Soliman and Perseda* became a Pembroke's property, and 1592, when it was entered upon the Stationers' Registers.

While Peele and his collaborators appear to have made little if any change in Kyd's construction and plot, palpable evidences of other diction and vocabulary than Kyd's are very apparent from the beginning of Act I. Scene iii. onwards to line 113 in Act I. Scene iv.; and again, in Act II. Scene ii., beginning at line 201 and continuing to line 247, as well as Act II. Scene ii., from the beginning onwards to line 92. Act IV. Scene ii. and Act V. Scene iii. appear to have been largely overwritten by Munday. In the former scene the words " prejuditiall to their muliebritie " and " incrochest upon my familiaritie " have a suggestively Crackstonian flavour, while quite foreign to our conception of Kyd. Piston's bastard Spanish, *Basolus Manus* for *beso los manos*, is put into the mouth of Crackstone by Munday in *Fidele and Fortunio* :

Basilus codpiece for an old *manus.*

The phrase "the braginest knave in Christendom," spoken also by Piston, is utterly unlike Kyd's vocabulary and manner, while Munday frequently coins such superlatives. Crackstone says of himself :

> think I am the perplexionablest man that lives at this day.
> . . . .
> Thou art the comfortablest fellow that ever I did see.

The mock Latin quoted by Piston :

> O extempore, O flóres,

and by Basilisco :

> O coelum, O terra, O maria, Neptune,

treats learning with a flippancy not elsewhere indulged in by the "home bred" but ardent Senecan, Kyd, though frequently displayed by Munday's comic characters.

Act II. Scene i. of *Fidele and Fortunio* begins as follows :

> Enter Captain CRACK-STONE, *disguised like a schoolmaster, in the apparell of Pedante, with a book in his hand.*
> Softe, for it is night, I must not make any noyse I trowe :
> Me thinkes this apparell makes me learnd,
> Which of all these Starres doo I knowe.
> Yonder is the green Dog, and the blew Beare,
> Harry Horners Girdle, and the Lyons eare.
> Me thinkes I should spowt Lattin before I beware,
> *Argus mecum insputare ?*
> *Cur Canis tollit poplitem,*
> *Cum mingit in parietem ?*
> Alice tittle tattle Mistres *Victoriaes* maid :
> If I speake like the Schoolmaister, shee will never be afraid.
> As soon as she opens the doore to let mee in :
> With my *Ropericall aliquanci* I will begin.
> *Swinum, Velum, Porcum. Graye-goosorum Jostibus Rentibus, dentibus, losadishibus,* come after us.

While it is critically apparent that a number of passages in *Soliman and Perseda,* including the Piston and Basilisco scenes, were materially altered from Kyd's version, and now fairly evident also that some of the alterations were made by Peele, Munday, and possibly others, working for the Admiral's company, between the beginning of 1589 and the end of 1590, there are portions of the Piston and Basilisco scenes in which the character of the braggart Basilisco is sustained with a quality of imaginative humour, and in lines exhibiting a sweep and fluency of diction, quite impossible to Munday at his best, as well as to any other known writer of the period with the exception of Shakespeare, to phases of whose early comedies these passages bear an alluringly suggestive resemblance.

In Act I. Scene iii., for instance, Kyd's original hand appears to have been almost completely overwritten by Peele and Munday in collaboration, the comic Piston and Basilisco lines being overwritten by Munday, and the remaining lines, to a lesser extent, by Peele. From line 65, however—where Basilisco is first introduced in this scene —onwards to about line 149, Munday's matter has been greatly improved, and very probably by Shakespeare. If these lines be critically read in conjunction with Act I. Scene i. of *Love's Labour's Lost*, the Shakespearean flavour of the former, as well as a distinct dramatic relationship between Armado and Basilisco, are strongly suggested.

A still more noticeable dramatic analogy long recognised, but unaccounted for by critics, is revealed by a comparison of the Basilisco of Act v. Scene iii., from line 64 to the end of the scene, with the Falstaff of *Henry IV., Part I.*, Act v. Scene i., from line 121 to 144; Act v. Scene iii., from line 30 to line 64; and Act v. Scene iv., from line 111 to 132.

It has been shown that *Soliman and Perseda* was a property of the Admiral's company between about the beginning of 1589 and the end of 1590 ; several correlative facts indicate that it was transferred to Pembroke's company at the end of 1590, when a new reorganisation of companies took place. *The Spanish Tragedie*, which was a Henslowe-Alleyn property in 1592, was entered upon the Stationers' Registers by Abell Jeffes in this year. *Soliman and Perseda*, of which we find no mention in Henslowe's *Diary*, was entered at the same time by Edward White. It appears that Burbage dealt with White in such matters at this period, while Alleyn dealt with Jeffes. The possession of *Soliman and Perseda* by Pembroke's men, in from 1591 to 1593, is further indicated by the facts that Shakespeare, in the composition of *King John* early in 1591, parodied one of its lines as follows :

> Knight, knight, good mother, Basilisco-like.

It has now been made evident that *The Rare Triumphs of Love and Fortune* is an early play of Kyd's, written in or before 1582, and very probable that *Soliman and Perseda*, in its first form, and under a different title, was a still earlier composition. I will now endeavour to indicate the probability that *The Taming of a Shrew*, in its original form, pertained also to Kyd's fourteener period, and that it intervened between *The Historie of the Soldan and the Duke of* ―― and *The Rare Triumphs of Love and Fortune*. In view of the fact that the two plays here mentioned were performed at Court by Derby's men in 1580 and 1582, it may be reasonably inferred that the play entitled *A Storie of* ――, presented by this company in the intervening year, was also one of Kyd's now known plays in an early form rather than a lost play. Kyd's plays were much more likely, from their value as company properties, to be hidden as his work by the repeated revision of later hands, than to have been lost to the stage by disuse. The caption, " A Storie of ———," would be rather incongruous if applied to *The Spanish Tragedie, The First Part of Jeronimo, Titus Andronicus,* or *Hamlet,* supposing that any of these plays were then in existence. It could reasonably have been used, however, for *The Taming of a Shrew* as *A Storie of the Taming of a Shrew,* if this play was then extant, as it seems very probable that it was.

While all of Kyd's plays were more or less overwritten, and some of them so frequently and for so long a period, that only expert analysis has recognised his work in them, no one of his plays presents so difficult a critical problem as *The Taming of a Shrew* and its latest revision as *The Taming of the Shrew.* This is due to the fact that it was a very early play in its original form, and evidently pertained to the fourteener period; that it also was a very popular play, its long-continued popularity leading to more frequent revivals and revisions, and by a greater number of hands, than any other of his plays. Had Greene and Nashe never made their allusions to " vainglorious tragedians," " who get Boreas by the beard and the heavenlie bull by the dewlap," and to the ewe, " whose fleece was as white as the hairs that growe on Father Boreas chinne, or as the dangling dewlap of the silver bull," it is very doubtful that internal evidence, or such meagre literary history of the play as we have hitherto possessed, would ever have enabled critics to recognise Kyd's authorship of an early form of this play. With these hints to guide us, however, and with our now developing knowledge of Kyd's early dramatic work and affiliations, as well as a clearer understanding of the manner in which plays as stage properties were revised again and again, irrespective of their original authorship, a critical examination of *The Taming of a Shrew* reveals sufficient traces of Kyd's overwritten hand, as substrata, fully to confirm the ascription indicated by his critical dramatic contemporaries. I find, as a rule, that humorous passages in fourteener plays were usually written in doggerel lines of approximately the same length, the fourteener evidently being regarded as too formal a measure for humorous purposes, Greene's *Sir Clyamon* and Chapman and Munday's *Fidele and Fortunio* being typical of this usage. With the exception of the lines spoken by Crackstone and a few lines here and there linking the Crackstone passages with the remainder of the play, all of this play was written by Chapman, whose lines are, however, slightly overwritten by Munday, especially in the Pedante passages. Most of Chapman's passages are written in fourteeners, while nearly all of the Crackstone lines—which are Munday's—are in doggerel. When, then, we find such doggerel lines in comic portions of an early Shakespearean play, as we do, for instance, in the dialogue in Act III. Scene i. of *The Comedy of Errors*, we may be reasonably certain that such lines are pre-Shakespearean, and that they were retained with little or no change from an old fourteener base, especially when, as in this particular instance, the diction and the farcical quality of the humour are so unlike anything we readily recognise as Shakespeare's. The large number of such doggerel lines still present in the clownish portions of *The Taming of a Shrew* indicate its early fourteener form and its original composition in the late 'seventies, or early 'eighties, of the sixteenth century.

The inferential history of this play, previous to its

notice by Greene and Nashe, appears to be that it was originally written by Kyd, and evidently from a still older base,[1] in the fourteener period, and probably in 1581, when it was presented as *A Storie of the Taming of a Shrew*; that it was revived and revised by him and possible collaborators—in the comic parts—at intervals, until 1587, when he ceased to write for the stage; and that it was again revised by Marlowe between 1587 and 1589, in which year it evidently passed from Marlowe's hands, he becoming stage poet for the new Strange's company at this time, and George Peele succeeding him in this capacity with the Admiral's men. After this the history of this play is more definitely traceable.

When the allusions of Greene and Nashe to *The Taming of a Shrew* were written, it was evidently still in Burbage's and Marlowe's hands as a company property, and in a form somewhat differing from the version we now possess, in which there is no mention of the ewe " whose fleece was as white as the hairs that grow on Father Boreas' chinne," nor of the " dangling dewlap of the silver bull." The passage which in the earlier version contained these expressions in the present version reads:

> Sweet Kate, lovelier than Diana's purple robe,
> Whiter than are the snowy Apennines,
> Or icy hair that grows on Boreas' chin!
> Father, I swear by Ibis' golden beak,
> More fair and radiant is my bonny Kate.

As the " snowy Apennines " line appears also in *Soliman and Perseda*, which antedates Marlowe's *Tamburlaine*, where the " snowy Apennines " are also mentioned, we may assume that, at least in this instance, the phrase was

[1] Gascoigne's *Supposes*, which was published in 1572.

suggested to Marlowe by Kyd's earlier use of it. In this same passage, however, we have the line:

> Father, I swear by Ibis' golden beak,

which has been regarded as an incorrect application of an idea used by Marlowe in *Tamburlaine*:

> A sacred vow to him and heaven I make,
> Confirming it with Ibis' holy name.

The " golden beak " line was evidently due to a revision by another hand after Marlowe had ceased to write for the company owning his manuscript. The distinction noted here, where, in the first instance, Marlowe evidently reflects Kyd, and in the second, a later reviser ignorantly reflects Marlowe, offers us a solution of the large number of Marlowan, and at the same time pseudo-Marlowan passages in this play. Seeing that many of the Marlowan reflections in *The Taming of a Shrew* are traceable to two plays composed by Marlowe at a later date, it is probable in some of these instances, as in the first instance noticed above, that Marlowe reflects his acquaintance with the MSS. of Kyd that he found among Burbage's properties when he succeeded him as company poet. It is very evident however that Marlowe's two plays are copied in several grandiloquent instances by a later reviser who worked for theatrical interests with which Marlowe was not now connected as company poet, but who still owned his MSS. of *Tamburlaine* and *Faustus* as company properties. Now we know that Marlowe was connected with the Burbages, who owned *The Taming of a Shrew* from 1587 until 1589, when Greene and Nashe made their critical allusions to Burbage's company, its writers and properties. We know also that he was connected with Pembroke's company, who owned this play from 1591 to 1594, when it became a Chamberlain's property. In whose possession, then, was this play between 1589 and the end of 1590, *i.e.* from the time Strange's company was formed, and Marlowe became their company poet, until Burbage and Alleyn parted at the end of 1590 ? Undoubtedly in the hands of Alleyn and the Lord Admiral's men, who during this period also owned *Tamburlaine* and *Faustus*. It was evidently now revised by Peele and some of his assistants, who it is likely, at the suggestion of Alleyn— who had a taste for grandiloqeunt phrases—incorporated such phrases in an indiscriminate and stage-carpenterlike manner from two of their Marlowan properties. *The Taming of a Shrew* becoming a Pembroke's property at the end of 1590, was again very thoroughly revised by Marlowe; his revision of this period, however, not being included in the Quarto published in 1594, but continuing unpublished, as a stage property, until its publication in 1623, in the First Folio, as *The Taming of the Shrew*. In the thirty years intervening between Marlowe's death, in 1593, and 1623, it was evidently slightly revised at least twice, and possibly thrice, by Shakespeare : once in 1594, when the old play was sent to press; and again in or about 1597; and again possibly in from 1607-8. It was still later revised by Beaumont and Fletcher after Shakespeare had retired from the stage, and they had succeeded him as writers for the Burbage interests. Traces of their work are plainly recognisable in this play, from which all evidence of Kyd's hand, except his basic plot, had long since been eliminated when they revised it for the last time.

Had this play not been preserved in an earlier form it

would now be difficult, if not impossible, to convince critics that Kyd ever had the remotest connection with it ; and the indicative allusions of Greene and Nashe in 1589 to a still earlier form would have remained quite meaningless to us if we now possessed only the version of the First Folio. I have no hesitancy in affirming that Marlowe's hand is plainly recognisable in both the earlier and later versions, in both of which there are also traces of Peele's and Munday's hands, and in the latter even overwritten traces of Chapman's.

In the present much overwritten state, and with the nebulous literary history of

> *The First Part of Jeronimo,*
> *The Spanish Tragedie,*
> *Titus Andronicus,* and
> *Hamlet,*

any attempt to indicate the order of production of Kyd's originals must necessarily be inferential or conjectural, though it seems reasonably certain that all of them were produced in their earliest forms some time between 1580, when *The History of the Soldan and the Duke of* —— was produced by Derby's men before the Court, and 1587, when Kyd retired from theatrical work. A number of striking dramatic analogies between *Soliman and Perseda,* the scene of which is cast in Rhodes and Constantinople, and the *Spanish Tragedie,* the scene of which, in an earlier form—if we may judge by Ayrer's German translation— was also placed in Constantinople, lead me to infer that the latter play in its earliest form was produced *not long after* the first production of *Soliman and Perseda* in its original form as *The Historie of the Soldan and the Duke of* —— in

1580, and was the play mentioned by Jonson in the Induction to *Cynthia's Revels* in 1601 as " the old Hieronimo as it was first acted." It will be noticed that Jonson, who was born in 1572-3, and cannot have been more than from nine to twelve years of age when " the old Hieronimo " was first produced, does not reflect his own knowledge in the passage quoted, but puts this reminiscent allusion into the words of one older than himself. " Another, whom it hath pleased nature to furnish with more beard than brain, prunes his mustaccio, lisps, and, with some score of affected oaths, swears down all that sit about him : ' That the old Hieronimo, as it was first acted, was the only best and judiciously penn'd play of Europe.' " The fact that we owe our current conceptions of the literary and stage history of this play largely to its recorded performances in Henslowe's *Diary* tends to distort our judgment regarding the period at which its reputation and popularity were first established. In the 'nineties, during which it was so frequently presented upon Henslowe's stages, it had declined into a revisionary aftermath of its much earlier and greater stage success, which, Jonson's allusion shows, was then being flatteringly compared with its latter-day vogue in an altered form. This, as well as other contemporary references to this always very popular play, indicate that it had already reached the zenith of its popularity during the years that its creator, Kyd, was still connected with the stage preceding 1587. As such allusions always refer to a single and never to a double or two-part play, it appears to be improbable that Kyd wrote two plays upon the subject of Hieronimo, one a comedy and one a tragedy, yet it is very evident that " the old Hieronimo as it was first acted " was materially altered by Kyd's own revisions, between the time of its first production in the early 'eighties, and 1587, when he left the stage. Let us now consider its further alterations by other hands in later years.

Between 1587 and the beginning of 1589 all of Kyd's plays remaining Chamberlain-Admiral's properties were subject to be revised by their stage poet, Marlowe. I find no trace of Marlowe's hand in *Titus Andronicus* or *Hamlet*, though a few slight but overwritten traces of his revisionary hand in both of the plays now known as *The First Part of Jeronimo* and *The Spanish Tragedy*, which, in the form that Kyd left them in 1587, were, I opine, then still one and the same play, *i.e.* the " old Hieronimo," with Kyd's final revisions.

Upon the formation of Lord Strange's company of adult actors early in 1589, when the old Burbage-Alleyn properties, and the recently purchased Oxford's properties, were divided between Strange's men at the Curtain and the Admiral's men at the Theatre, it appears likely that both *Titus Andronicus* and *Hamlet* went with Marlowe to Strange's men,[1] and that Kyd's *Hieronimo*, remaining an Admiral's property, was materially altered between 1589 and the beginning of 1592 by Peele and his assistants—its first division into two plays being made in this interval, one part becoming known as *Don Horatio* or *The Spanish Comedie*, and the other as *Jeronimo* or *The Spanish Tragedie*; but both of them containing matter expanded from Kyd's *Hieronimo*. After the beginning of 1591, when Burbage and Alleyn separated, and Strange's and the Admiral's

---

[1] It is not improbable that *Hamlet* may have been an Admiral's property at this period, from characteristic traces of Chapman's hand still in the play.

KYD AND HIS PLAYS 215

men combined under Alleyn and Henslowe as Lord Strange's company, these two plays are presented upon Henslowe's boards as old plays, and frequently upon consecutive days; *The Spanish Comedie* apparently being of an introductory nature to *The Spanish Tragedie*. The last recorded performance of *The Spanish Comedie* was on June 20, 1592, and of *The Spanish Tragedie*—at this period—on January 22, 1593. The former play never reappears under the titles of *Don Horatio* or *The Spanish Comedie*; while the latter, in a revised form, is presented as a new play under the title of *Jeronymo* on June 7, 1597, and on twelve occasions thereafter by October 11, in the same year. We have evidence in Henslowe's *Diary* that it was still further revised by Jonson in 1601, when Henslowe paid him £2 for additions; and again in 1602, when he paid him for further additions.[1]

When the Strange-Chamberlain's men left Alleyn and Henslowe for Burbage in the middle of 1594, while they retained among their properties the MS. of *Don Horatio* or *The Spanish Comedie*, they had already apparently disposed of *The Spanish Tragedie* to either Alleyn or the Admiral's men, who had it revised and presented as a new play in 1597. Some time between this date and the end of 1599 or beginning of 1600, *The Spanish Comedie* was obtained fraudulently by Jonson and Marston, who were now writing for the Children of the Chapel, and revised by Marston into the play now known as *The First Part of Jeronimo*, and presented upon this company's boards.

[1] As Jonson was evidently connected with the Admiral's company while it played at the Curtain between 1590 and 1592, it is likely he was with them at a still earlier date and also had a hand in the early revisions of *The Spanish Tragedie*.

As this followed so soon upon the recovery of *The Famous Victories* by the Burbage's men from the Lord Admiral's writers, and Shakespeare's dramatic reflections upon them in *Henry IV., Part II.*, and *Henry V.*, it was evidently Jonson's reprisal for their late defeat and their exposure in a similar affair.

In 1604 Marston published his *Malcontent*, dedicating it to his friend Jonson. In the Induction he informs us by pointed inference that the King's men—formerly the Strange-Chamberlain's men—in revenge for the theft of their *Jeronimo* (*The First Part of Jeronimo*) by the Children of the Chapel, had some time between 1600 and 1604, in turn, appropriated their property, *The Malcontent*, and presented it upon their own stage. The fact that Henslowe now paid Jonson for new additions to *The Spanish Tragedie*, as well as for a play entitled *Richard Crookback*—in all £12 —infers that he and the Admiral's men were tacitly allied with Jonson in his measures against Shakespeare's company.

This history should now make it very clear that the Children of the Chapel never possessed nor acted the Admiral's company's *Spanish Tragedie* (their *Jeronimo*), and that the only *Jeronimo* they had stolen was the Strange-Chamberlain's play of *Don Horatio*, or *The Spanish Comedie*, which they altered into *The First Part of Jeronimo*, but which in its pristine state was clearly " the old Hieronimo as it was first acted." In *The First Part of Jeronimo* Andrea is a living character ; in *The Spanish Tragedie* he is a ghost. There can be little doubt that he was a living figure in Kyd's original play.

Marston's characteristic rhymes and diction are now more apparent in this much revised and overwritten play than any of the earlier hands, including Kyd's, few of

KYD AND HIS PLAYS 217

whose unaltered lines remain in the play, though his phraseology and vocabulary are still apparent. Only one of Kyd's original fourteeners now remains in the play, but this is twice repeated, and in both cases as though quoted *from an original form of the play.* Act II. Scene i. lines 28–31 read :

> Tis sayd we shall not answer at next birth
> Our fathers fawltes in heaven ; why then on earth ?
> Which proves and showes, that which they lost by base Captivitie,
> We may redeeme with honored valiansie.

These lines of Kyd's are spoken by the King of Portugal, and are repeated almost verbatim by his son, Balthezer, in Act III. Scene i. lines 89–92 :

> Foure precious lines, spoke by our fathers mouth,
> When first thou camst embassador ; these they are :
> 'Tis said we shall not answere at next birth
> Our Fathers faults in heaven, why then on earth ?
> Which proves and showes that what they lost by base Captivity,
> We may redeeme by wonted Valliansie.

That even this one fourteener should remain after the play's many revisions, during its probable quarter of a century's stage life, suggests its original composition during, or very near to, Kyd's fourteener period. One slight trace of Marlowe's hand, altered by Marston, appears in the lines :

> Hast thou worne gownes in the University,
> Tost logick, suckt Philosophy.

Similar words and ideas are used by Marlowe in *Edward II.*, and also in both *The Taming of a Shrew* and *The Taming of the Shrew.* The opening lines of Act I. Scene i. of *The Taming of a Shrew* are plainly Marlowe's :

> Welcome to Athens, my beloved friend,
> To Plato's schools and Aristotle's walks ;
> Welcome from Sestos, famous for the love
> Of good Leander and his tragedy,
> For whom the Hellespont weeps brinish tears.

Act I. Scene i. of *The Taming of the Shrew* is also Marlowe, little if at all altered; here we have the same academic reflections:

> Glad that you thus continue your resolve
> To suck the sweets of sweet philosophy
> . . . . .
> Or so devote to Aristotle's checks
> As Ovid be an outcast quite abjured,

and in Act IV. Scene vi. of *Edward II.* :

> Make trial now of that philosophy,
> That in our famous nurseries of arts
> Thou suck'dst from Plato and from Aristotle.

Titus Andronicus and *Hamlet* have both been so drastically overwritten, the former by Peele, and the latter by Shakespeare, that it is impossible now more than to approximate the date of Kyd's originals between about 1583 and 1587. *Hamlet* evidently continued as a Burbage-Alleyn and Burbage property from 1589, when it is alluded to by Greene and Nashe, until its first publication in 1603, and in a further revised form for years afterwards. The fact that Peele revised *Titus Andronicus* into *Titus and Vespasian* early in 1592 suggests the probability that it was in Burbage's hands from 1589 to the end of 1590, and became a Strange-Admiral's property at the division of the properties early in 1591. In the form of *Titus and Vespasian* the play evidently lacked its former popularity, as it was again revised by Peele into its present form, early in 1594, for the Earl of Sussex's men, who were combined with a remnant of the Queen's men between 1590 and 1594. The version of this play that was translated into German was probably the same as the version first revised by Peel, in 1592, into *Titus and Vespasian*, taken in this year or

KYD AND HIS PLAYS

in 1590 by Richard Jones and Robert Brown to the Continent, with other Burbage-Alleyn plays. Shakespeare had no hand whatever in *Titus Andronicus* in its present form, which is the same as that presented by Sussex's men, for whom it was revised by Peele in January 1594. That a *Titus Andronicus* was in existence from five to ten years earlier than our first knowledge of the present play, and that it was exceedingly popular, are attested by Jonson in his *Bartholomew Fair* (1614), where he writes:

> He that will swear, *Jeronimo* or *Andronicus* are the best plays yet, shall pass unexcepted at here, as a man whose judgment shows it is constant, and hath stood still these five-and-twenty or thirty years.

As both *Titus Andronicus* and *Hamlet*, as Kyd left them, were evidently written during the last few years that he was connected with the stage, *i.e.* between about 1584 and 1587, it is not improbable that his schoolfellow, Lodge, who also wrote for the Burbage-Alleyn interests in this interval, collaborated with Kyd in one or both of these plays. Slight traces of Lodge's hand, which have been mistaken by Mr. J. M. Robertson for Greene's, are still discernible in *Titus Andronicus*. Greene was far too busy from 1583 to 1592 managing the dramatic production for the Queen's company to collaborate with a rival dramatist for the benefit of his company's chief competitor.

CHAPTER VIII

CHAPMAN AS A PRE-SHAKESPEAREAN

IT has now been made apparent that a large proportion of the successful plays bought by the London theatrical companies between the early 'seventies of the sixteenth century—when we gain our first knowledge of James Burbage and his theatrical activities —and 1623, when the First Folio of Shakespeare's plays was published, were subjected, as company properties, to frequent re-writings or revisions by other hands employed for this purpose, and whose own original plays, if they proved popular, were in turn subjected to similar treatment by their successors as company poets.

When Shakespeare entered upon his servitorship to Burbage, in from 1586 to 1587, for a period of two years, his relations to Burbage and his Theatre were apparently somewhat similar to those we find Dekker holding with the Lord Admiral's men at the age of eighteen, in 1595, as an assistant to the company poets, and training for a dramatic rather than an histrionic career, though he evidently functioned in both capacities during his inceptive years.

In Chapman's early *Histriomastix*, written towards the

CHAPMAN

end of 1593, Shakespeare is reminiscently alluded to as an "artist's prentice" during his servitorship, though then, *i.e.* in 1593, being caricatured as Postehaste, the company poet for Sir Oliver Owlet's company, a reflection of the capacity he filled with Pembroke's company at this period.

Considering Shakespeare's aptitude, we may infer that soon after his engagement by Burbage he was employed by his superiors in the company's dramatic work in making such subsidiary revisions in old properties as we find Dekker engaged in under Chapman's direction in 1595, in the revision of *Sir Thomas More*. It is likely that during the first few months of Shakespeare's servitorship with Burbage he served Kyd and Lodge, preceding Marlowe's régime as company poet. His progress in such work must have been rapid, as we are assured by the strictures of Greene and Nashe against him, as early as from 1588 to 1589, that his judgment as an "upstart reformer of arts" was then being angrily resented, though followed, by his supercilious detractors.

Shakespeare's revision of *Sir Thomas More*, some time between its purchase by Alleyn from Oxford's company early in 1589 and the end of 1590, indicates that it was a property of Lord Strange's company in this interval, who took it with them to Alleyn and Henslowe when they left Burbage at the end of 1590.

With the formation of Pembroke's company, shortly following the separation of Burbage and Alleyn, Shakespeare's dramatic standing in the Burbage organisation appears to have been enhanced, as his first known play, which was written for this company, was produced in the spring of this year. This was a re-writing of *The Trouble-*

some Raigne of King John, an old Queen's company's property by Lodge and Green, that with other Queen's plays had come to Pembroke's men at the time of the reorganisation of companies at the beginning of this year.

The procedure he followed in writing *King John* is typical of the bulk of his dramatic work, in being the rewriting of a company property written by earlier hands that he and his company had bought or inherited from another company. This was the custom in use among London theatrical companies for years before and after Shakespeare's day, and was followed by all the company poets of the time.

A critical examination of the sources of the thirty-seven plays usually published as Shakespeare's in the most comprehensive editions of his works, shows that at least twenty-seven, and possibly more, of these plays are based upon extant or recorded, but now lost, dramatic originals written by earlier hands. All of these old plays were evidently properties of Shakespeare's company at the time his re-writings or revisions were made. These twenty-seven plays were as follows :

> *King John.*
> *The Comedy of Errors.*
> *Henry VI., Part I.*
> *Henry VI., Part II.*
> *Henry VI., Part III.*
> *Love's Labour's Won* (*All's Well* in an early form).
> *The Two Gentlemen of Verona.*
> *The Taming of the Shrew.*
> *Richard III.*

Henry IV., Part I.
Henry IV., Part II.
Henry V.
The Merchant of Venice.
The Merry Wives of Windsor.
Twelfth Night.
Much Ado about Nothing
Measure for Measure.
Titus Andronicus.
Hamlet.
Othello.
King Lear.
Macbeth.
Timon of Athens.
Cymbeline.
Henry VIII.
Pericles.
The Tempest.

The remaining ten plays, none of which can be definitely traced to a concrete dramatic original; are based either upon some lost original; upon extant stories in prose or verse, such as Lodge's *Rosalind,* Greene's *Pandosto,* Brooke's *Romeus and Juliett,* Chaucer's *Troylus and Cryseyde,* or else upon *Holinshed's Chronicles, Plutarch's Lives*; or, as in the cases of *Midsummer Night's Dream* and *Love's Labour's Lost,* upon a composite of several sources; the plots of these ten plays in their present forms being presumably Shakespeare's own, except in the instance of *Troilus and Cressida,* where added plot and action by Dekker and Chettle were left incorporate by Shakespeare in his last revision of the play for publication in 1609.

These ten plays of Shakespeare's own probable plotting are as follows :

> *Love's Labour's Lost.*
> *Richard II.*
> *Midsummer Night's Dream.*
> *As You Like It.*
> *Romeo and Juliet.*
> *Troilus and Cressida.*
> *Julius Cæsar.*
> *Antony and Cleopatra.*
> *Coriolanus.*
> *The Winter's Tale.*

When Shakespeare, as Burbage's bonded servitor and dramatic apprentice, first began to essay dramatic composition, his native vocabulary as a Stratford grammar-school youth cannot have been very extensive, and was probably more limited than Greene's when he began his dramatic career, and, as I have indicated, borrowed so freely from John Studley's English translations of Seneca. Shakespeare, in the same manner as Greene, Dekker, Jonson, and other such dramatic beginners, naturally enlarged his vocabulary through contact with the old plays by many hands, and of varying vocabularies, that he found in his company's property box, and used for years afterwards as the structural bases for his own dramatic work.

I have already shown that the originals of the following four plays, composed or else re-written from still older bases by Lodge and Greene individually, or in collaboration, came to Shakespeare's hands as properties of Pembroke's company at the end of 1590, or early in 1591, and that

the old *King Leir* came to his hands as a Chamberlain's property in 1594 :
> *Henry VI., Part II.,*
> *Henry VI., Part III.,*
> *Richard III.,*
> *King John,*
> *King Lear* ;

that the first three named were re-written by Marlowe, and *King John* by Shakespeare, at this period; Shakespeare, a year or two later, again slightly revising the first four, and in 1605 re-writing *King Leir* into *King Lear.*

I have also outlined the literary history of Kyd's
> *Taming of a Shrew,*
> *Titus Andronicus,* and
> *Hamlet.*

While Shakespeare almost completely re-wrote *King John, King Lear,* and *Hamlet,* his revisionary work was very subsidiary to that of Marlowe's in *Henry VI., Parts II. and III., Richard III.,* and *The Taming of the Shrew* ; and neither of them had any hand in the final revision of *Titus Andronicus,* which was revised by Peele and his assistants, for Henslowe's stage.

In such re-writing and revision Shakespeare's suggestible and receptive mind would naturally acquire from Kyd, Greene, and Lodge the use of words absent from his own natural vocabulary, yet his indebtedness of this nature to these three writers is much less noticeable than his numerous and undoubted accretions from Chapman, even at his earliest period of composition, which antedates current knowledge of the inception of Chapman's literary activities by three to four years. Chapman's appearance upon

London's literary horizon has hitherto been dated, at the earliest, in from 1593 to 1594; yet Shakespeare distinctly reflects his diction and vocabulary in plays written as early as from 1591 to 1592, as well as in his revision of *Sir Thomas More* in from 1589 to 1590.

The very evident verbal influence exercised by Chapman's early dramatic productions (hitherto unknown) upon Shakespeare's work from the beginning to the end of his dramatic career was due in the first place to the fact that at the time he commenced to engage actively in dramatic composition he worked largely upon Chapmanian models, purchased by Alleyn from Oxford's company in 1589, and inherited by, or sold to, Pembroke's company at the reorganisation of companies and re-distribution of properties that took place at the end of 1590. His re-writing and improvement of these early Chapman-Munday plays, in which he retained much of Chapman's vocabulary, evidently first aroused Chapman's resentment. The continuity and bitterness of his hostility in turn led Shakespeare to a more interested and intensive study of his later productions; and for a period, from about 1595–6, when he wrote the fifth or Rival Poet book of sonnets, reflecting Chapman, until about 1599, during which Chapman assailed the simplicity of his diction in contradistinction to his own highly latinised style in such lines as :

> And though to rhyme and give a verse smooth feet,
> Uttering to vulgar palates passions sweet ;
> Chance often in such weak capricious spirits,
> As in nought else have tolerable merits,

Shakespeare appears deliberately to have emulated Chapman's more learned vocabulary and diction in all of his poems and plays produced at this immediate period; the seventh book of sonnets, *Troilus and Cressida*, *The Lover's Complaint*, and the revision of *All's Well that Ends Well*, all worked upon at this time, illustrating his success in this apparently deliberate effort. His company's recovery of the stolen play of *The Famous Victories* and of the Admiral's writers' revision of Greene's and Lodge's version of it at this time, and Shakespeare's revision of it into *Henry IV., Part II.*, *Henry V.*, and *The Merry Wives of Windsor*—all hasty work in which he left extensive substrata of the earlier hands—tended also now greatly to accentuate the Chapmanian, and distort the Shakespearean, flavour of his productions. His emulation of Chapman's diction and vocabulary in *The Lover's Complaint* was so realistic that a learned professor has gravely ascribed the poem to Chapman, an ascription in which he has been supported by the stylistically acute but historically and critically erring Mr. J. M. Robertson, who ascribes the Chapmanian tone of Shakespeare's work at this period to congenial collaborative relations with Chapman, who, in fact, was then one of the leading writers for Burbage's principal theatrical competitor, and recently engaged with Peele and Jonson in re-writing a stolen Burbage property for Henslowe's boards.

In *Shakespeare's Sonnet Story*, pp. 380–94, I have demonstrated Shakespeare's reasons for the production of *The Lover's Complaint* at this time. The almost complete absence from such a long poem, of harsh consonantal rhymes, such as merit and spirit, elect and deject, vent and went, exempt and contempt, state and hate, etc., so characteristic of Chapman at this period, and the presence of even a few lines so clearly

Shakespeare's, and so unlike Chapman both in spirit and expression, as :

> Storming her world with sorrow's wind and rain.
> . . . .
> O most potential love! vow, bond, nor space,
> In thee hath neither sting, knot, nor confine,
> For thou art all, and all things else are thine.
> . . . .
> O father, what a hell of witchcraft lies
> In the small orb of one particular tear!
> . . . .
> O cleft effect! cold modesty, hot wrath,
> . . . .
> Love lack'd a dwelling and made him her place.
> . . . .
> Whose white weighs down the airy scale of praise.
> . . . .
> O, how the channel to the stream gave grace!
> Who glazed with crystal gate the glowing roses
> That flame through water which their hue encloses,

should have precluded the ascription to Chapman of a poem printed as Shakespeare's with his Sonnets in 1609, in the first eight verses of which he so clearly foreshadows his conception, later dramatised in the state and person of Ophelia. Such a literally specious, but biographically and historically untenable ascription, illustrates the danger of dependence upon the letter alone in Shakespearean criticism. Such an unusual and disagreeable poem as *The Lover's Complaint* was not likely to have been written by a poet of Shakespeare's art, merely as a literary *tour de force*. The primary function of literary criticism is to understand a writer's meaning.

When Chapman and Munday sent *Fidele and Fortunio, or The Two Italian Gentlemen*, to press in 1584, it is very likely that they had—as was customary—made a further revision of it for the stage, and that it was from this revision rather than from the published play that Shakespeare's *Two Gentlemen of Verona* was written. It is not unlikely also that the old Queen's company's property, *Felix and Filomena*, presented before the Court in 1585, and probably written by Greene, was now a Pembroke's property, acquired along with *The Troublesome Raigne of King John, Henry VI., Parts II. and III., The Famous Victories of Henry V., The True Tragedie of Richard III., James IV., Locrine*, and others at this time (1590–1), and that Shakespeare used both *The Two Italian Gentlemen* and *Felix and Filomena* as bases in the construction of *The Two Gentlemen of Verona*. I agree with Mr. J. M. Robertson in his recognition of traces of Greene's work in this play, but only as substrata.

At the same time that Pembroke's men acquired Chapman and Munday's *The Life and Death of Thomas Lord Cromwell* (1591), they apparently also became possessed of *The Two Italian Gentlemen*, or a revision of it retained for stage purposes when the play was published. I have shown that very shortly before this, Shakespeare, while still with Strange's men, revised an extensive passage of Chapman's work in *Sir Thomas More*. As this is the earliest extant specimen of Shakespeare's revisionary work, and is written in his own autograph, a consideration of the manner in which he revised Chapman may guide us in recognising a Chapmanian substrata, or revision, in printed plays where a similar evidence of Chapman's vocabulary exists.

In the Chapman passage in *Sir Thomas More* that he revised, Shakespeare evidently found a number of new words and phrases, only a few of which are found again in plays that do not suggest a Chapmanian base; about six of which are again to be found in plays indicating an original base by Chapman, and ten of which never appear in plays attributed to Shakespeare; yet all but one of which are frequently to be found in Chapman's poems and plays. Of this list, seventeen in all, in the eighty-two verse lines examined, the ten never again to be found in a Shakespearean play are as follows: topt, transportation, quelled, forwarn, a god on earth, enstalls, appropriate, inhumanity, shark on you, momtanish. The last word is not found elsewhere than in *More*; " state of men " is not found in Shakespeare, but " state of man," which is common in Chapman, is found only in four Shakespearean plays, all of which strongly smack of a Chapmanian base: *Henry V.*, *Macbeth*, *Henry VIII.*, *Julius Cæsar*.

The following words and phrases—plodding, ravenous fishes, supposition, ruff, strong hand (in the sense used in *More*), and innovation—are all frequently used by Chapman, but, except in three instances, are used by Shakespeare only in plays in which further evidence indicates a hand in the original base by Chapman and Munday, or Chapman alone.

" Plodding " is used once only by Shakespeare, and then in *Love's Labour's Lost*, which, while not indicating a base by Chapman, was revised by Shakespeare in 1595, largely as raillery upon Chapman's *Shadow of Night* theories. " Ravenous fishes " is used only once and in a non-Chapmanian play, *Titus Andronicus*; its presence there, however, may indicate that Chapman may have given Peele, with whom he was then associated, some slight collaborative help in his work upon the play, or that Peele borrowed the phrase. " Supposition " is to be found in

The Comedy of Errors, All's Well, in its early form, and *Much Ado about Nothing*; the former two strongly suggestive of Chapman, and the latter slightly so. "Ruff" is to be found in *All's Well, Henry IV., Part II.*, and *Pericles,* all exhibiting a Chapman base; and also in *The Taming of the Shrew,* in which Chapman's collaborative revisionary hand is quite probable, between the beginning of 1589 and the end of 1590. "Strong hand," in the sense used in *More,* is to be found in *The Comedy of Errors* and *Hamlet,* the former displaying substrata of Chapman's and Munday's. Its use in *Hamlet* is probably due to the presence of some Chapman matter while Shakespeare worked upon his revision. "Innovation," meaning trouble, rebellion, or agitation, which is the sense in which Shakespeare interpreted it when he evidently first found it in *Sir Thomas More,* and in which he always afterwards uses it, is found in *Henry IV., Part I.,* where it is accompanied by another Chapmanian word, "hurly-burly"; in *Othello,* where it means trouble, or agitation; and in *Hamlet,* where the meaning which Shakespeare always gives this word appears definitely to indicate that he here referred to Essex's rebellion, and that it was because of something to do with this outbreak that the Lord Chamberlain's men were compelled to travel in 1601. Chapman nearly always afterwards uses the word in its modern connotation, of change from a static condition.

In addition to *The Two Italian Gentlemen* and *Thomas, Lord Cromwell,* it now appears very probable that a number of other Oxford properties, written or revised by Chapman and Munday, were bought or inherited by Pembroke's company from the Burbage-Alleyn interests at the end of 1590.

We have so far left unaccounted for the provenance and former stage-ownership of :

>   *The Comedy of Errors.*
>   *Love's Labour's Won (All's Well* in an early form).
>   *The Merchant of Venice.*
>   *The Merry Wives of Windsor.*
>   *Twelfth Night.*
>   *Measure for Measure.*
>   *Othello.*
>   *Macbeth.*
>   *Timon of Athens.*
>   *Cymbeline.*
>   *Henry VIII.*
>   *Pericles.*
>   *The Tempest.*

There is little reason to doubt that all, or most, of these plays were founded upon older dramatic bases that were properties of the Burbage-Alleyn interests before the end of 1590; of the old Queen's company, from which so many plays came to Pembroke's company at this time; or of Oxford's company, whose properties were bought by Alleyn in 1589, and later sold to Strange's and the Admiral's men.

The presence of traces of Munday's and Chapman's work as substrata in the following plays, or of Chapman's peculiar vocabulary, leads naturally to the inference that their originals were Oxford's company's properties, and in some manner the collaborative work of these two writers; or else that some of these plays were revised by Chapman or Munday between 1589 and the end of 1590, while they were Admiral's properties; most of them being sold to Pembroke's men at the latter date, and others still later

CHAPMAN

on to their successors, the Lord Chamberlain's men or the King's men :

>   *The Comedy of Errors.*
>   *Love's Labour's Won* (the early form of *All's Well that Ends Well*).
>   *Macbeth.*
>   *Timon of Athens.*
>   *Henry VIII.*
>   *Pericles.*

The Comedy of Errors.

It is unlikely that the earliest form of *The Comedy of Errors* was an original work of Chapman's and Munday's, and much more probable that the traces of their hands in it are due to revision. The large amount of pre-Shakespearean matter in this play, in the form of fourteeners and doggerel, strongly suggests its original form as a fourteener play of the type of *The Two Italian Gentlemen,* and its date of production in the 'sixties or 'seventies of the sixteenth century. In from 1582 to 1583, when the formation of the old Queen's company caused the temporary disruption of Leicester's men, and the elimination of Warwick's and Derby's men, Leicester's company was restored, and the new Lord Hunsdon's company formed from the men that were left of the two defunct companies ; and probably from some members of the Children of St. Paul's (now become men), as this company also disappears from all records in this year. The Children of St. Paul's had now performed before the Court once or twice a year for many years past, making their last appearance there on December 26, 1581, for which they were paid on April 24, 1582.

As nothing further is recorded concerning them in City, Court, or provincial records until 1585, when Thomas Giles was authorised to take up twenty boys to form a new St. Paul's company, the first Court appearance of which was on February 18, 1588, it is apparent that the older company had ceased to exist in 1582. It appears very probable that *The History of Error*, presented before the Court by the Children of St. Paul's on New Year's Day 1577, was an early form of *The Comedy of Errors*, which was absorbed as a property along with some of the company owning it, either by the Burbage organisation or by Oxford's company. My reason for this inference is that I find slight but significant traces of Kyd's hand in the play; fairly extensive passages by Lodge which are slightly overwritten by Chapman, as well as a number of Chapman's characteristic couplets, which show that his work is later than the fourteener period to which *The Two Italian Gentlemen* pertains, and evidently of the period of *Sir Thomas More*, or later. Seeing that Oxford's company and the Admiral's company, through the arrangement between Burbage and Laneham, held much the same relations to each other between 1585 and 1589 that existed between Strange's and the Admiral's companies between the beginning of 1589 and the end of 1590, in the interchange or intersale of properties; and that Kyd and Lodge were with Burbage and Alleyn and the Admiral's men from 1585 to 1587, while Chapman and Munday were with Oxford's men during the same period, and later, and with the Admiral's men from 1589 to the end of 1590, it would be very natural for revisionary work by these four men, as well as by Marlowe and Peele, to have been still existent in a number of the plays inherited by Pembroke's from these earlier companies in 1590–1. To sum up, then, I find in *The Comedy of Errors* faint and overwritten traces of Kyd's hand ; fairly extensive remains of Lodge's work overwritten by Chapman, whose hand is revealed by his characteristic vocabulary. I also find traces of Chapman's hand in a number of his characteristic rhymed couplets, some of which appear to overwrite lines by Kyd. Munday's work is also recognisable in most of the doggerel lines spoken by the Dromios.

From these apparent facts I judge that this play came to Burbage from the Children of St. Paul's in about 1582–3, as a fourteener play, when it was revised by Kyd; that Lodge revised it some time between 1585 and 1587 into pentameters, when he produced *The Wounds of Civil War* for the Admiral's company ; that it became an Admiral's property in 1589, and was revised again by Munday and Chapman, working under Peele, some time before the end of 1590, when it came to Pembroke's company and to Shakespeare, who, in turn, slightly revised the former revisions, besides adding new matter of his own that bespeaks a very early period in his work.

The unusual word " disannul " in Act I. Scene i. of *The Comedy of Errors*, and which is found elsewhere only in *Henry VI., Part III.*—erroneously ascribed by Mr. J. M. Robertson to Greene, who, being continuously in the employment of the Queen's company from 1583 to 1590, never can have worked upon Burbage-Alleyn properties in this interval—appears in a Lancastrian passage that is indubitably by Lodge, Greene's collaborator in the three *Henry VI.* plays. Mr. Robertson, for whose stylistic acumen I have a high respect, frequently errs, however, in imputing Lodge's matter to Greene, of whose company affiliations he is apparently in the dark. He is similarly in error in ascribing to Marlowe Lodge's very characteristic lines in the opening passage of *Henry VI., Part I.*, as follows :

> Hung be the heavens with black, yield day to night !
> Comets, importing change of times and states,
> Brandish your crystal tresses in the sky,
> And with them scourge the bad revolting stars
> That have consented unto Henry's death !

as well as his correspondingly liturgical lines in Anne's lamentation in *Richard III.*, Act I. Scene ii. :

> Set down, set down your honourable load—
> If honour may be shrouded in a hearse,—
> Whilst I a while obsequiously lament
> Th' untimely fall of virtuous Lancaster.

A comparison of these two passages with his composition in *The Troublesome Raigne of King John*, Part II., Scene vi. :

> Set down, set down the load not worth your pain !
> Fordone I am with deadly wounding grief :
> Sickly and succourless, hopeless of any good,
> The world hath weari'd me, and I have weari'd it,

written two to three years earlier, not only corroborates the identity of Lodge's hand in the later plays, but indicates the inception and development of his liturgical idea.

A further comparison of these passages by Lodge with Act I. Scene i. of *Richard III.*, which is clearly Marlowe's composition, should serve definitely to differentiate Marlowe's from Lodge's dramatic style at this period :

> Now is the winter of our discontent
> Made glorious summer by this sun of York ;
> And all the clouds, that lour'd upon our house,
> In the deep bosom of the ocean buried.
> Now are our brows bound with victorious wreaths ;
> Our bruised arms hung up for monuments ;
> Out stern alarums changed to merry meetings,
> Our dreadful marches to delightful measures.

The slight traces of Kyd's hand that I notice in *The Comedy of Errors* are, first, the word " carcanet," repeated from Kyd's *Soliman and Perseda*—the earliest use of the word that I find, and certainly earlier than Chapman's use of it, to whom it is ascribed by Mr. J. M. Robertson. The next reflection of Kyd's hand is the reference in Act II. Scene i. to the elm and vine:

> Thou art an elm, my husband, I a vine,

which is also repeated from a Kyd play, *The Spanish Tragedie*; its dramatic use being original with Kyd, who obtained it from the story of Soliman and Perseda in *The Courtlie Controversie of Cupid's Cautels*. It is not to be found elsewhere, and the lines in which it appears in *The Comedy of Errors* are accompanied by Chapman's characteristic consonantal rhymes:

> Be it my wrong you are from me exempt,
> But wrong not that wrong with a more contempt.
> . . . .
> Whose weakness, married to thy stronger state,
> Makes me with thy strength to communicate.

The name " Balthazar " is evidently also repeated from *The Spanish Tragedie*.

The rhymed doggerel lines in Act III. Scene i. are probably Munday's, as they strongly resemble similar matter in *The Two Italian Gentlemen*. In Act II. Scene i. Lucetta's sentiments concerning male control repeat those expressed by the subdued Kate in the closing scene of Kyd's much overwritten play, *The Taming of a Shrew*, which is the least altered passage in the whole play. These lines of Lucetta's are evidently Kyd's matter overwritten by Chapman, whose largely unique vocabulary and characteristic rhymed couplets are noticeable here and there nearly all through *The Comedy of Errors*, as for instance :

> Who, every word by all my wit being scann'd,
> Wants wit in all one word to understand.

I know of no other poet of this immediate period who so frequently rhymes the word " scanned." In *Sir Thomas More* he writes :

> Uppon this little borde is dayly scande
> The health and preservation of the land.

Other characteristic lines of Chapman's in *The Comedy of Errors* are :

> Do their gay vestments his affections bait ?
> That's not my fault ; he's master of my state.
>
> . . . .
>
> When the sun shines let foolish gnats make sport,
> But creep in crannies when he hides his beams.
>
> . . . .
>
> Indued with intellectual sense and souls,
> Of more pre-eminence than fish and fowles.

The following words and phrases in *The Comedy of Errors* are all characteristic of Chapman : Statutes, bloods, excludes, confiscate, unspeakable, vapours, procrastinate, maw, controls, pre-eminence, intellectual, souls, accords, dame, servitude, adversity, spurns, discourses, vestments, state, defeatures, jewel, enamelled, incorporate, consecrate, contaminate, adulterate, digest, digestion, strumpeted, contagion, scanned, gravity, exempt, contempt, compact, vulgar, comment, estimation, distract, abject, credit, circumstance, shameless, strong hand. A number of these words have already been pointed out as evidence of Chapman's hand in *The Comedy of Errors* by Mr. J. M. Robertson.

Though the whole of Act I. Scene i. was originally Lodge's work, the least altered passage from his hand still remaining

CHAPMAN

in the play are lines 140 to 156, the words here—extremity, dire, mishap, dignity, advocate, hapless, hopeless, hap, honour, disannul—are all characteristic of Lodge. Ægeon's speech in Act v. Scene i., beginning

> Not know my voice!
> O time's extremity,

are also little altered. Lodge, however, is less recognisable by his vocabulary—which curiously resembles Chapman's in his early literary years—than by the dull uniformity of his measure and beat, the uninspiring quality of his diction, and the monotony of his end-stopped lines. In all of these three features he is unique among his contemporaries.

As the old *King Leir* is unadulterated Lodge, its lines may more safely be used as a gauge of his style than any of the remainder of his dramatic work, which is mostly collaborative with Greene: I find traces of Kyd's hand in Lodge's *The Wounds of Civil War*.

Shakespeare's work in *The Comedy of Errors* antedates 1592, when the evidence of the Oxford leases for the Crown Inn and the Tavern indicate that John Davenant had already married Anne Sackfeilde and taken her to Oxford. In June 1590, when her father, William Bird, the Mayor of Bristol, made his last written will, Anne Sackfeilde was still living with her mother at Hotwells, near Bristol, her putative father, Sackfeilde, evidently having recently died. *The Comedy of Errors*, which reflects her in the lines—

> I know a wench of excellent discourse,
> Pretty and witty; wild, and yet, too, gentle:
> There will we dine. This woman that I mean,
> My wife—but, I protest, without desert—
> Hath oftentimes upbraided me withal:
> To her will we to dinner,

was evidently written between June 1590 and about the beginning of 1592, at the latest, while Anne Sackfeilde was still unmarried. While the lines immediately preceding this passage, with Chapman's characteristic "strong hand," and ending with his equally characteristic rhymed couplet :

> For slander lives upon succession,
> For ever housed where it gets possession,

are evidently by Chapman and are unlike Shakespeare, there can be no doubt, however, that the thirteen lines following, describing the youthful tavern hostess, are by Shakespeare ; and little doubt that they reflect a personal interest ; being the first reflection of the Dark Lady of the Sonnets in any of his plays.

Love's Labour's Lost and *Love's Labour's Won*—the latter the early form of *All's Well that Ends Well*—were both written by Shakespeare shortly following the Queen's visit to the Earl of Southampton's seats at Cowdray and Tichfield, upon the occasion of her progress in the autumn of 1591. Both of these plays in their early forms are dramatic reflections of Shakespeare's impressions and observations upon these occasions, when he and his company, we may judge, were engaged by the young Earl to entertain the Queen ; both plays also reflect the Earl of Southampton's affairs at this period ; and the latter, in its revised form of *All's Well that Ends Well*, also reflects them in 1598.[1]

Though most of the story of *All's Well that Ends Well* is ultimately derived from the *Decameron*, and evidently

[1] See *Shakespeare's Sonnet Story*, pp. 404–22. Bernard Quaritch, London, 1922.

CHAPMAN

through the medium of Painter's *Palace of Pleasure* (1566), Shakepeare's play contains convincing evidence that it was founded upon an earlier dramatic original. A number of significant indications infer that this original was an Oxford's property, written by Chapman and Munday.

All of the archaic remains in the play strongly suggest their work. The Parolles part in the original play was doubtless written by Munday; Parolles being, in his early form, one of his typical braggarts, such as Crackstone in *The Two Italian Gentlemen*, or his revision of Basilisco in *Soliman and Perseda*. The first fifty lines of Act II. Scene iii. are evidently Munday's and Chapman's work, little if at all altered by Shakespeare. Lafeu's words in this scene:

> Lustig, as the Dutchman says:

which are so inappropriate to the courtly gentleman presented by Shakespeare in this character, are clearly a vestige of the old Oxford play, as well as a reference to another Oxford property probably recently presented. Jacob van Smelt, a Dutchman in Munday's *The Weakest Goeth to the Wall*, uses the word for the English "lusty."

Though this play was largely re-written by Shakespeare in 1598, at his most Chapmanesque period, the very large number and the nature of the words characteristic of Chapman in the older portions of the play indicate their retention by Shakespeare from an older base rather than his adopted use at this early period of so many such words from Chapman, many of which do not appear again in Shakespeare's works, and those to be found, as a rule, only in other plays strongly suggesting a Chapman base.

The divergent and rival company connections of Greene and Chapman, all through their concurrent careers, naturally negative the probability, or even possibility, of Mr. Robertson's suggestion that Greene had any hand in this play, as well as his further quite untenable inference that Greene and Kyd collaborated.

The lines which Mr. Robertson finds so suggestive of Greene :

> Ere twice the horses of the sun shall bring
> Their fiery torcher his diurnal ring ;
> Ere twice in murk and occidental damp
> Moist Hesperus hath quench'd his sleepy lamp ;
> Or four and twenty times the pilot's glass
> Hath told the thievish minutes how they pass ;
> What is infirm from your sound parts shall fly,
> Health shall live free, and sickness freely die,

are neither Shakespeare's nor Greene's, but clearly Chapman's. In three of these lines there are five words never again used by Shakespeare and four never used by Greene ; while four of them, and other forms of the fifth, are frequently used by Chapman. These words are : torcher, diurnal, murk, occidental, Hesperus. The old-fashioned quality of the lines is much more likely to have been original with Chapman than with Greene, whose somewhat similar lines probably reflect Chapman, who preceded Greene as a writer for the stage by several years. It is still more likely that the lines from *Hamlet* :

> Full thirty times hath Phoebus' cart gone round
> Neptune's salt wash and Tellus' orbed ground,
> And thirty dozen moons with borrowed sheen
> About the world have times twelve thirties been,
> Since love our hearts and Hymen did our hands
> Unite commutual in most sacred bands,

preceded Chapman's lines in the original of *Love's Labour's Won*, and also Greene's similar lines in *Alphonsus of Arragon.*

CHAPMAN

Yet, I find nothing in what remains of Kyd's work that suggests his hand in these lines from *Hamlet*. I cannot find that he ever uses the word "Tellus," or "commutual," nor do I find anything in his verses remotely resembling this metre. Shakespeare, also, never elsewhere uses these two words, nor indulges in this metre, while Chapman frequently uses "Tellus," and "commutual" is like a word of his coinage. This would infer, then, that Shakespeare may have introduced these lines, for their dramaturgically archaic quality, from some play of Chapman's among his company's properties, or that Chapman at some time had a hand in *Hamlet*. The former appears the more probable as Shakespeare in this same scene paraphrases a passage from *Queen Dido*, though the latter is not improbable. *Hamlet* may have been an Admiral's company's property between 1589 and the end of 1590, or have been in Oxford's company's hands temporarily between 1585 and 1589, when it is likely a similar interchange of plays took place between them and the Admiral-Chamberlain's men, that we find later in use between Strange's and the Admiral's men.

The large proportion of once used and rarely used words from Chapman's vocabulary in *All's Well*, and the presence of traces of Munday's collaborative work, clearly indicate its original as one of the Oxford's properties, retained or procured by the Burbages when they parted with Alleyn in 1590.

Macbeth and *Macdobeth*.

A few significant indications concerning the literary history of *Macbeth*, combined with very convincing internal evidence, have led me to the conclusion that in its earliest form this play was also written by Munday and Chapman for Oxford's company some time before 1589. Such evidence seems also to infer that it became an Alleyn-Henslowe property in 1591, and was probably revised in or about 1595–6 for some one of the companies that Henslowe financed other than the Admiral's company; such as the Queen's company, Pembroke's men, or the Worcester-Oxford combination, and that some time before 1605–6 it became a property of Shakespeare's company, when it was revised into approximately its present form. I say approximately because of the probable fact that it was somewhat revised by post-Shakespearean revisers after Shakespeare had retired from London.

That a play upon the subject of Macbeth existed years before Shakespeare's, and that it was not then owned by his company, is indicated by two facts: first, that Kempe, the actor, who was a member of Shakespeare's company from 1594 to about 1601–2, in his *Nine Days' Wonder*, in 1600, writes: " I met a proper upright youth, only for a little stooping in the shoulders, all heart to the heel, a penny poet, whose first making was the miserable story of Mac-doel, or Mac-dobeth, or Mac-somewhat." Had this been a Lord Chamberlain's play Kempe's allusion would not have been so indefinite. Had it been an Admiral's company's play we would doubtless have had some notice of it in Henslowe's *Diary*.

Could we learn for which company Anthony Munday wrote in 1595–6, we would probably know the company that owned the earlier form of *Macbeth* at that date. Munday was one of the most prolific ballad-writers of the time, and a number of his ballads appear to have been written and published by him concurrently with the stage presentation of plays upon the same subject, either as an advertising device to popularise such plays, or as a means of profiting in the sale of ballads by their dramatic vogue.

A ballad upon the subject of *Macdobeth* was registered in the year 1596, from which I infer the probability that *Macbeth* was being presented at that time by some company with which Munday was connected as a writer. Faint suggestions of Munday's hand and undoubted evidence of Chapman's hand are still apparent in the diction, while portions of the plot follow the lines of *Sir Thomas More* and *Thomas Lord Cromwell*, in the fact that the protagonists in all three cases are rapidly advanced in honours at the beginning of the plays, the announcement of their new dignities being conveyed to them by their noble friends, acting as messengers of their sovereigns. All three quickly attain the height of their fortunes and as quickly decline. Much of the play is Chapman, transposed and improved by Shakespeare in about the same manner as he revised and transposed the passage in *Sir Thomas More*.

The short-lined rhymes of the witch passage that comprises Act I. Scene i. are plainly by the same hand as the similar rhymes in Act IV. Scene i., the vocabulary and matter of which clearly reveal George Chapman as the author. In the scansion of the first eight lines of Act I. Scene i. :

> FIRST WITCH. When shall we three meet again,
> In thunder, lightning, or in rain ?
> SEC. WITCH. When the hurly burly's done,
> When the battle's lost and won.
> THIRD WITCH. That will be ere set of sun.
> FIRST WITCH. Where the place ?
> SEC. WITCH. Upon the heath.
> THIRD WITCH. There to meet with Macbeth,

we appear to have evidence that this act and scene pertained to the play in its earlier form of *Macdobeth*. The scansion of the eighth line being falsified by the omission of the letters " do."

Act I. Scene i., though doubtless, like most of the remainder of the play, written over a base by Chapman, now shows little of his hand, even as substrata, and no evidence whatever of Shakespeare's. It is very probable that both Act I. Scene ii. and Act III. are post-Shakespearean. A comparison of the witch lines of Act IV Scene i., which are early and evidently Chapman's, with those of Act I. Scene iii., reveal the latter as probably post-Shakespearean work.

The first evidence of Shakespeare's hand in *Macbeth* is in Act I. Scene iii., where Macbeth and Banquo enter; from this to the end he overwrites a base by Chapman, and also from here onward to the end of Scene vii. A slight idea of the manner in which Shakespeare adapted or transposed Chapman's original may be gained by a comparison of a few lines from Chapman's *Cæsar and Pompey* with lines in *Macbeth* employing the same metaphor, now transposed by Shakespeare, as follows:

>I have no spur
>To prick the sides of my intent, but only
>Vaulting ambition, which o'erleaps itself
>And falls on the other.

Cæsar and Pompey:

>What think you, lords, that 'tis ambition's spur
>That pricketh Cæsar to these high attempts?

The dialogue from the beginning of Act II. Scene i. to line thirty-two appears to have been original with Shakespeare, but from the beginning of the passage reading:

>Is this a dagger which I see before me,

CHAPMAN

down to line sixty-three, he clearly re-wrote a Chapman base; the following words and phrases are distinctly Chapman's: "a false creation," "dudgeon gouts of blood," "witchcraft celebrates pale Hecate's offerings,"

> Hear it not, Duncan, for it is a knell
> That summons thee to heaven, or to hell,

and in Scene ii., "drugg'd their possets," "surfeited grooms," "brain-sickly," "smear the sleepy grooms with blood."

> I'll *gild* the faces of the grooms withal,
> For it must seem their *guilt*.

The "gild" and "guilt" used here are used elsewhere by Chapman. Substrata of Munday's are reflected in Shakespeare's:

> The multitudinous seas incarnadine,
> Making the green one red.

In 1598 Munday uses a similar phrase in *The Death of Robert Earl of Huntingdon*:

> The multitude of seas died red with blood.

Act IV. Scene i. is Chapman slightly altered by Shakespeare, and probably a post-Shakespearean reviser. The short-lined rhymes are indubitably Chapman, unaltered. Lines 50 to 61 are almost unaltered Chapman, the same idea expressed in very similar terms being found elsewhere in his works. Act IV. Scene i. lines 50 to 61:

> Though you untie the winds and let them fight
> Against the churches; though the yesty waves
> Confound and swallow navigation up;
> Though bladed corn be lodged and trees blown down;
> Though castles topple on their warders' heads;
> Though palaces and pyramids do slope
> Their heads to their foundations; though the treasure
> Of nature's germins tumble all together,
> Even till destruction sicken; answer me
> To what I ask you.

Chapman's *Histriomastix*, Act v.:

> . . . . teach thy fiers
> To climbe the toppes of houses; and thy mines
> To blow up Churches in th' offended skye;
> Consume whole groves and standing fields of Corne,
> In thy wild-rage, and make the proud earth groane
> Under the weight of thy confusion.

Chapman's *Shadow of Night*:

> Convert the violent courses of thy floods,
> Remove whole fields of corn, and hugest woods,
> Cast hills into the sea, and make the stars
> Drop out of heaven, and lose thy mariners.
> So shall the wonders of thy power be seen,
> And thou for ever live the planets' queen.

Act IV. Scenes ii. and iii., though probably greatly expanded by Shakespeare, appear to have had some Chapmanian base. The sleep-walking scene in Act v. Scene i. appears to be entirely by Shakespeare. From Act v. Scene ii., onward to the end of the play, Shakespeare overwrites Chapman, except in one or two notably original passages, such as lines 16 to 28, in Act v. Scene v.:

> Wherefore was that cry?
> The queen, my lord, is dead.
> She should have died hereafter;
> There would have been a time for such a word.
> To-morrow, and to-morrow, and to-morrow,
> Creeps in this petty pace from day to day,
> To the last syllable of recorded time;
> And all our yesterdays have lighted fools
> The way to dusty death. Out, out, brief candle!
> Life's but a walking shadow, a poor player
> That struts and frets his hour upon the stage
> And then is heard no more: it is a tale
> Told by an idiot, full of sound and fury,
> Signifying nothing.

That *Macbeth* contains a large amount of non-Shakespearean matter, either as substrata or post-Shakespearean revision, or both, will clearly appear by comparing its metrical characteristics with those of *Othello*, composed about a year earlier, and with *Antony and Cleopatra*, which appeared about a year later. While the metrical indications of their periods of composition approximate closely in the case of *Othello* and *Antony and Cleopatra*, they both differ very widely from those of *Macbeth*.

Timon of Athens.

It would be a work of supererogation to add further to the exhaustive and convincing evidence advanced by Mr. J. M. Robertson, that Chapman's revised and unrevised hand is present, and in a large measure, in *Timon of Athens*. In view of the foregoing history and argument regarding the acquisition by Shakespeare's company of a large number of Chapman's old plays, between 1589 and 1591, it should now also be unnecessary further to rebut his automatically disproved theory of collaboration between Shakespeare and Chapman. As in the case of *Sir Thomas More, Cromwell, The Two Italian Gentlemen*, and other Chapman and Munday plays in Oxford's properties, the original of *Timon of Athens* evidently also came into the possession of Shakespeare's company at or about 1589 to 1591. The mention of " critic Timon " by Shakespeare in *Love's Labour's Lost*, in about 1591–2, suggests his company's possession of Chapman's *Timon* at that time. Shakespeare's *Timon*, like his *Macbeth, Henry IV., Part II.,* and *Henry V.*, still retains extensive substrata from the dramatic base he worked upon, largely, we may judge, because of hasty work. It has frequently been suggested that his work upon *Timon of Athens* was left unfinished and completed by another hand, or hands. I entirely agree with this. As Mr. Robertson has already recognised, we have in the speech of Flavius, the steward, in Act IV. Scene ii., unadulterated Chapman. The sentiments expressed are the same, and the language similar to that in Scene xiii. in *Sir Thomas More*, in which More bids farewell to his family and servants, including Catesbie, his steward. This resemblance strongly suggests the original composition of Chapman's *Timon* near to that of *More*, and indicates it as an old Oxford's property. Had Shakespeare finished his revision of Chapman's *Timon* it is most unlikely that he would have left in his revision large unrevised passages by Chapman.

Henry VIII. and *Pericles*.

Strong evidence exists in the plot, action, and vocabulary of these plays, and also in rhymed couplets in *Pericles*, suggestive of Chapman, that they were both developed, and probably through several revisions, from original Chapman or Chapman-Munday bases. The jealous and bitter character of Bishop Gardiner developed in *Henry VIII.* follows the model already forecast in his presentations in *Cromwell* and *More*. This leads me to infer that Munday and Chapman also produced an early play upon Wolsey which remained a Henslowe-Alleyn property, and which, in conjunction with *Cromwell*, was revised in 1601-2 by the Henslowe-Alleyn writers into *The Life and Death of Cardinal Wolsey*. Chapman's early vocabulary is quite as noticeably present in *Henry VIII.* and *Pericles*, as in the plays already examined, with the exception of *Timon* and *Macbeth*.

The Two Italian Gentlemen is the earliest play in which

I find Chapman's hand, and the first in which I find collaboration between him and Munday. As it was published in 1584, it was probably produced from two to three years earlier. Bodenham, the compiler of *England's Helicon*, ascribes to " shepherd Tony " (Anthony Munday) verses from it correctly ascribed to Chapman by Allot in *England's Parnassus*. An examination of this play reveals the fact that only the Crackstone passages are Munday's work, and that the remainder of the play is Chapman's. Lacking the facts above to guide us, it would have been very difficult to recognise Chapman's style in this play by comparing it with his later work ; even with *Cromwell* and *More*, only from three to six years later. This difficulty is increased by the facts that this play alone, of his now recognised work, is written entirely in fourteeners, doggerel, and short rhymed measures, with no pentameters to compare with his later work, and that only inceptive traces of his later, very characteristic vocabulary are here present. It was the presence of one such word in *The Two Italian Gentlemen*—" pitfall "—combined with the significant resemblances between the conjurations of Medusa here, and the witches in *Macbeth*, that first led me to suspect Chapman's substrata in that play. The word " pitfall " appears only once in Shakespeare, in the lines from *Macbeth*, Act IV. Scene ii. :

> Poor bird ! thou'ldst never fear the net nor lime,
> The pitfall nor the gin.

The structure of this and other lines in the same scene that suggest the fourteener period ; the common use in *The Two Italian Gentlemen* and in *Macbeth*, and not elsewhere in Shakespeare, of the word " pitfall " ; the common use in these two plays, and not elsewhere, of the word "fillet," and in both instances used in magical conjurations, lead me to infer the probability that Chapman and Munday's *Macdobeth*, in its first form, was a fourteener play, and pertained to about the same period as *The Two Italian Gentlemen*. The use of the word "searoom" in *The Two Italian Gentlemen*, and again only in *Pericles*, may similarly indicate a very early form of that play also. The part taken by Medusa in *The Two Italian Gentlemen*, which evidently followed Chapman's study of witchcraft and the black arts in such books as Reginald Scott's *The Discoverie of Witchcraft*, marks the beginning of the element of the supernatural that Chapman develops in certain plays, such as *Charlemagne, Bussy D'Ambois, Macdobeth*, and probably other lost plays. As Chapman's writing of *The Two Italian Gentlemen* preceded the publication of Scott's book by a few years, it is probable that he had already studied some of the numerous foreign and English authorities that Scott mentions as his sources. Such a list of spirits as Medusa mentions—Nettabor, Temapttor, Vigilator, Somniator, Astarot, Berliche, Buffon, Amachon, Suchon, Sustani, Asmodeus—implies a study of this nature upon Chapman's part. Other fairly distinctive words of Chapman's found in this play are: posset, found only in *Macbeth, The Merry Wives*—both plays with a Chapman base—and *Hamlet*. The large number of Chapman's characteristic words I find in *Hamlet* are due, either to the fact that Shakespeare in his revisions of this play derived such words from Chapman's copy at hand, or else that Chapman had a revisionary hand in the play between 1589 and the end of 1590, when it may temporarily have been an Admiral's property. "Swindge" is also found here and in all of Chapman's work, and seldom elsewhere.

CHAPMAN

The word "dame" for lady is found here a number of times; no poet of the period uses this word with Chapman's frequency. "Liklihood," found here twice, is indicative of Chapman always in a Shakespearean play. "Gazers eyes," found five times in this play, and frequently in Chapman's early work. In *Histriomastix* it occurs in the lines :

> Ile have a Jewell Amatist
> Whose beauty shall strike blind the gazers Eye.

"The world runnes on wheels," found several times here, was later used as the title of a play by Chapman; physic, physician, shrouds, precepts, parables (the latter found only in *The Two Gentlemen of Verona*), gudgion, catterwalling (found only in *Twelfth Night* and *Titus Andronicus*). This very limited list makes it apparent that Chapman had not then developed his vocabulary to any large extent, and had not yet entered upon the coinage of neologisms. The growth of his vocabulary was probably hastened by his early work upon his Homeric translations, which, the use of certain words appears to indicate, began in about 1585-8, at the latest. The word "ostent," which I regard as a coinage of Chapman's, and which naturally appears frequently in his Homeric translations, is used for the first time in *Sir Thomas More*, if its presence in *Pericles* does not indicate substrata of a still earlier date.

The Life and Death of Thomas Lord Cromwell evidently came to Burbage's hands as a Pembroke property in 1591. It was published in 1602 by Henslowe's and Alleyn's writers as an obsolete property, they having now incorporated its substance concerning Cromwell into the *Life and Death of Cardinal Wolsey*, which was written for Henslowe's stage by Chettle, Munday, Drayton, and Smith, between June 1601 and May 1602. It was published by William Jones, whose publications of plays are all Henslowe-Alleyn plays, and who never published a Burbage property. Much internal evidence in *Henry VIII.* suggests that *Cardinal Wolsey* later on became a Burbage property, and was re-written by Burbage's writers into *Henry VIII.*, after Shakespeare had retired from active work. It appears very probable also that the *Wolsey* compiled by the four writers mentioned above was based upon an old Chapman-Munday play concerning Wolsey, as well as upon their *Cromwell.* While there is no evidence of Chapman's late hand in *Henry VIII.*, as it now appears, there is very strong evidence in phrase and vocabulary that the play was built upon an early Chapman base or bases. *The Cromwell parts of " Henry VIII." are plainly taken from the old play of " Cromwell,"* and evidently were conveyed there through their absorption into *Wolsey* in 1601-2. Dr. Samuel Johnson, and others equally authoritative in their days, to the contrary, notwithstanding, I cannot believe that a single line of Shakespeare's exists in this partisanly Protestant and political play, which is basically as strongly suggestive of Munday's and Chapman's work as it is totally unlike Shakespeare's.

The use by Shakespeare in Act II. Scene i. of *The Two Gentlemen of Verona*, of the four following fourteeners spoken by Speed, and his concluding words admitting that he had found these lines in print, appear to indicate their retention from an earlier fourteener base, which was probably either a revision by Chapman and Munday of their *Two Italian Gentlemen*, or the Queen's company's *Felix and Filomena*, portions of the stories of both of which plays are incorporated in *The Two Gentlemen of Verona* :

For often have you writ to her, and she, in modesty,
Or else for want of idle time, could not again reply ;
Or fearing else some messenger, that might her mind discover,
Herself hath taught her love himself to write unto her lover.
All this I speak in print, for in print I found it.

Thomas Lord Cromwell was evidently revised several times between about 1583, when it was first produced by Munday and Chapman, and the time the Burbages sold it to Henslowe and Alleyn some time before 1602 Its last revision for the Lord Chamberlain's men was made by Thomas Dekker, whose hand is plainly recognisable in the choruses, as well as in the comic passages in which Hodge appears, where Munday's hand is overwritten. Despite its several revisions, Chapman's early hand is still apparent in most of the lines spoken by Cromwell, whose characterisation and career practically repeat those of Sir Thomas More, in the play of that name, produced about three years later by Munday and Chapman. A very casual comparison reveals a common authorship in the two plays.

Sir Thomas More.

The fortunate preservation of the original MS. of this play written in Munday's hand, as well as additions or revisions by a number of later hands, including Shakespeare's, affords us an idea of the probable state of the average dramatic MS. by the time their last owners sent them to press. As in *Cromwell*, Chapman's hand is to be found mostly in the lines spoken by the protagonist; though it appears also in other portions of the play, as in Lincoln's speech beginning :

Come gallant bloods, you, whose free soules doo scorne,

and ending with the characteristic lines :

Since justice keeps not them in greater awe
Weele be our selves rough ministers at lawe,

256 CHAPMAN

Chapman's hand, though overwritten at times by Munday, is also apparent in the utterances of Shrewsbury and Surrey. The most characteristic passage of Chapman's in the play is in Scene viii., beginning at line 1410:

    Enter Sir THOMAS MOORE, *his lady, daughters,* MR. ROPER,
    Gentlemen, and servaunts, as in his house in Chelsey.

MOORE. God morrowe good sonne Roper, sit good Madame,
uppon an humble seate, the time so craves,
rest your good hart on earth, the *roofe of graves.*
You see the floore of greatnesse is uneven,
the Cricket and high throane alike neere heaven.
Now daughters, you that *like to braunches spred,*
and give best shaddowe to a private house :
Be comforted my Girles, your hopes stand faire,
vertue breeds gentrie, she makes the best heire.

BOTH DAU. God morrow to your honor.

MOORE. Nay, good night rather,
your honor's creast-falne with your happie father.

RO. Oh what *formalitie,* what *square observaunce*
lives in a little roome, heere, *publique care,*
gagges not the eyes of slumber : heere, fierce riott,
ruffles not proudely in a coate of trust,
whilste like a Pawne at Chesse, he keepes in ranck
with Kings and mightie fellowes, yet indeed
those men (tha)t stand on tip toe, smile to see
him *pawne his fortunes.*

MOORE. True sonne
Nor does the wanton tongue heere skrewe it selfe
into the eare, that like a vise, drinkes up
the iron instrument.

LADY. we are heere at peace.

MOORE. Then peace good wife.

LADY. ffor keeping still in compasse, (a straunge poynte
in *times newe navigation,*) we have sailde
beyond our course.

MOORE. Have doone.

LADY. we are exilde the Courte.

MOORE. Still thou harpste on that,
Tis sinne for to deserve that banishment,
but he that nere knewe Courte courtes sweete content.

LADY. Oh but deare husband.

MOORE. I will not heare thee wife,
The *winding laborinth* of thy *straunge discourse,*
will nere have end. Sit still, and, my good wife,
entreate thy tongue be still: or credit me,
thou shalt not understand a woord we speake
weele talke in Latine.
Humida vallis raros patitur fulminis ictus.
More rest enjoyes the subject meanely bred,
then he that beares the Kingdome in his head.
Great men are still Musitians, else the world lyes,
they learne lowe (noates) straines after the noates
that rise.

RO. Good Sir, be still your selfe, and but remember,
How in this *generall Courte of short liv'de pleasure*
the worlde, *creation* is the *ample* foode,
that is *digested* in the *maw of tyme.*
If man him selfe be subject to such ruine,
How shall his garment then, or the *loose pointes,*
that tye *respect* unto his *awefull place* :
avoyde distruction ? / Moste honord father in lawe,
the blood you have bequeath'de these severall hartes
to nourishe your *posteritie,* stands firme
As as with joy you led us first to rise
So with like harts weele lock *preferments eyes.*

MOORE. *Close them not then with teares, for that ostent,*
gives a wett signall of your discontent.
If you will share my fortunes, comfort then.
an hundred smiles for one sighe : what, we are men.
Resigne (wett) wett passion to these weaker eyes,
which prooves their sexe, but grauntes nere more wise.
Lets now *survaye our state* : Heere sits my wife,
and deare esteemed issue, yonder stand
my loving Servaunts, *now the difference*
twixt those and these. Now you shall heare me speake,
like Moore in melanchollie. / I conceive, that Nature
hath *sundrie mettalles,* out of which she frames
us *mortalles,* eche in *valuation*
out prizing other. Of the finest stuffe,
the finest features come, *the rest of earth,*
receive base fortune even before their birthe.
Hence slaves have their creation and I thinke
Nature provides content for the *base minde,*
under the whip, the burden and the toyle,

their *lowe wrought bodies drudge in pacience.*
As for *the Prince,* in all his *sweet gorgde mawe,*
and his *ranck fleshe* that *sinfully renewes
the noones excesse in the nights daungerous surfeits,
what meanes or miserie from our birth dooth flowe,*
Nature entitles to us, that we owe.
But we beeing subject to the *rack of hate,*
falling from happie life to *bondage state
having seene better dayes,* now know the lack
of glorie, that once rearde eche high fed back.
But that in your age did nere viewe better,
challendge not fortune for your *thriftlesse debter.*

CATESBIE. Sir, *we have seene farre better dayes,* then these.
MOORE. I was the patrone of those dayes, and knowe,
those were but *painted dayes,* only for showe,
then greeve not you to fall with him that gave them.
Pro hæris generosis servis gloriosum mori.
deare Gough, thou art my *learned Secretarie,*
you Mr. Catesbie *Steward of my house,*
the rest (like you) have had fayre time to growe
in *Sun-shine of my fortunes.* But I must tell ye,
Corruption is fled hence with eche mans office.
Bribes that make open *traffick twixt the soule,
and netherland of Hell,* deliver up
their guiltie homage to their second Lordes
then *liu(in)g thus untainted, you (are) well
Trueth (is) no Pilot for the lan(d) of hell.*

The words, phrases, and lines italicised above display many of the peculiarities of mind, diction, and vocabulary that so definitely distinguish Chapman's thought and style from those of all of his contemporaries, and render his lost work so readily recognisable to those who know him well. Here we have his neologisms, his harsh consonantal couplets, one of his characteristic puns, his reflections upon unfortunate birth so common with him; his honest steward, to be found in *Bussy D'Ambois* and *Monsieur D'Olive,* as well as in *All's Well* and *Timon*; his virtuous learning and poverty and vicious wealth; and, withal, his very distinctive vocabulary.

CHAPMAN

As *Sir Thomas More* exhibits Chapman's literary idiosyncrasies more clearly than either of the earlier plays examined, so the following still later play (1593), though materially altered by Marston in 1599 and containing collaborative lines by Nashe from 1593, displays in a more palpable manner his accentuating peculiarities of vocabulary, mind, and style at this period.

Histriomastix in its early form, though possibly written some months earlier, was finished by Chapman and Nashe after the death of Marlowe, on May 30, 1593. It reflects the attempt of Raleigh, Harriot, and others with whom Marlow and Roydon were associated, to set up an academy in London, which was apparently ended by the murder of Marlowe, and the plainly factitious investigation of the orthodoxy of his fellow-members instituted by Sir Robert Cecil after that mysterious and sinister event. It also reflects Shakespeare and Pembroke's company and their impecunious condition—reported by Henslowe to Alleyn— in which they returned to London some time in August, when they were compelled to pawn their apparel for their charges. Harriot, the astronomer, is Chrisoganus; Southampton, Lord Mavortius; Florio, Southampton's Italian tutor, is the Italian lord, Landulpho; and Shakespeare is Posthaste, the poet for Sir Oliver Owlet's company. Lines directly alluding to Shakespeare and his *Troilus and Cressida* were introduced by Marston in 1599, as a renewed attack upon Shakespeare.

The fact that Chapman and Nashe, in the late summer of 1593, were both interested in Marlowe's literary remains—coupled with a slight and overwritten trace of Nashe's hand in an attack upon Shakespeare in the lines from *Histriomastix* quoted below, some of which repeat similar slurs cast by Nashe in collaboration with Greene a couple of years earlier—led me to suggest that Nashe collaborated with Chapman in this play, but that his lines had been largely obliterated by Marston's revision. Nashe's early strictures appear to be repeated in the following lines :

> O age, when every Scriveners boy shall dippe
> Profaning quills into Thessaliaes spring ;
> When every artist prentice that hath read
> The pleasant pantry of conceipts shall dare
> To write as confident as Hercules ;

I have now found very convincing evidence in other lines in this play that Nashe worked with Chapman upon it in 1593. Shortly before Greene died, Nashe wrote, in conjunction with him, *The Old Wives' Tale*, in which the following verses are his :

> *Enter the* HARVEST-MEN *singing, with women in their hands.*

FRO. Soft ! who have we here ? our amorous harvesters.
FAN. Ay, ay, let us sit still, and let them alone.

> *Here the* HARVEST-MEN *sing, the song doubled.*
>
> Lo, here we come a-reaping, a-reaping,
> To reap our harvest-fruit !
> And thus we pass the year so long,
> And never be we mute.
>
> [*Exeunt the* HARVEST-MEN.]

In an earlier scene the harvest-men also appear :

> *Enter the* HARVEST-MEN *a-singing, with this song double repeated.*
>
> All ye that lovely lovers be,
> Pray you for me :
> Lo, here we come a-sowing, a-sowing,
> And sow sweet fruits of love ;
> In your sweet hearts well may it prove !
>
> [*Exeunt.*]

CHAPMAN

The Old Wives' Tale was the last thing in which Greene and Nashe collaborated in 1592. Greene died early in September of this year. About a year later, when Chapman composed his early *Histriomastix*, Nashe was now collaborating with him when he wrote similar harvest verses for this play :

The harvest-folkes Song.

Holyday, O blessed morne !
This day Plenty hath beene borne.
Plenty is the child of Peace ;
To her birth the Gods do prease.
Full crown'd Mazors Bacchus brings,
With liquor which from grapes hee wringes.
Holliday, O blessed morne !
This day Plenty hath ben borne.
Holliday, let's loudly cry,
For joy of her nativity.
Ceres, with a bounteous hand,
Doth at Plenties elbo stand,
Binding mixed Coronets
Of wheat which on her head she sets.
Holliday, O blessed morne !
This day Plenty hath bin borne.
Holliday, let's loudly cry
For joy of her nativity.

The very obvious identity of the style of these two sets of quaintly natural verses ; Nashe's connection at this time with Chapman ; the utter unlikeness of these verses to anything ever written by Marston or Chapman, the only other hands in *Histriomastix*, appear fully to warrant the conclusion that they were written by Nashe.

While very slight traces of Chapman's overwritten hand are discernible also in *Julius Cæsar, The Merchant of Venice* (in the Casket scene), *Othello,* and *The Tempest,* this may be due in some instances to Chapman's revision of originals during his connection with the Admiral's men in 1589 and 1590, or to Shakespeare's use of Chapman's MSS. of other plays in making his revisions. In the cases of *Julius Cæsar* and *The Tempest*, however, the evidence strongly suggests Chapmanian bases. The presence of the word " elbow " and the peculiar expression, twice repeated, " let's loudly cry," in the verses by Nashe quoted above, indicate the probability that in *Julius Cæsar* Shakespeare worked upon an original of Chapman's in which Nashe had collaborated. Mr. J. M. Robertson has called attention to the following questionable lines in this play which are certainly neither Shakespeare's nor Chapman's, as they never use the contraction " let's " for " let us," nor would be likely to write such dramatic nonsense :

>   Stoop, Romans, stoop,
> And let us bathe our hands in Cæsar's blood
> Up to the elbows, and besmear our swords :
> Then walk we forth, even to the market-place,
> And waving our red weapons o'er our heads,
> Let's all cry " Peace, freedom and liberty ! "

Nashe is the only writer of this period that collaborated with Chapman who ever uses the contraction noticed, and to whom lines so dramatically weak can logically be attributed.

As Jacob Ayrer's *Die Schöne Sidea*, upon which it has been suggested by Tieck that much of the incident, as well as the expression, of *The Tempest* are based, was in all probability, like the remainder of Ayrer's publications, built upon an English original, taken to Germany in 1590 or 1592 by Richard Jones and Robert Browne, from the Burbage-Alleyn stock, it is probable that it was an early form of Chapman's original for *The Tempest*, and that the spiritual affinity that has frequently been noticed between Cerimon in *Pericles*, and Prospero in *The Tempest*, may indicate Chapman's two originals as of about the same early period and evidently Oxford's properties. Such traces of Chapman's hand as are now discernible in *The Tempest* consist of vocabulary altogether. The Masque in its present form is clearly neither Chapman's nor Shakespeare's, most of it being evidently post-Shakespearean, and probably by Beaumont or Fletcher. Yet something resembling the Masque in a simpler form appears to have been an integral part of an earlier base. The following short-lined verses, spoken by Juno and Ceres, as well as the concluding lines of Iris' speech, and the dance of the reapers and nymphs, all bear a significant resemblance to the verses of the harvest-men by Nashe in *The Old Wives' Tale*, and also to the harvest-folks' song and scene in the early *Histriomastix* (1593), in which Ceres with sheaves, and Bacchus with grapes, appear :

JUNO. Honour, riches, marriage-blessing,
Long continuance, and increasing,
Hourly joys be still upon you !
Juno sings her blessings on you.

CERES. Earth's increase, foison plenty,
Barns and garners never empty ;
Vines with clustering bunches growing ;
Plants with goodly burthen bowing ;
Spring come to you at the farthest
In the very end of harvest !
Scarcity and want shall shun you ;
Ceres' blessing so is on you.

Enter certain Nymphs.

You sunburn'd sicklemen, of August weary,
Come hither from the furrow, and be merry :

>Make holiday ; your rye-straw hats put on,
>And these fresh nymphs encounter every one
>In country footing.
>
>*Enter certain Reapers properly habited : they join with the Nymphs in a graceful dance.*

The resemblance between these verses and the harvest scene of which they form a part, and Nashe's similar verses and harvest scenes in *The Old Wives' Tale* and *Histriomastix*, infers the probability that the early *Fair Sidea* was revived and revised by Chapman and Nashe at the same time and for the same company for which the early *Histriomastix* was written, which was evidently the Children of the Chapel, for whom Nashe, at the same period, finished *Queen Dido*. There is in all of the verses quoted from these three plays a lyric simplicity and quaintness, not likely to be found in three sets of verses, in three different plays, by three separate hands ; and they all sing the praises of harvest-time, and in much the same strains. It seems likely, then, that the more artificially pastoral flavour of most of the verses in the Masque in *The Tempest*, with their greater erudition and numerous classical allusions, displaced or greatly altered a more natural harvest scene, with simpler songs and dances by reapers and nymphs, in an earlier form of the play, some vestiges of which still remain.

CHAPTER IX

PEELE'S HAND IN
SIR THOMAS MORE

OUR past knowledge of Peele's connection with the stage, as well as of his affiliations with the dramatic companies, has been as fragmentary and indefinite as it has hitherto been concerning Munday, Chapman, Kyd, Marlowe, Greene, Lodge, and Nashe; as well as of Shakespeare previous to 1594, and of Jonson previous to 1597.

A brief survey of Peele's acknowledged and ascribed dramatic work may throw some new light upon such affiliations. His first play, *The Arraignment of Paris*, which was composed at Oxford, was presented before the Court by the Children of the Chapel in 1581, and was sent to press in 1584, being printed by Henry Marsh. A second pastoral play, entitled *The Hunting of Cupid*, of a similar nature, judging by a few passages from it which survive in *England's Helicon* and *England's Parnassus*, was entered for publication upon the Stationers' Registers in 1591. There is no record either of its stage presentation or of its publication, yet it probably reached both, as Drummond of Hawthornden records it as one of the books read by him in 1609. No copy is now known to survive. Its license for entry upon the Stationers' Registers being made in the name of Richard Jones, indicates it as an Alleyn property in 1591. It appears probable that it was originally written for the Children of the Chapel, and that Peele was still connected with them in from 1582–3, when they disappear from the records for about four years.

Of extant plays ascribed or ascribable to Peele his *David and Bathsabe* was evidently the next in order of composition. As this play is not mentioned in Henslowe's *Diary* and was published in 1599 by Adam Islip, while all of Peele's other publications from 1589 onwards were made through channels that issued Admiral's and Alleyn-Henslowe's properties—such as Richard Jones, Abel Jeffes, and Edward Alde—it becomes evident that *David and Bathsabe* was composed before 1589, and for a company that Peele worked for between 1582–3, when the Children of the Chapel disappear from the records, and 1589, when he joined Alleyn and the Admiral's men. There can be little doubt that this was either the Children of the Chapel or Oxford's company. The fact that Peele, Chapman, and Munday all joined Alleyn and the Admiral's men in 1589, when Alleyn bought Oxford's properties, may infer that the three poets came from Oxford's men at this time; but the fact that *David and Bathsabe* appears never to have been an Admiral's nor an Alleyn property may indicate it as a play of the Children of the Chapel, as this was the only other London company at that time with which Peele may have been connected.

When Alleyn and his brother bought Oxford's properties in the spring of 1589, Lord Strange's new company of adult actors was evidently forming. At about this same time we find Greene and Nashe casting slurs at Marlowe and Shakespeare, and also alluding critically to

Kyd's plays, but beginning to praise Peele as a writer and Alleyn as an actor, and also to link their names. It was at this time that Marlowe left the Admiral's men and became stage poet for Strange's men, and that Peele succeeded him in that capacity with the Admiral's men, with Munday and Chapman as his assistants.

Less than two years later, at the end of 1590, when Burbage and Alleyn parted, and Shakespeare and Marlowe remained with Burbage and the newly formed Pembroke's company, Peele accompanied Strange's and the Admiral's men to Alleyn and Henslowe, and continued with this amalgamation as company poet under their successive titles of Lord Strange's men, the Earl of Derby's company, and the Lord Chamberlain's men, until the middle of 1594, when the Lord Chamberlain's men returned to Burbage; the Admiral's men in the company now becoming the nucleus of a new company, known thereafter for several years as the Admiral's company.

Peele's hand as substrata in Shakespeare's *Henry V.*, which I have already indicated as being re-written from the Admiral's company's play of the same title, presented upon Henslowe's boards for the first time in November 1595, gives us fairly definite evidence that he still continued as their company poet at that time.

The date of Peele's death is not at present known, but it must have occurred some time between November 1595 and September 1598, when Meres, in his *Palladis Tamia*, mentions his previous decease.

In the new light of Peele's continuous connection as company poet with Edward Alleyn and the Admiral's men under their various titles, from 1589 until his death some time between the end of 1596 and the middle of 1598, it becomes extremely probable that most, if not all, of the plots and fragments of plots of plays presented upon the Admiral's company's boards between 1589 and *circa* 1596–8, which are now preserved at Dulwich College or the British Museum, would be likely to show at least some traces of Peele's directive hand, in his capacity of company poet. Guided by this induction, a careful examination of the writing in *Sir Thomas More* classified by Professor Greg as hand C; of the plot of *The Second Part of the Seven Deadly Sins* (Dulwich College MS. XIX. and XX.), and of *Fortune's Tennis* (British Museum Addit. MS. 10449/5), with the only examples of Peele's handwriting we possess (British Museum MS. Lansd. 99 Fol. 151 and (British Museum Addit. MS. 21432 Fol. 9a), has led me irresistibly to the conclusion that in hand C in *Sir Thomas More*, and the similar writing in the two Admiral's company's plots mentioned, we have added and more natural and characteristic examples of Peele's Italian hand.

In order to guide the general reader who may wish to make his own comparison of these several manuscripts and form his own judgment, I will briefly indicate a few of the salient resemblances between Peele's acknowledged holographs and the manuscripts under consideration.

It is necessary that one making a comparison should know that the writing classified as hand C in *Sir Thomas More* includes two very distinct caligraphic styles: one, an old English hand, which is confined nearly altogether to the text in the hand C portions of the play. This hand, from the apparent facility that Peele exhibits in its use, was evidently his usual and ordinary writing when composing or transcribing. In the only examples of Peele's acknowledged handwriting that we possess, we have on such old English writing to compare with the text he transcribed in *Sir Thomas More.*

Hand C's other — and for our present purpose more important—style is a well-formed, and, in the capitals, a somewhat ornate Italian hand. This latter hand Peele uses in *More* only for stage directions, and the names of the characters in the play. In the plots of *The Seven Deadly Sins* and *Fortune's Tennis,* he uses this hand only.

If this second caligraphic style of hand C be compared with that of Peele in his letter to Lord Burghley, letter by letter, starting with A and on through the alphabet, a very convincing similarity will become apparent. Only one slight discrepancy will appear, and that in the letter *h,* lower case. The slightly different *h,* which is usual in hand C and in the plots, is due to the evident fact that Peele here wrote more naturally and more quickly than in the carefully written letter to Burghley; and, in writing more naturally and rapidly, unconsciously reverts slightly in his *h*'s to his own more natural and usual old English hand; but only in this particular letter, which frequently follows a capital T, that approximates more nearly to the old English T than any of his other capitals. In spite of this slight reversion to type, it will be found that he at times, in the plots, uses the same form of *h* that he uses in the Burghley letter.

Aside from the palpable similarity of the shape of the letters, both capitals and lower case, in the Burghley letter and in hand C and the plots, an indication of the greatest significance, in the opinion of the present writer, is the fact that all of these manuscripts, including the Burghley letter, exhibit the same indiscriminate use of both a Greek ϵ and an Italian *e,* as well as the occasional use of the Old

English ♃. Such a distinctive habit would be most unlikely in the hands of two different men.

In pursuing his professional labours in his work upon the *More* MS. and the two plots mentioned, Peele evidently wrote rapidly, and to a large extent subconsciously, so far as the formation of his letters was concerned. He wrote also without any deep personal interest or feeling being involved, and in the plot of *The Seven Deadly Sins* endeavoured to get as much matter as possible into a limited amount of space, the necessary compression here being more important than the beauty of his caligraphy.

In the letter to Burghley, on the other hand, in which he supplicates help from the unimaginative and tight-fisted old Lord Treasurer — who scoffed at Queen Elizabeth's gift of £50 to Spenser for *The Faerie Queen* in the phrase, " fifty pounds for a song "—he wrote under an emotional strain, and with evident anxiety to make a favourable impression. His hand, however, apparently revolting involuntarily from the enforced servility of the epistle, gives a stilted height to the letters above the line and a flourish to the letters below the line, in forming which he makes liberal use of the space at his disposal.

If the reader will compare the general shape and effect of the word " Messenger " in the fifteenth paragraph or section of the plot of *The Seven Deadly Sins* with the same word—used only once—in the letter to Burghley, he will find convincing evidence of the identity of the hand in both manuscripts. A significant similarity is also evident when the little word " and " in the stage directions, " Enter Sir Thomas More *and* his man," is compared with the letters ' a n d ' in the word " Englandes " in the Burghley letter. A further comparison of the capitals where possible, especially the capital A's, D's, E's, and M's, and of each of the lower case letters in turn, should leave no doubt in any mind that the writing ascribed to hand C in *More*, as well as of the two plots examined, was executed by George Peele in his capacity of company poet for the Admiral's men.

One of J. P. Collier's alleged discoveries in Lord Ellesmere's papers was a certificate giving a list of sharers in the Blackfriars Theatre in 1589, all of them being represented at that date as members of the Queen's company. As this list included Peele, who I have shown was an Admiral's man at that time, as well as the two Burbages and Shakespeare, who were then Lord Strange's men—no one of the four ever at any time being a Queen's man—and as the Blackfriars was not used as a theatre between 1584 and 1597, the fabricated nature of Collier's discovery becomes very apparent.

The use made by Collier of the phrase, "a life contemplative," in the verses he entitles *The Hermit's Speech*, the MS. of which, in Peele's handwriting and signed with his initials, he claimed to possess, appears to indicate that he found the phrase in Chettle's revisionary portion of the *More* MS., and that the Hermit's, as well as the Gardener's and the Mole-catcher's speeches, are of the same spurious character as the list of the Blackfriars sharers. Dyce published the certificate mentioned, in his *Account of George Peele and his Writings*, prefaced to his edition of Peele's works (London: Routledge, Warne & Routledge, 1861), but questions its authority. Though he also published the three speeches mentioned, his curt reference to them in his Preface, and the fact that he uses an extract from Collier's *History of English Dramatic Poetry* as an

Introduction, instead of writing his own, appears to infer tacit doubts on his part regarding their authenticity.

In view of the fact that Collier, before he embarked upon his career of invention, was probably the most acute and productive Shakespearean worker of his time, his strange aberration is explainable only upon the tolerant hypothesis that much learning had made him mad. The historically important and critically conclusive fact concerning the problems of the composition and revisions of *Sir Thomas More*—of Peele's identity as the writer of the script ascribed to hand C by Mr. Greg—appears to have been easily within Collier's grasp had he not previously devoted his abilities to laborious inventions which the developments of this fact completely destroy.

Shortly after Richard Simpson's announcement of his discovery of Shakespeare's composition and handwiting in the MS. of *Sir Thomas More*, Collier noticed and announced his recognition of a likeness between the handwriting of Peele's letter to Lord Burghley and that of the scribe recently classified as hand C; but owing to his former inventions his announcement fell on deaf ears, and later paleographical authorities who may have investigated the matter appear to have allowed their judgment to be distorted by the fact that the resemblance was a suggestion of Collier's. It appears very probable that his inventions for over two decades previously, especially those noticed above regarding the Peele holographs he claimed to possess, deterred his further investigations in this instance.

In the light now thrown upon Peele's dramatic affiliations in and after 1589, there appears to be a foundation of truth in some of the stories told of him in *Merrie Conceited Jests of George Peele*, published in 1627. One of these

PLATE IV.

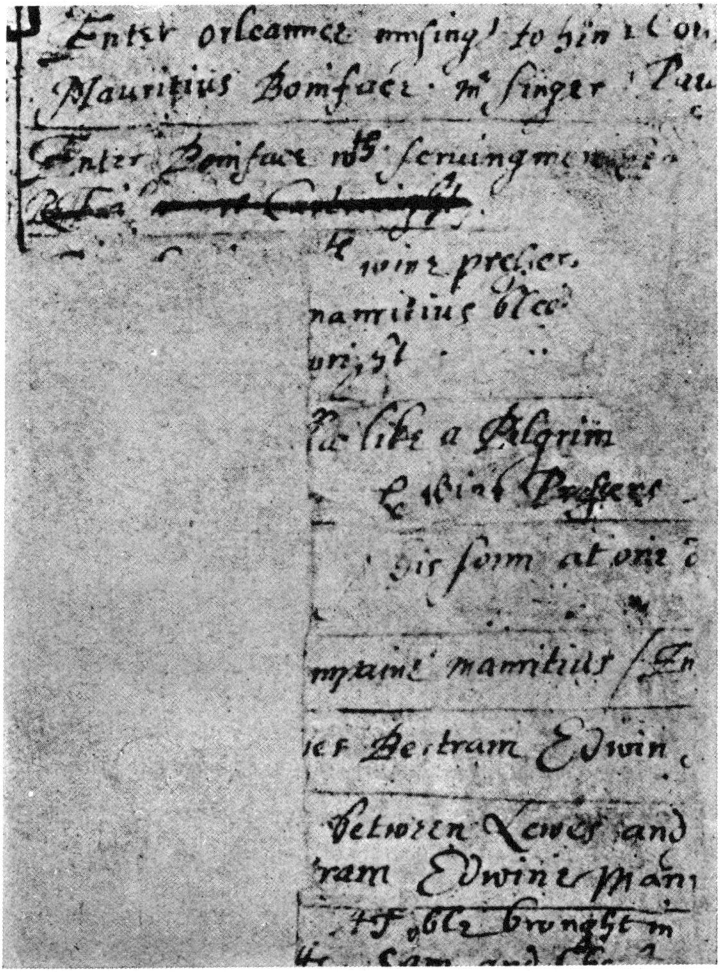

PART OF THE PLOT OF A LOST PLAY—*FORTUNE'S TENNIS*.
B.M. Add. MS. 10449/5.

stories gives an account of a trick played by Peele upon a company of players at Bristol, as well as upon the Mayor, by the use of a "certain history of *The Knight of the Rhodes."* The only play of this period dealing with Rhodes is Kyd's *Soliman and Perseda,* which I have shown came to Peele's hands as a company property of the Admiral's men early in 1589, and left his hands late in 1590, when it was taken over by Pembroke's company. If the story related was true, as it appears to have been, the Mayor of Bristol victimised by Peele was William Bird, father of Anne Davenant of Oxford, whose term of office covered the two years during which Peele and the Admiral's men possessed *Soliman and Perseda* as a property. Another suggestion of actual fact concerning Peele in these jests is the mention of his lost play of *The Turkish Mahomet and Hiren the Fair Greek,* which indicates the same period; this play being also presented upon the Admiral's boards in this interval.

INDEX

Admiral's Company, the Lord, 8, 9, 14, 22, 23, 34 n., 40, 42, 46, 48, 50, 51, 54, 64–70, 78, 80, 81, 91, 107, 108, 132, 133, 136, 180, 181, 182, 185, 188, 199, 202, 209, 214, 216, 232–43, 262, 266, 268
A Farewell, 200
Agamemnon, 71, 89
Agamemnon (Seneca's), 139
A Groat's-worth of Wit, 9, 13, 18, 26, 35, 59, 63, 64, 68, 94, 127, 174
Albion's England, 164
Alcius, 135
Alde, Edward, 266
Alde, John, stationer, 113
Allen, Dr., of Rheims, 113
Alleyn, Edward, 9, 14, 22, 23, 25, 28, 35, 36; as "Roscius" and company's "Cæsar," 37, 38, 42, 43, 44, 46, 49; as "famous Ned Alleyn," 50, 66, 67, 70, 95, 97, 106, 111, 115, 121, 185, 199, 221, 226, 266–67–68
Alleyn, John, 23, 41, 43, 46, 50, 115
Alleyn's Papers, 163
Allot, Robert, 116
All's Well that Ends Well, 227, 230, 240, 243
Alphonsus of Arragon, 26, 139, 143, 144, 146, 161, 169, 195, 242
Anatomy of Absurdity, 3, 36, 39
"Anthony the Poet" (Munday), 67
Antony and Cleopatra, 3, 224, 249
Ariodante and Genevora, 186
Arraignment of Paris, The, 14, 62, 63, 135–143, 265
Arundel's players, Lord, 19
A Storie of —— (The Taming of a Shrew ?), 195, 207
As You Like It, 224
Aubrey, John, 83

"*Ave Cæsar*," 38
Ayrer, Jacob, 198, 212, 262

Bartholomew Fair, 219
Battle of Alcazar, 195, 200
Beaumont, Francis, 263
Bentley, ——, 39, 185
Bentley and Knell, 185
Blind Beggar of Alexandria, The, 78, 112, 146
Boar's Head Tavern, the, 46, 47
Bodenham, John, 116, 119, 251
Braynes, John, 45 n.
Bristol, 239
British Sidanen, 118
Brooke, Professor C. F. Tucker, 102
Brown, Ford K., 130 n.
Browne, Robert, 43, 44, 46, 91, 108, 219, 262
Burbage, James, 1, 8, 10, 11, 13, 16, 17, 18, 19, 20; his pugnacity, 28, 29, 31, 33, 40, 41; his stubbornness, 42, 51; defies the Mayor, 54, 61, 70, 96, 106, 111, 116, 121, 126, 184, 187, 220, 221, 267
Burbage, Richard, 16, 17, 23, 25, 115, 181
Burghley, Lord, 19, 51, 73, 126, 269, 270, 273
Bussy D'Ambois, 252

Cæsar and Pompey, 246
Campion, Edmund, 113
Castle, William, 18
Cavendish, Thomas, 163
Cecil, Sir Robert, 130
Chamberlain's company, Lord, 8, 12, 17, 22, 23, 27, 28, 31, 32, 33, 34 n., 53, 64, 65, 67, 77, 78, 79, 80, 81, 83, 88, 89, 90, 91, 92, 97, 98, 104, 108, 110, 111, 115, 121, 125, 181, 188, 214, 225, 231, 232, 235

INDEX

Chambers, R. W., 67 n., 102, 103
Chandos portrait of Shakespeare, 40
Chapman, George, 3, 10, 14, 15, 47, 62, 63, 84, 85, 86, 91, 105, 106, 108, 112, 116, 117, 119, 125, 132, 161, 182, 183, 186, 194, 208, 212, 225, 226–64, 265, 266
Charlemagne, 112, 200, 201, 202, 252
Chettle, Henry, 87, 89, 105, 106, 107, 108, 109, 110, 121, 253, 272
Children of St. Paul's, the, 14, 45, 50, 233
Children of the Chapel, 14, 24, 45, 62, 124, 135, 143, 215, 264, 265, 266
Cholmley, John, 56
Cobham, Lord, 78
Coldocke, Francis, 198
Collier, John Payne, 47, 271–72.
Comedy of Errors, 72, 92, 116, 208, 222, 230, 231, 232, 233, 234, 235, 237, 238, 239
Comedy of Umers, 86
Contention, The, 37, 60, 61, 71, 154, 156
Coriolanus, 224
Cornelia, 196
Courtlie Controversie of Cupid's Cautels, 196, 198, 237
Cowdray, 240
Crawford, Charles, 120
Creede, Thomas, 75, 77, 80
Crosse-Keys, the, 27, 48, 51, 91, 93, 97, 98
Crown Tavern, 239
Curtain, the, 17, 22, 28, 34 n., 44, 45, 46, 48, 55, 83, 199; as "the Green Curtain at Shoreditch," 214
Cymbeline, 181, 182, 223, 232
Cynthia's Revels, 213

Dark Lady of the Sonnets, the, 1
Davenant, John, 239
David and Bathsabe, 266
Death of the Earl of Huntingdon, The, 247
Decameron, The, 240
Defense of Cony-Catching, The, 69
Dekker, Thomas, 71, 72, 81, 82, 84, 87, 88, 89, 106, 107, 108, 110, 121, 122, 124, 125, 178 n., 220, 221
Delphrygus, 68
Denmark, 170

Derby's company, the Earl of, 32, 33, 184, 185, 186, 187, 188, 190, 191, 195, 233
Description of Liparen, The, 178
Die Schöne Sidea, 262
Discoverie of Witchcraft, 252
Distracted Emperor, The, 200
Doctor Ffostes (Marlowe's *Doctor Faustus*), 66, 210
Doneoracio (Don Horatio), 66
Drake, Sir Francis, 200
Drayton, Michael, 121, 253
Droeshout engraving, 40
Drummond of Hawthornden, 265
Dulwich College, 37
Dutton, John, 185
Dutton, Laurence, 185
Dyce, Alexander, 136, 178, 272

Edward I., 109, 115, 149
Edward II., 31, 37, 91, 108, 110, 150, 217, 218
Edward III., 31, 37, 38, 71, 90, 92, 108, 109, 157
Elizabethan stage, 5
Elizabeth, Queen, 240
Encomium Lauri, 178, 179
England's Helicon, 116, 119, 120, 251, 265
England's Parnassus, 116, 120, 251, 265
English College in Rome, 114
" English Seneca," 30, 138
English Villanies, 110
Ephemeris Chrisometra, 131
Epistle to the Gentlemen-Scholars, 182
Essex, Earl of, 93
Every Man in his Humour, 86, 144
Every Man out of his Humour, 86

Faerie Queene, The, 164, 270
Fair Sidea, The, 264
Famous History of John of Gaunte, The, 180
Famous Victories of Henry V., The, 74, 75–90, 110, 146, 216, 227, 229
Farmer, J. S., 103
Felix and Filomena, 229, 254
Fidele and Fortunio, 62, 91, 92, 105, 116, 117, 119, 120, 126, 136, 194, 202, 203, 208
Fleay, F. G., 64, 86, 110, 119, 136, 144, 165
Fleetwood, William, 19, 20, 55

276 INDEX

Fletcher, John, 263
Florio, John, 110
Folio, The First, 60, 72, 220
Fortune's Tennis, 268–69
Four Kings, The, 136
Fourteeners, 63, 136
Foxe's *Book of Martyrs*, 122
Friar Bacon and Friar Bungay, 65, 144, 146, 147, 168
Furnival, Dr. F. J., 102, 104

Game of Cards, 135
Gentlemen-Scholars, 5, 29, 30, 31
George-a-Greene, 143, 145, 163, 168, 169
Giglot, 148
Giles, Thomas, Master of St. Paul's boys, 46 n.
Greene, Robert, 1, 3, 9, 10, 12, 13, 25, 26, 29, 35, 36, 38, 39, 59, 61, 62, 63, 64, 65, 69, 70, 82, 94, 96, 126, 127, 135, 137–82, 187–90, 191, 195, 207, 209, 212, 218, 219, 221, 222, 224, 225, 227, 229, 235, 239, 241, 242, 265, 267
Greg, Professor, 268

Halliwell-Phillipps, J. O., 19, 21
Hamlet, 4, 30, 77, 90, 191, 198, 206, 208, 212, 214, 219, 222, 223, 225, 231, 242, 252
Harriot, Thomas, 130, 131
Harvey, Gabriel, 63, 177, 178, 179
Hathaway, Richard, 181
Hatton, Sir Christopher, 55, 74
Heneage, Sir Thomas, 76
Henry III., of France, 24
Henry IV., Part I., 74–76, 77, 78, 79, 80, 82, 92, 222, 231
Henry IV., Part II., 74, 79, 80, 82, 155, 156, 172, 216, 222, 227, 231, 249
Henry V., 14, 33, 71, 72, 74, 78, 79, 80, 81, 82, 84, 87, 89, 153, 216, 227, 230, 249
Henry V., the Admiral's company's, 14, 83, 85, 125, 153, 155, 267
Henry VI., Part I., 14, 24, 59, 61, 62, 66, 95, 96, 123, 146, 166, 167, 222, 229, 236
Henry VI., Part II., 37, 60, 61, 155, 156, 222, 224, 229
Henry VI., Part III., 37, 59, 60, 61, 141, 175, 222, 224

Henry VI., The Three Parts of, 61, 65, 71, 81, 145, 146, 150, 157, 164, 181
Henry VIII., 223, 230, 233, 235, 250, 254
Hercules (Seneca's), 139
Hermit's Speech, The, 271
Hero and Leander, 182
Heywood, Thomas, 104, 105, 106, 107, 124
Historie of the Soldan and the Duke of ——, 195, 196
History of Error, The, 234
History of Love and Fortune, A, 186
Histriomastix, 129, 131, 132, 182, 220, 248, 261, 263, 264
Holland, John, 59, 60, 61
Honest Whore, The, 122
Honour of the Garter, 130
Hotwells at Bristol, 239
Householder's Philosophie, The, 30, 191
Humorous Day's Mirth, A, 86
Hunting of Cupid, The, 265
Hyde, John, 20
Hymns to the Shadow of Night, 129, 130, 131, 248
Hyppolytus (Seneca's), 139

Isle of Dogs, The, 182

Jack Drum's Entertainment, 182
James IV., 75, 76, 78, 146, 150, 168, 229
Jeffes, Abel, 206, 266
Jeffes, Humphrey, 59, 60, 61
Jeronymo, 66, 215
Jew of Malta, The, 66
Johannes Factotum, 127
John-a-Kent and John-a-Cumber, 67, 103, 115, 116, 117, 118, 119, 121
Johnson, William, 185
Jones, Richard, 43, 44, 46, 91, 199, 219, 262, 266
Jones, William, 121 n., 146, 254
Jonson, Ben, 3, 72, 83, 84, 85, 87, 89, 107, 121, 125, 213, 215, 216, 219, 224, 227
Julius Cæsar, 183, 224, 230, 261, 262
Juvenal, young, 64

Kempe, William, 16, 115
"King and Kaiser," 142

INDEX 277

King John, 72, 73, 92, 100, 167, 206, 222, 224, 229
King Lear, 223, 224, 225
King Leir, 163, 164, 165, 167, 168, 180, 181, 239
King of Scots, 130
King of the Fairies, The, 68
Knell, ——, 185, 186
Kyd, Thomas, 11, 12, 27, 30, 31, 59, 65, 66, 71, 90, 105, 130, 138, 152, 186, 187, 188, 189, 191, 192, 194–219, 221, 224, 265, 273

Lamb of God, The, 63, 145
Lancastrian scenes, 152
Laneham, Henry, 44, 45, 48, 55, 57, 83
Laneham, John, 55, 185
Leicester, Earl of, 184
Leicester's company, Earl of, 16, 17, 22, 42, 46, 55, 115, 185, 187
Life and Death of Cardinal Wolsey, 250, 253, 254
Life and Death of Thomas Lord Cromwell, 91, 92, 116, 117, 119, 120, 121, 122, 229, 231, 249, 253, 255
Locrine, 64, 76, 77, 142, 146, 150, 160, 161, 168, 172, 173, 174, 176, 181, 229
Lodge, Thomas, 12, 13, 61, 64, 82, 145–83, 189, 219, 221, 222, 224, 225, 227, 235, 238, 239, 265
Longshankes (Peele's *Edward I.*), 67
Looking Glass for London, The, 61, 65, 75, 144, 145, 150, 157, 164, 168, 174
Love's Labour's Lost, 3, 92, 100, 128, 205, 222, 224, 230, 232, 240
Love's Labour's Won, 92, 233, 240, 242
Loyalty and Beauty, 135
Lucrece, 100
"Lukewarm blood," 154
Lyly, John, 63

Macbeth, 2, 72, 92, 116, 117, 223, 230, 232, 233, 243, 249, 251, 252
Macdobeth, 243, 244, 245, 252, 253
Mahomet, 67
Malcontent, The, 216
Malmutius Donwallow, 181
Marlowe, Christopher, 10, 11, 12, 24, 25, 27, 30, 35, 48, 59–62, 65, 66, 70, 71, 76, 81, 90, 97, 101, 109, 124, 130, 148, 150, 152, 153, 156, 157, 161, 162, 182, 183, 195, 199, 208, 210, 217, 218, 221, 224, 236, 265, 267
Marston, John, 3, 66, 84, 121, 125, 132, 215, 216, 217, 261
Martin Marprelate controversy, 50, 52, 126
Martin's Month's Mind, 179
Massacre at Paris, The, 24, 66
Master of the Revels, 51
"Mr. Maxton, the new poet," 67
Measure for Measure, 223, 232
Medea (Seneca's), 139
Menaphon, 3, 29, 30, 31, 34, 36, 127, 135, 178, 182, 191
Merchant of Venice, The, 223, 232, 261
Merchant Taylors' company, 186, 188, 189, 190, 197
Meres, Francis, 83
Merrie Conceited Jests of George Peele, 272
Merry Wives of Windsor, The, 74, 78, 89, 222, 227, 232, 252
Midsummer Night's Dream, A, 76, 77, 92, 224
Much Ado About Nothing, 119, 182, 186, 222, 231
Mucidorus, 146, 151, 161, 166, 167, 168, 171, 174, 175, 176, 180
Mulcaster, Richard, 188, 189, 191
Mulcaster's boys. See Merchant Taylors' company
Muly Molloco, 67
Munday, Anthony, 12, 14, 47, 62, 92, 103, 106, 111, 112, 113, 116, 117, 119, 120, 121, 122, 128, 186, 187, 194, 205, 208, 212, 228, 229, 231, 235, 241, 251, 253, 265, 266

Nashe, Thomas, 1, 3, 9, 10, 12, 13, 18, 26, 29, 31, 34, 35, 36, 43, 63, 64, 65, 82, 94, 95, 96, 126, 138, 183, 189, 190, 191, 207, 209, 212, 218, 221, 260, 263, 264, 265, 267
Never Too Late, 37, 38, 40, 161, 165
Newton, Thomas, 139
Norris, Sir John, 200
Northumberland, Earl of, 130
Notable Discovery of Cozenage, A, 169
Nowell, Thomas, 113

Œtæus (Seneca's), 139

278 INDEX

Old Wives' Tale, The, 63, 64, 65, 96, 145, 163, 168, 175, 177, 179, 180, 260, 261, 263, 264
Orlando Furioso, 65, 68, 69, 122, 144, 146, 150, 168, 171, 176
Othello, 223, 231, 232, 249, 261
Ovid's Banquet of Sense, 129
Oxford, the Earl of, 113, 114
Oxford's company, the Earl of, 14, 23, 34 n., 46, 47, 50, 91, 92, 109, 114; Oxford's boys, 115, 118, 119; as pigmies, 125, 180, 181, 186, 201, 226, 241, 243

Palace of Pleasure, Painter's, 241
Palladis Tamia, 267
Pap with a Hatchet, 46 n.
"Particularities," 153
Pasquil and Katherine, 182
Pastoral Comedy of Robin Hood and Little John, A, 180, 181
Pedlar's Prophecy, 75
Peele, George, 12, 14, 36, 37, 38, 39, 59, 61, 62, 64, 65, 66, 67, 70, 78, 80, 81, 85, 87, 90, 94, 97, 105–8, 125, 129, 130, 137, 143, 195, 200, 201, 205, 209, 212, 218, 219, 227, 265–273.
Pembroke, the Earl of, 73
Pembroke's company, the Earl of, 13, 14, 32, 59, 60, 64, 69, 70, 72, 74, 76, 77, 90, 91, 93, 124, 133, 144, 181, 210, 211, 221, 222, 224, 229, 231, 232, 235, 267
Pericles, 223, 231, 232, 233, 250, 252, 253, 263
Perimedes the Blacksmith, 27, 57, 161, 169
Perkyn, John, 185
Perrot, Sir John, 73
Pierce Pennilesse, 82, 93
Plague, the, 94
Planetomachia, 28, 165, 173
Pollard, A. W., 67 n.
Pope, Thomas, 115
Porter, Henry, 109
Printemps d'Iver, 198
Puckering, Lord Keeper, 12, 130

Queen Anne's men, 47, 109
Queen Dido, 24, 182, 243, 264
Queen's company, the, 9, 12, 13, 17, 19, 28, 34 n., 46, 54, 55, 57, 59, 60, 62, 63, 64, 65, 69, 70, 72, 74, 97, 143, 146, 151, 152, 157,

163, 180, 181, 185, 187, 218, 222
Quip for an Upstart Courtier, A, 63, 145

Raleigh, Sir Walter, 130
Rankin, William, 181
Rare Triumphs of Love and Fortune, The, 190, 192, 193, 194, 195, 202, 206
Repentance of Robert Greene, The, 143
Reply to Stephen Gosson's School of Abuse, 152
Richard II., 92, 224
Richard III., 33, 37, 71, 74, 76, 77, 92, 150, 157, 164, 224, 236
Robertson, Mr. J. M., 219, 227, 229 235, 237, 238, 242, 249, 250, 262
Romayne Life, The, 120
Romeo and Juliet, 182, 224
Rosalynde, 148, 167 n.
Rose Theatre, 9, 24, 47, 56, 84, 93, 98, 111, 242, 249, 250, 262
Roydon, Matthew, 129, 130, 161

Sackfielde, Anne, 239, 240
Sackfielde, William, 239
Sarrazin, Professor G., 189
Satiromastix, 83
Schoell, Professor L., 99 n., 112
Scott, Reginald, 252
Second Part of the Seven Deadly Sins, The, 268–69, 270.
Sejanus, 72, 161
Selimus, 142, 146, 163, 168, 171, 176, 195
Seneca, 139, 189
Seneca, his Tenne Tragedies, 30 n., 139
"Shakescene," 18, 26
Shakespeare, Hamnet, 16
Shakespeare, Judith, 16
Shakespeare, William, 1, 2, 6, 11, 13; as a serving man, 19; his early acquaintance with Marlowe, Edward Alleyn, and Richard Burbage, 25; his two years' servitorship, 34–35; as Thersites and Mullidor, 40; as company poet, 59, 62, 72, 77, 80, 81, 89, 92, 95, 98, 101, 106, 113, 115, 126, 128, 129; as Postehaste, 132, 150, 153, 157, 164, 165, 181, 191, 216, 219, 220, 221; as

INDEX

"artist's prentice," 224, 226, 227, 228, 231, 240, 246, 265, 267
Sheffield's company, the Earl of, 23, 43, 44
Shepheard, Tony (Anthony Munday), 120, 121
Sidney, Sir Philip, 48
Simpson, Dr. Percy, 124
Simpson, Mr. Richard, 26, 29, 40, 99, 100, 101, 102, 129, 272
Sinclair, John, 59, 60
Sion College, 131
Sir Clyamon and Sir Clamydes, 62, 63, 135–43, 160, 161, 165, 194, 208
Sir Giles Goosecap, 187
Sir Oliver Owlet's players, 132
Sir Thomas More, 9, 35, 52, 67, 87, 99, 100, 103, 108–37, 221, 229, 231, 238, 249, 250, 253, 255, 268, 272–73
Slaughter, William, 185
Soliman and Perseda, 192, 193, 195, 196, 198, 199, 237, 241, 273
Southampton, the Earl of, 25, 240
Southampton, Lady, 76
Spanish Comedie, The, 66, 84, 215
Spanish Tragedie, The, 66, 184, 191, 193, 196, 197, 198, 199, 206, 207, 212, 214, 215, 216, 237
Spedding, James, 102
Spencer, Gabriel, 59, 60, 61
Spencers, The, 108, 109
Spenser, Edmund, 164
Standen, Mr., 93
Stanyhurst, Richard, 177, 178
Stationers' Registers, 33, 76, 77, 79, 82, 109, 118, 136, 145, 146, 163, 166, 180, 181, 265
Stowe's Chronicle, 185
Strange News from Purgatory, 62, 63, 179
Strange's company, Lord, 8, 13, 24, 27, 34 n., 50, 58, 59, 62, 65, 69, 70, 115, 132, 144, 181, 185, 214, 267
Strange's company of acrobats, Lord, 23
Studley, John, 138–40, 142, 224
Stukeley, Tom, 200
Sussex's company, Earl of, 9, 13, 32, 34 n., 54, 63, 66, 91, 97, 143, 144, 218, 219

Tamber Cam, 163
Tamberlen, 66
Tamburlaine, 24, 25, 30, 66, 163, 195, 200, 209, 210
Taming of a Shrew, The, 31, 32, 33, 73, 75, 77, 90, 191, 193, 206, 208, 209, 217, 225, 237
Taming of the Shrew, The, 32, 207, 217, 218, 222, 231
Tannenbaum, Dr. Samuel, 104, 105, 224
Tarleton, Richard, 185
Tears of Peace, The, 131, 132
Tempest, The, 183, 223, 232, 261, 262, 263, 264
Theatre, the, 17, 20, 22, 28, 34 n., 44, 45, 97, 185, 214
Thompson, Sir E. Maunde, 67 n., 99
Tilney, Edmund, Master of the Revels, 52, 102, 125, 126, 127, 185
Timon of Athens, 72, 92, 116, 117, 223, 232, 233, 248, 249
Titus Andronicus, 24, 32, 66, 90, 91, 192, 193, 199, 206, 212, 214, 218, 219, 222
Titus and Vespasian, 66, 77, 90, 126, 141, 163, 218, 225, 230, 253
Topcliffe, Richard, 113
Tragedy of the Guyes, The, 24, 66
Troilus and Cressida, 71, 87, 89, 132
Troublesome Raigne of King John, The, 37, 72, 73, 76, 146, 147, 164, 165, 166, 168, 222, 229, 236
True Tragedy of the Duke of York, The, 94
True Tragedie of Richard III., The, 37, 60, 61, 71, 74, 75, 76, 81, 82, 146, 164, 165, 166, 181, 229
Turkish Mahomet and Hiren the Fair Greek, The, 67, 200, 273
Twelfth Night, 223, 232, 253
Two Gentlemen of Verona, The, 33, 92, 197, 222, 229, 237, 253
Two Italian Gentlemen, The, 228, 231, 233, 241, 250, 251, 252, 253, 254

Valdrako, 28, 57
Venus and Adonis, 25, 100
Venus Tragedy, 28, 173
Virgin Martyr, The, 178

Wallace, Professor C. W., 41
Walsingham, Sir Francis, 185

INDEX

Warner, William, 130
Wars of the Roses 61, 74, 157
Warwick's company, the Earl of, 185, 187, 233
Weakest Goeth to the Wall, The, 116, 117, 119
White, Edward, 206
Willobie his Avisa, 129, 131
Wilson, J. Dover, 67 n.
Wilson, Robert, 185
Winter's Tale, The, 224
Wise Man of Westchester, The, 67, 118

Wood, Anthony, 83
Worcester's company, the Earl of, 22, 34, 43, 44, 47, 48, 97, 109
Wotton, Henry, 196, 198
Wounds of Civil War, The, 152, 180, 235
" W. P.," 39
" W. S.," 64, 160

Yeoman of Her Majesties Chamber, 56
Yorkist scenes, 152, 153
Yver, Jacques, 198